JUL 2 0 2009

The media's watching Vault!
Here's a sampling of our coverage.

"For those hoping to climb the ladder of success, [Vault's] insights are priceless."
– *Money* magazine

"The best place on the web to prepare for a job search."
– *Fortune*

"[Vault guides] make for excellent starting points for job hunters and should be purchased by academic libraries for their career sections [and] university career centers."
– *Library Journal*

"The granddaddy of worker sites."
– *U.S. News & World Report*

"A killer app."
– *The New York Times*

One of Forbes' 33 "Favorite Sites."
– *Forbes*

"To get the unvarnished scoop, check out Vault."
– *Smart Money Magazine*

"Vault has a wealth of information about major employers and job-searching strategies as well as comments from workers about their experiences at specific companies."
– *The Washington Post*

"Vault has become the go-to source for career preparation."
– *Crain's New York Business*

"Vault [provides] the skinny on working conditions at all kinds of companies from current and former employees."
– *USA Today*

JUL 2 0 2009

156

HIGH SCHOOL
CAREER BIBLE

HIGH SCHOOL
CAREER BIBLE

VAULT EDITORS

For information about permission to reproduce selections from this book, contact Vault.com Inc.150 W. 22nd St. New York, New York 10011-1772, (212) 366-4212.

Library of Congress CIP Data is available.

ISBN 10: 1-58131-539-2

ISBN 13: 978-1-58131-539-4

Printed in the United States of America

Acknowledgments

We are extremely grateful to Vault's entire staff for all their help in the editorial, production and marketing processes. Vault also would like to acknowledge the support of our investors, clients, employees, family and friends. Thank you!

Table of Contents

Visit Vault at **www.vault.com** for insider company profiles, expert advice,
career message boards, expert resume reviews, the Vault Job Board and more.

VAULT CAREER LIBRARY

ix

Visit Vault at **www.vault.com** for insider company profiles, expert advice, career message boards, expert resume reviews, the Vault Job Board and more.

VAULT CAREER LIBRARY

xi

V/\ULT CAREER LIBRARY

Visit Vault at www.vault.com for insider company profiles, expert advice, career message boards, expert resume reviews, the Vault Job Board and more.

VAULT CAREER LIBRARY   xiii

Visit Vault at www.vault.com for insider company profiles, expert advice, career message boards, expert resume reviews, the Vault Job Board and more.

VAULT CAREER LIBRARY   xv

Introduction

Hey there, early bird! If you are reading this guide, you are way ahead of the game in terms of your career. Many people don't start thinking about what they want to do "when they grow up" until after college—according to studies by the National Association of Colleges and Employers (NACE), less than 60 percent of college students applied for a job before graduation. Getting a jumpstart on your career is a wise decision, as you will have a better idea of what's out there and how to get what you want.

So, relax. As a high school student or recent graduate, the world will not end if you don't have a concrete career goal just yet. Almost everybody has difficulty figuring out what to do with the rest of their lives, and thinking about it now puts you in good standing when you start the process of finding that first "real" job.

This Vault guide will help you get a leg up on planning your future and will assist you in narrowing your career search by giving you an overview of popular professions. It also has some important advice for when you start applying for jobs.

Start with your guidance or college counselor

Every high school has at least one guidance or college counselor. And talking to your school's counselor is a good place to start making plans for your future, whether you want to go to college or jump right into a career. School counselors will have information on colleges and pre-professional schools and programs, and will probably talk to you about what you like to do and how you can turn your interests into a career. Your counselor can also help you put together all the materials you'll need to apply to college or to your first internship or job.

Attend college fairs

The best way to start any career is an education. College is not only a great place to learn about your chosen profession, but also a great place to learn about yourself. College fairs bring together lots of representatives from different colleges who want to talk to you about their programs. Attending a college fair will give you a better sense of what's out there and help you decide what college to attend—as well as give you some valuable contacts for when you start applying!

Work experience already?

The best way to get a job is to have a job. Work experience of any kind will help you get your first "real" job. Working during school or over the summer, as well as participating in co-ops, internships and volunteer projects all provide valuable experience. Even if you hate your summer job, you'll know what you don't want to do and have narrowed down your career options. You'll also be in a better position when it's time to move on to your next job. The perfect candidate has more than a perfect GPA and diploma from a great school; he/she also has good leadership skills, is a good problem-solver, and can communicate with and relate to co-workers and customers alike.

Don't stress

All that said, don't stress too much about choosing your first job. Gone are the days of working 40 years at one company and leaving with a gold watch; today's job market is much more fluid—most professionals starting their careers today will work in at least five different industries or functions before they retire. For a generation of young, curious and versatile students, that is an exciting prospect.

Good luck!

The Team at Vault

Visit Vault at www.vault.com for insider company profiles, expert advice, career message boards, expert resume reviews, the Vault Job Board and more.

VAULT CAREER LIBRARY   1

CAREER ADVICE

Resumes

Where to Begin

Rule number one: Employers don't really, truly care what you did at your last job. They care about what you can do for them. They wonder about your potential for future success working for them. And your resume must answer these questions.

As Shannon Heidkamp, recruiting manager for a division of Allstate Insurance says, "People need to ask themselves 'What value can I offer this prospective employer?'" The before-and-after samples on the following page tell potential employers what skills each employee used, what tasks he/she accomplished and what honors he/she garnered—skills, tasks and honors that can be applied to future jobs. Specific job openings, whether advertised through newspaper ads, Internet sites or inter-office memos, come with specific job descriptions. If you find out about the job through a friend, ask for a copy of the job description. Your job is to meet those requirements by listing your qualifications that most closely meet these prerequisites.

Ten seconds

Studies show that regardless of how long you labor over your resume, most employers will spend 10 seconds looking at it. That's it.

Because of the masses of job searchers, most managers and human resource employees receive an enormous number of resumes. Faced with a pile of paper to wade through every morning, employers look for any deficiency possible to reduce the applicant pool to a manageable number. Thus, your resume must present your information quickly, clearly, and in a way that makes your experience relevant to the position in question. That means condensing your information down to its most powerful form.

So distill, distill, distill. Long, dense paragraphs make information hard to find and require too much effort from the overworked reader. If that reader can't figure out how your experience applies to the available position, your resume is not doing its job.

Solve this problem by creating bulleted, indented, focused statements. Short, powerful lines show the reader, in a glance, exactly why he/she should keep reading.

Think about how to write up your experience in targeted, clear, bulleted, detail-rich prose.

It's what you did, not what your name tag said

Resumes should scream ability, not claim responsibility. Employers should be visualizing you in the new position, not remembering you as "that intern from Chase." While some former employers can promote your resume by their mere presence, you don't want to be thought of as a cog from another machine. Instead, your resume should present you as an essential component of a company's success.

Visit Vault at **www.vault.com** for insider company profiles, expert advice, career message boards, expert resume reviews, the Vault Job Board and more.

VAULT CAREER LIBRARY   5

Computer and Internet Technician

Before:

Primary duties: Computer repair and assembly, software troubleshooter, Internet installation and troubleshooting, games.

After:

Primary duties:

- Assembled and repaired Dell, Compaq, Gateway, and other PC computers
- Analyzed and fixed software malfunctions for Windows applications
- Installed and debugged Internet systems for businesses such as Rydell's Sports, Apple Foods and Eric Cinemas

Theater Marketing Intern

Before:

Responsibilities included assisting with artist press releases, compiling tracking sheets based on information from reservationists and box office attendants, handling photo and press release mailings to media, assisting in radio copywriting, and performing various other duties as assigned.

After:

Experience includes:

- Wrote artist press releases that contributed to an increase in sales by 23%
- Compiled and maintained mailing list of 10,000—Cambridge Theater's largest ever list
- Handled press relase mailings to *Anchorage Daily News*, and Fox Four Television
- Contributed to copywriting of promotion radio commercials for selected events

Think broadly

Applicants applying for specific job openings must customize the resume to for each position. Many job-hunters, particularly those beginning their careers, apply to many different jobs.

A person interested in a career in publishing, for example, might apply for jobs as a writer, proofreader, editor, copywriter, grant proposal writer, fact-checker or research assistant. The applicant may or may not have the experience necessary to apply for any of these jobs. But you may have more skills than you think.

When considering the skills that make you a valuable prospect, think broadly. Anybody's who's worked a single day can point to several different skills because even the most isolated, repetitive jobs offer a range of experience. Highway toll collection, for instance, is a repetitive job with limited variation, but even that career requires multiple job skills. Helping lost highway drivers read a map means "Offering customer service in a prompt, detail-oriented environment." Making change for riders translates as "Cashiering in a high-pressure, fast-paced setting." But unless these toll-booth workers emphasize these skills to prospective employers, it'll be the highway life for them.

Selected history

A lot of things happen in everyone's day, but when someone asks "How was your day?" you don't start with your first cough and your lost slippers. You edit. Resumes require that same type of disciplined, succinct editing. The better you are at controlling the information you create, the stronger the resume will be.

When editing your history to fit the resume format, ask yourself, "How does this particular information contribute towards my overall attractiveness to this employer?" If something doesn't help, drop it. Make more space to elaborate on the experiences most relevant to the job to which you are applying.

Similarly, if information lurks in your past that would harm your chances of getting the job, omit it. In resume writing, omitting is not lying. If some jobs make you overqualified for a position, eliminate those positions from your resume. If you're overeducated, don't mention the degree that makes you so. If you're significantly undereducated, there's no need to mention education at all. If the 10 jobs you've had in the last five years make you look like a real-life Walter Mitty, reduce your resume's references to the most relevant positions while making sure there are no gaps in the years of your employment.

Visit Vault at **www.vault.com** for insider company profiles, expert advice, career message boards, expert resume reviews, the Vault Job Board and more.

VAULT CAREER LIBRARY

7

Cover Letters

The Importance of the Cover Letter

Despite the fact that companies consistently demand that applicants submit cover letters along with their resumes, many job seekers still believe the cover letter to be nothing but a mild formality. Sometimes they don't bother sending a cover letter at all or just one-paragraph notes, quickly belted out with little thought.

The cover letter is your first chance to have a conversation with your prospective employer, to tell him/her who you are, why you're contacting him/her, and to explain any inconsistencies or peculiarities about your resume. It's a brief, one-sided conversation, of course, but one you should enter.

When you send a poor cover letter, you send the message that you can't get the job done, even when quality is essential. Unless you enjoy sitting around in the house ducking calls from bill collectors, that's not the kind of message you want to send.

Too short is too bad

Many people send one paragraph, two- or three-sentence throwaway notes in place of real cover letters. Or they confuse the cover letter with a dashed-off note, such as the fax coversheet. A cover letter should have three to four paragraphs, no paragraphs over six lines long, with the longest one being the middle one or two, and the shortest one being the final, summation paragraph. The idea is to make the document brief and easily readable while still demonstrating a professional, thoughtful manner.

Silliness

In attempt to let their personality and humor soak through the cotton-bound paper, many applicants try to make their cover letters funny. But these attempts rarely work. You have no way of knowing if your prospective boss shares your sense of humor. More broadly speaking, the cover letter offers a sample of your ability to conduct business-like communications. Clowning around can disguise your professionalism.

Poor grammar and, mispelings

No one wants to make grammatical or spelling errors, but applicants nevertheless consistently submit cover letters with small, thoughtless, yet deadly errors.

Many problems slip through because people have a difficult time seeing the mistakes in their own writing. So ask someone else to proofread the cover letter for you. If that's not possible, read the document aloud, slowly and word by word. Every time you make a correction, read the whole document over again. Writers make many mistakes during the final editing process as they make corrections, particularly with tense and word placements. Spell checks can also be typo insinuaters, causing writers to change misspelled words into wrong words, as demonstrated by one cover letter writer who boasted that "Referees are available on request."

Visit Vault at **www.vault.com** for insider company profiles, expert advice, career message boards, expert resume reviews, the Vault Job Board and more.

VAULT CAREER LIBRARY   9

Clichés put egg on your face

It goes without saying that the best way to sound unremarkable and insincere is to fill your cover letter with clichés. So if that's what you were planning, go back to square one and get busy as a beaver at putting together a collection of original thoughts instead of a collection of those same old employee buzzwords. Even if those buzzwords represent honest information you are trying to relay, remember, the road to hell is paved with good intentions. The best way to express your desires is to say how you really feel. True statements run circles around clichéd phrases. So if you come up with the real McCoy, take a bow, because you're moving in the right direction faster than a speeding bullet.

Pontificating with immoderately labored interpretive phraseologies (that is, writing overdone sentences)

Sometimes, in an effort to impress, writers go overboard. How many times have you seen someone strain to play it cool, only to crash and burn after misusing an impressive-sounding word? In an attempt to sound intelligent, cover letter writers regularly produce sentences that use big, impressive, but unfamiliar words. The resulting mistakes cause embarrassment for both the reader and writer, and ensure prompt dismissal of your application. (Even if the reader understands your meaning, she may be put off by your pretentiousness.)

Egomaniacal tone

A golden rule for cover letter writing: Make sure that by the time you've finished your writing, the person most impressed by your letter isn't you. This is an opportunity for you to give employers an idea of who you are, what you've accomplished and how you can contribute to their company. Nobody likes a self-absorbed narcissist, and even fewer people want to work with one. The best way to avoid such errors is to avoid unqualified, grandiose statements and assumptions about how impressed your reader will be with you.

It's the sentiment that counts

When you tell potential employers why you're interested in working for them and their companies, be sincere. Don't bother pouring on a bunch of flattering statements. If you're interested in a position or company, just say why.

Okay:

- "Cymad's increasing stake in the booming semiconductor market makes this position intriguing indeed."

- "I've admired your company's products for some time, especially the Nibok 5000."

No good:

- "You have the most fabulous company ever and it would be the culmination of my life dream to work with you."

- "I would DIE to work at Microdex."

Interviews

Getting Ready

Would a seasoned attorney stride into a courtroom on the day of an important case without having considered every angle of the case? Would a professional climber arrive in Kathmandu without provisions and maps of Mount Everest? Nope. If you want to sway the jury or reach the summit, you've got to go into the big event prepared. The same is true of going into an interview. Preparation is an essential part of the interview process and one that it is easy to overlook or shortchange.

According to polls, most job candidates spend less than an hour preparing for their interviews. No one is going to make you prepare for an interview, least of all the people who will be asking the questions, so it's up to you to get ready on your own.

Unprepared interview subjects often give poor interviews, says Clift Jones, an account director at Bozell Worldwide Advertising. "One of the biggest mistakes people make is to come in with no agenda. They don't know why they want the job, anything about the unique strengths of the company or why they'd be a good match. They're eager and little else. It's much more impressive if they've put a lot of thought into what they want from a situation and what they have to offer before they come in."

By preparing for the interview you'll be doing yourself a favor. Remember: More time spent in preparation means less anxiety on the day of the interview. It's a relief to have something relevant to say, a cogent question on your tongue, a collection of stories underscoring specific elements of your prodigious competence, when the interviewer's anticipatory eyes fall on you and it's your turn to speak.

In addition to alleviating pre-interview stress, being prepared has several other benefits:

- It shows the interviewer that you care enough about the position, the company and the industry to research its current status and future;

- It suggests that once you're hired your preparation, you will be equally as sound for meetings and assignments;

- It shows respect for the interviewer and the company for which he or she works;

- It provides more opportunities for you and the interviewer to have a meaningful conversation in which you can find common ground.

Research

Research is a vital preparation tool. Over time, companies, like countries, develop distinct cultures and inner languages. In some cases the language of a corporation or industry can become so specialized that an outsider will have trouble understanding it. The job candidate who learns an organization's lingo well enough to speak it during the interview just might, like a long-lost relative, be embraced with a cry of, "He's one of us!" and welcomed into the fold.

Where can someone find this kind of insider knowledge? Vault produces a series of profiles and surveys on organizations that can help the information-hungry interviewee. Other user-friendly, if more company-friendly, sources of information include the packets prepared for a company's stockholders. Any stockbroker will send you these, provided you assure them of your interest in someday purchasing stocks through them. A company's human resources, treasury or public relations office will be happy to send you an annual report (which will include a company's financial, marketing, and product report), a prospectus (which includes a list of the CEO and major players), or a 10K report (which contains a company's historical and financial information).

Visit Vault at **www.vault.com** for insider company profiles, expert advice,
career message boards, expert resume reviews, the Vault Job Board and more.

VAULT CAREER LIBRARY 11

Trade magazines (or "the trades"), industry insider magazines, can apprise you of current events, hirings and firings, trends, and other relevant issues. Libraries, career centers and web sites can also be valuable information-gathering places. Spending a day at the library is an especially good way to get the job search going if you're just starting out.

Perhaps the most direct way of getting the real skinny on a company is to talk to someone who works there. Speaking to someone in a position similar to the one in which you're interested can give you vital insights into the company's modus operandi and expose some of the rats in its cellar—or executive suites. If you don't know anyone who's had experience at the company, you might ask around to see if you have any less obvious connections to the industry or a parallel field.

As in other areas of the job search, it's a good idea to treat your preparation for the interview as a job. You might, for example, want to keep a notebook for observations on the companies with which you've interviewed. Or, you might collect the information you gather in an interview folder. Not only will this give you some practice—a warm-up in the organizational skills important in any job—but it will also help you focus and take the preparation process a little more seriously. Some especially important things to remember are the names, numbers and extensions of any contacts with whom you've spoken, the dates and times when those contacts occurred, lists of reasons why you're interested in a particular organization, and potential obstacles or drawbacks associated with a company.

Review your resume

Before the interview, your resume is probably going to be the only thing the interviewer knows about you. In most cases, whoever is going to interview you will have that resume close at hand and might even have memorized key elements of it, so it's important you to be totally familiar with what you've written. Take some time to review what you've done and to observe how it's represented. If you haven't updated your resume in a while, you might discover serious omissions. Maybe you've left off an important experience, or maybe you've forgotten about an experience that could take center stage during the interview. If you can't remember something on your resume, your interviewer may think you are lying.

Check the dates of past jobs for any gaps you might be asked to explain. If you were out searching for the last living grizzly bear in Arizona for those few months when you weren't working, spend some time thinking about how you can turn this to your advantage in the interview. Those tracking skills might prove your passion, bravery and tenacity, for example. Just as importantly, this offbeat experience might help you establish a connection with your interviewer and give him or her an insight into your character.

Consider doing some role playing as you review your resume. Try stepping outside yourself and look at your resume hypercritically, as an employer looking to hire you would. Based on your resume, try imagining questions you'd ask yourself and reasons for not hiring yourself. Once you've imagined the on-paper preconceptions this person likely has of you before you meet him, you can come up with an effective plan for exceeding these expectations face to face.

Because computers play such a vital role in the workplace, it's a good idea to review before the interview exactly which programs you know. If you have experience with any of the programs the company uses, you can make an immediate positive impact on the organization. If you're particularly ambitious, you can give yourself this computer advantage by finding out which programs the company uses and familiarizing yourself with them before the interview.

Emotional preparation

Even if you've made yourself into a walking tome of facts and figures, computer programs and trade lingo, you might not make a good impression unless you're emotionally prepared for the interview. In a mad rush to do whatever you have to do to land a job, you may not take the time to ask yourself how you really feel about this job.

The interview is as much a forum for you to find out if the company and the job fit your needs as it is for the company to discover whether or not you're right for them. You may have to give up some aspects of your dream job, but the goal is to sacrifice as little as possible. What do you want from a job? What are you good at doing? What do people compliment you on?

In the ideal situation, the interviewer and the interviewee are equally interested in finding a perfect fit. Look out for yourself. Ask hard questions about work conditions, drawbacks and low points. If asked tactfully and backed up with research, well-directed questions of this sort won't offend a responsible interviewer. After all, a happy employee is going to be more productive than someone who hates his job.

But if you choose unwisely the first time, don't worry—jobs are no longer forever. People change careers nowadays about as often as their hairstyles. Chances are, even the person who interviews you, if he or she hasn't been living in a cave with blind fish, will understand that you probably won't be with the company for life. Gone are the days of the 1950s "company man" who signed up after college and stayed on until he retired. Nevertheless, choosing a job and career right the first time saves a lot of time and angst.

At the Interview

Controlling jitters and tension

The prospect of sitting alone in a room with a stranger and talking about yourself can be terrifying. You certainly don't want the stress to overwhelm you. If an interviewer's strongest impression of you at the end of the interview is the sweat on your brow, quiver in your voice and the twitches in your limbs, you're in trouble. Here's how to put things in perspective.

Remember:

- Someone at the organization likes you and thinks you have a chance to contribute. You haven't been called in to be tortured—you have a real shot at getting hired.

- If this interview doesn't work out, you will have another one. There are a lot of jobs out there.

- Every interviewing experience you have will prepare you to do better in the next one.

- The person sitting across from you was once sitting on the hot seat just like you, and she survived and got the job even though her voice trembled a bit and her knees knocked a little. Everyone's been through the situation and knows what it's like.

- Just like everyone else, this person interviewing you has friends and casual acquaintances with whom she hangs out. She isn't always so formal. Try to connect with your interviewer on a human level, without being too goofy and informal.

Some interviewing don'ts

The truth is, if you've gotten an interview, you already have some quality or experience that interested your prospective employers. The job, to some degree, is now yours to lose. Here are some final tips to help you avoid that fumble.

In an interview, do not:

1. Blame poor performance on past employers, workplaces, bosses or co-workers. Even if you worked for Satan in Hell, make an attempt to say something pleasant or neutral, such as, "I met many interesting sinners," or "It was a really hot industry."

Visit Vault at **www.vault.com** for insider company profiles, expert advice, career message boards, expert resume reviews, the Vault Job Board and more.

VAULT CAREER LIBRARY   **13**

2. Discuss personal or academic pursuits, unless you're still clearly in the small talk portion of the interview, someone asks you about these directly, or it you can relate them to the position for which you are interviewing. Hobbies like mountain climbing show persistence.

3. Appear too eager to discuss matters of compensation, hours or vacation time. These are legitimate questions, but they should take a back seat to discovering whether or not you and the job are a good fit.

4. Show bad posture: Don't slouch, tap your feet or splay your legs or arms.

5. Let nervousness alter your actions: Don't fumble with objects in your hand, rearrange your hair, jiggle pocket change or chew gum.

6. Let your message get muffled: Don't slur, don't drop your eyes or speak too quickly.

7. Fail to have questions when the time comes.

8. Run on too long with answers to questions. Be aware of how the interviewer is responding to what you're saying. If you catch him or her looking bored or staring at you with a glazed or unfocused look, it's probably time to stop talking. If they want to find out more about what you were talking about, they'll ask you to continue.

9. Fail to answer the question you're asked.

10. Forget to smile! Remember, you're there at their invitation.

Shmoozing/Networking

What does schmoozing sound like to you? Maybe it sounds smug, unctuous, oily, slimy. It sounds, quite frankly, like "oozing." Schmoozing is far from slimy, but "oozing" actually isn't a bad description of what a schmoozer does. A schmoozer slides into opportunities where none are apparent, developing friendships from the slightest of acquaintances. Through formless, oozy, schmoozy actions, a schmoozer moves slowly but inexorably towards his or her goals.

What is schmoozing? Schmoozing is noticing people, connecting with them, keeping in touch with them—and benefiting from relationships with them. Schmoozing is about connecting with people in a mutually productive and pleasurable way—a skill that has taken on new importance in our fragmented, harried, fiber-optic-laced world.

Schmoozing is the development of a support system, a web of people you know who you can call, and who can call you, for your mutual benefit and enjoyment. Schmoozing is the art of semi-purposeful conversation: half chatter, half exploration. Schmoozing is neither project nor process. It's a way of life.

Who You Know Matters

"I tell my clients that 15 percent of jobs are filled through the newspaper, 5 percent are filled through companies like mine, and 80 percent are filled through word-of-mouth," says Beth Anrig, the owner of Beth Anrig and Associates, a job placement service in Connecticut. Anrig places individuals in positions in a wide variety of industries, ranging from banking to publishing. "Do you know how most jobs are filled?" Anrig asks. "A manager asks a couple of people if they know anyone good."

We've moved past the point where we expect that jobs will be mainly filled through company recruiting and advertising.

According to widely cited statistics, 75 to 80 percent of all job seekers find their new position through referrals; most openings never see the light of day (or newsprint). By schmoozing, you make word-of-mouth work in your favor. You can learn about a variety of industries and make friends and contacts upon whom you can call for career advice or assistance. Now how to do it?

Schmoozing When in School

If you're still in school, you have golden schmoozing opportunities all around you. Many students forget that there are numerous people at their school who already know them and are predisposed to want them to succeed—their teachers.

If you think your history teacher only knows about the French Revolution, think again. He's probably pretty savvy about life in this century, as well.

Another important reason to get to know your professors is for recommendations. Most colleges require at least two teacher recommendations in their application. Make sure to choose teachers who really know you, inside and out of the classroom. You don't want to choose a teacher who only knows you as the quiet kid in the back who does pretty well on pop quizzes. You want the teacher who can talk about your enthusiasm and personality, as well as performance.

Make sure you are on a first-name basis with each and every one of your teachers. Most teachers only see students out of class when they're begging for extensions on papers or explaining how they slept through the midterm. Your schmoozing should come as a welcome change.

Introduce yourself to your teacher at the beginning of the semester. Tell him/her you're looking forward to taking the class, and if you're majoring (or thinking about it) in the subject, let him/her know that, too. If you have any questions about

Visit Vault at **www.vault.com** for insider company profiles, expert advice, career message boards, expert resume reviews, the Vault Job Board and more.

VAULT CAREER LIBRARY 15

something in class or are curious about something you've read, ask. But make sure to ask non-class-related questions, as well. How did they get interested in geometry? Are they doing any research of their own? If so, what?

Because, after all, you ultimately want to get a job and/or go to college after you graduate, ask your teacher for advice about that, too. What have other students in his/her subject done after graduation? What does the teacher recommend you do?

Tap alumni resources

Alumni already have a point of similarity with you. Ron Nelson points out, "Just having that little thing like a school connection takes you from 'Who the hell are you and why are you calling me?' to 'Oh, OK, you went to Vanderbilt, too, what can I do for you?' It's not a big thing, but it's enough."

Tamara Totah, the former headhunter for The Oxbridge Group, also recommends using alumni contacts from your school, although she cautions that you should never directly ask them for a job. "The minute they hear that they get worried," she says. "Talk to them about what different opportunities may be available in the industry. People will spend 30 minutes with you. They know how tough it is."

The Informational Interview

It's not a job interview—exactly. But it does get you face-to-face with someone in an industry that interests you. Informational interviews are an invaluable opportunity to learn about the inside scoop into the career field that interests you. Many people are prepared to spend 10 minutes to an hour of their time talking to those looking for a job, assessing their skills and background, and giving them some pointers in breaking into their chosen field.

Says Beth Anrig, "I tell all my clients that the best thing to do is to set up informational interviews." One caveat: "never call them that," she says. Informational interviews sound too much like interviews, and that sounds like asking for a job. Everyone is over-networked, in the official sense. No one has the time anymore to do something that is just like a job.

So don't frame the "informational interview" as any kind of interview. Instead, say that you want to talk with them, or get coffee or chat. Your goal is to have a conversation, not an interview. Ask semi-personal questions: What got you started in this industry? What other careers did you consider? Are you happy in your choice? At the same time, talk honestly and openly about your own career aspirations, and why the industry in question appeals to you. If you click, keep the person abreast of your career progress and decisions.

Informational interviews serve other purposes, too. They are also a way to talk to people about a college that interests you. Alumni love to talk about their alma maters, and love to talk to people who want to hear

Internships

The Importance of Interning

If you're reading this book as a high school student or recent high school graduate, you're in good shape—many college students don't begin thinking about careers until late in their senior year or (gasp) after graduation. If you're one of the early birds, make sure you take advantage of your time by getting experience through a summer and/or school-year internship.

What is an internship?

An internship is a sort of trial run at a company—and one of the best ways to test out a potential career field or employer. Internships can last two weeks or a full year, though most of them are for a three-month period or so. Most internships take place over the summer, though others may be available over the fall or spring semester or of a duration of your choosing. Similarly, the majority of internships are full time, though some are part time.

Why do an internship?

You might be tempted just to take a job to earn money. There's nothing wrong with that—but there's so much more right with doing an internship. For example, if you want to break into a field that's tough to crack, like entertainment, advertising or politics, the very best way to get a job in the field is to have interned in it. Not only will you have great experience on your resume, but you'll also meet plenty of contacts and potential mentors. Similarly, interning at a top company puts you on the fast track to getting a full-time offer from that firm—or one of its competitors! Most large companies are much more likely to hire a former intern than someone "right off the street." Even if you don't end up working for your employer, you'll have some invaluable and difficult-to-obtain experience on your resume.

But I need to get paid!

Don't think that doing an internship means giving up on pay altogether. It's true that many internships are unpaid or only offer school credit—at the same time, these are often small, interesting organizations or companies in glamorous industries. But many others offer some kind of payment, from a stipend or travel allowance to a very generous salary. Others offer interesting perks, including travel and the chance to attend exclusive industry events.

Tips for applying to internships

Let's say you've found an internship that interests you. That's great! The first thing you should do is to follow all the instructions. Here's a short checklist of things you need to do when applying for internships.

- *Apply by the deadline.* A few months before the deadline is even better—a small organization might just take the first qualified intern who applies. Follow the instructions! If you're asked to provide a writing sample, don't send your photo portfolio. If you're asked to provide a reference, start canvassing your teachers.
- *Make sure your resume is up to date and thoroughly spellchecked.* If you've never written a resume, go to your school guidance center and ask for help. And ask an experienced professional or two whom you trust to review your resume. If you are applying for internships in different fields, you may need to have more than one version of your resume highlighting different experience. Make sure that your most current contact information is on the resume.
- *Don't ignore the cover letter.* Make a persuasive case in your cover letter, which should be tailored to each internship, that you really want to intern at the company. Do your research and be specific—and honest—about why the opportunity is right for you. Again, make sure you carefully proofread the cover letter. Let a trusted friend or teacher read it, as well.

Visit Vault at **www.vault.com** for insider company profiles, expert advice, career message boards, expert resume reviews, the Vault Job Board and more.

VAULT CAREER LIBRARY   17

- *Follow up.* If you're really interested in an internship, there's nothing wrong with a quick call or e-mail a few weeks after the application to let the organization know how interested you are. But don't pepper them with phone calls every day.

- *Carpe diem.* If you're really interested in an internship, but your qualifications aren't quite right, apply anyway and stress your real interest. Many organizations would rather have a truly excited and motivated intern than one that just meets the qualifications on paper.

- *Take experience over money.* You can always earn money. The window of opportunity for internships isn't eternally open. If you're really broke, consider taking a part-time job in order to work at the internship you really want.

Intern any time

Most companies with internships have formal programs during the summer, when they hire a number of college or high school students. However, many companies also hire during the school year, so if you're starting your senior year of high school, it's not too late to get that all-important professional work experience. Even if you're not jumping straight into the work world, colleges love work experience, especially internships! We can't stress this enough: if you can manage it financially, interning in a profession in which you have long-term interest is almost always more preferable than taking a paying job that has nothing to do with your interests. Years down the road, we're sure you'll agree that it was worth it.

For information on internship programs, refer to the *Vault Guide to Top Internships*, which has information on more than 750 top programs, and check out the Internship Board at www.vault.com for up-to-date listings.

Make Sure You Don't Blow Your Internship

Remember that scene in *Grease* when the Rydell High kids are singing about the summer? Danny "had me a blast," while for Sandy it "happened so fast." It seems a strange comparison, but many summer interns at America's leading companies describe their summers the same way. Not all experiences are quite so rosy, but in any case, young employees get both a feel for the corporate culture and a taste of the workforce during the course of these often finely crafted programs. Whether their time is spent doing substantive work that affects the company or just making Starbucks runs all summer, there is a goal in mind. Summer interns need to spend those precious weeks making a favorable impression in order to get that all-important full-time offer.

Granted, the reason that many summer programs are so carefully organized and lavish is so that interns will want to come back. In many programs, "you have to seriously mess up not to get [an offer]." Much more commonly, though, interns are not afforded such leeway, and need to be aware of what it takes to secure a full-time position. First and foremost, while the fate of the company may not hinge on the work interns produce, optimum effort must still be made on assignments. Simply put, no matter if it seems insignificant, "whatever work you do, make sure to do a good job," advises one recruiter. Satisfying this requirement may mean punching the clock after the summer sun has disappeared for the night. Most businesses do not take kindly to employees who leave a vapor trail out the door when the five o'clock whistle blows.

Also extremely important are the connections, however informal, made with established employees. This is especially true with mid-level and senior employees who have a say in who gets hired. Those who assume that a stellar academic record and a shiny pair of Ferragamo wing tips are a substitute for engaging conversation may be in for a rude awakening come Labor Day. Successful networking can be accomplished by working for a variety of people or through socialization inside the office.

Attendance at company social events, when offered, is an "important way to build personal relationships within the company," as well. Whether cruising the halls or knocking a few back at the local pub, a gregarious persona cannot be discounted—"office wallflowers just will not cut the mustard," says one corporate insider. On the other hand, there are limits; for instance, insiders at Goldman Sachs tell a cautionary tale wherein one investment banking associate who failed to get an offer was snubbed "as a result of excessive brown nosing."

At the same time, summer interns need to be careful about exposing, or more to the point imposing, their personality on their fellow employees. At some companies, for example, "you're not allowed to be rude to anyone—secretaries, the lady in the cafeteria, or whoever it is." Even fast-paced offices with a reputation for "screamers" may be averse to bringing in new people who will perpetuate a harsh culture. "Some summer interns behave completely inappropriately," says a source at a Wall Street firm. "One recent summer associate had a big mouth and she screamed a lot. She made enemies in only eight weeks, including some managing directors."

Of course, even when interns generally play their cards right, one wrong move may stand between them and a job offer. For instance, an insider tells Vault that one would-be full-timer was not asked back to his company after "arguing with a partner at a softball game about what position to play." Another inexplicably turned over an entire assignment to an unqualified subordinate. Perhaps the most extreme example involved an overly enthusiastic intern at one firm who, while on a company retreat, stripped off his clothes and hopped into the hot tub. That's a little too much information!

How to Take Advantage of Your Internship

The internship craze is reaching new heights. Nearly three-quarters of all college students do internships today as compared to 1 in 36 in 1980. These numbers have made many employers a bit uneasy. After all, these employers are, for the most part, getting all this labor for free, or at most a small stipend. Isn't there something a little bit wrong with that? Many employers think so. That won't stop them from taking the sweet deal, but they won't feel good about. That's where you—the intern—come into the picture. The intern has an extremely receptive and grateful audience at his internship, an audience that aims to please. Consequently, if the intern plays his cards well, he or she can do extraordinary things during a two- or three-month stint.

Be there first

At most internships, especially those that take place in the summer, the company or organization will have several interns for a particular time period. If possible, arrive a week or so before the other interns. First, you will get more individual attention in the beginning and consequently can establish yourself as the "favorite" intern. Second, you may be able to get the first pick of the assignments. Third, you may get the first pick of the desks, or wherever they will seat you. Employing this rule to its extremes, interns have been known to use this seemingly simple technique to get the later-arriving interns to become their "pseudo-interns"—farming out menial tasks to them so they can concentrate on more substantive work.

Look around

Once you get inside a company, you should not feel restrained by the department that you're working in—or even to your assigned supervisor. Figure out what you most want to do in the organization and schmooze the person who does it. A good way to do this is to ask them to lunch. A good line is: "I'm trying to absorb as much information as I can in this internship, and what you do seems particularly interesting. I wonder if you are available for lunch any time this week." They will almost always say "Yes." When they describe what they do at lunch, try to relate the skills that they employ to skills that you have.

For example, if they tell you about the press release they are writing for company X, slip in how that's similar to your school newspaper writing experience. Hopefully, they will then offer you a chance to draft a press release. If not, try to give them another nudge, but make it gently. "Oh, writing press releases seems like so much fun!" you can add, or something to that effect.

Visit Vault at **www.vault.com** for insider company profiles, expert advice, career message boards, expert resume reviews, the Vault Job Board and more.

VAULT CAREER LIBRARY   **19**

Never complain

When you are given menial errands to do, take it in good cheer. No one likes a whiner. If you feel like you must say something, couch it in humor. One State Department intern remembers telling his boss: "Although being a Deputy Assistant Secretary of Photocopying has its moments, I was wondering if I could do more substantive work here." It got his message across—and worked. Remember: As long as you do a few things that look impressive, you won't have to put on your resume that for 99 percent of the time you ran errands and photocopied stuff. So instead of complaining about your menial tasks—or even non-verbally complaining by acting dour—express an interest in doing substantive work, and be as specific as possible. Specificity shows interest.

Dressing for Success

Dressing for Interview Success

Though Henry Thoreau once warned us to "distrust any enterprise that requires new clothes," he never had corporate or business interviews. Here's how to make that critical first impression count.

Your rumpled manly fashion statement

Men are relying on the basics—with a twist. "Black is huge," says Andi Cohen, a fashion executive, who also mentions charcoal gray and navy as popular colors this season. Cohen says three-button suits and sports coats are in, but two-buttons are making a comeback. When shopping for the perfect suit, Cohen points out a few style trends to look out for: higher buttons, a narrow lapel and plain front pants. While men still can't go wrong with a basic white button-down shirt, French blue shirts continue to be almost unduly popular.

Keep fashion out of the interview

While pantsuits are increasingly acceptable even in the most conservative institutions for female work wear, the interview is not the time to be fashion forward. Wear a skirt suit in black, brown, navy or black-and-white houndstooth. The confident may choose to wear a red suit. Choose a button down shirt that fits smoothly underneath, or a shell. Remember that the interviewer may invite you to remove your jacket.

On the other hand, if you intend on wearing a pantsuit every day, you may wish to wear a pantsuit as a screening mechanism. A company that dings you for not wearing a skirt is probably not somewhere you want to work. At least you won't have to worry about having your skirt ride up.

Work Dress

"Casual" dress

The invention of the "casual" or "dress down" day has made the workplace a little more human-looking, brightening the assembly line of black suits and brown skirts, but it has also made life a little more confusing for the office workers who don't make the rules. Any experienced employee knows that a soft and friendly workplace is usually an optical illusion—office permissiveness always has a concrete wall in back of it. So for the touchy question of what to wear on "dress down" morning, the trick is to know how far you can go before you hit the wall. Here are three basic "zones" of casualness within which most businesses can be found; during your job interview, you may want to find out where that particular business sits.

"Business" casual

Basically, this means you can have a little sugar on your gruel. The most traditional businesses, such as law offices and financial institutions, practice this form of dressing down. Business casual clothes are almost the same as business clothes, but with splashes of color added.

- The skirt can be replaced with slacks or a dress, the dress shoes with casual pumps
- The shirt can be blue or pink, the jacket tan or another light color, the tie a little brighter and more playful

In other words, think like a Victorian going out for a day in the park (not like yourself in the same situation).

Visit Vault at **www.vault.com** for insider company profiles, expert advice,
career message boards, expert resume reviews, the Vault Job Board and more.

VAULT CAREER LIBRARY 21

"Dress" casual

This is perhaps the most confusing and perilous zone of all because it can only be described as "in-between." At the same time, it is where the majority of offices are located, including advertising firms, government agencies and medical offices.

- A vest or soft knits, including dresses, can replace the women's suit.
- A sport shirt with vest, sweater or jacket, and corduroy or patterned pants can replace the men's suit

"Relaxed" casual

Beware: life is still no slice of cherry pie at these places. However, your "weekend wear," including jeans and dignified single-colored T-shirts, may get some weekday exposure. Relaxed casual days happen at offices where there is little face-to-face contact with customers, such as high-tech firms, sales support teams and telemarketing operations.

- No ties or pantyhose. No, we insist!
- Khaki or denim skirt or pants, with crisp shirt, vest, blazer or cardigan for women.
- Jeans or khakis with denim or polo shirt, vest or sweater for men.

Remember, if you use one bit of aggressively casual clothing, like jeans, T-shirt or tank top (that was a joke), balance it with an equally strong bit of fanciness, such as a belt, nice shoes or a crisp shirt.

Thank You Letters

Thank You Notes: Always in Style

Are thank you notes a relic of a bygone era when workers wore starched white shirts and neatly pressed suits to work every day?

Many job hunters think so. But they're wrong, say employment experts. According to Vault's exclusive Interview Manners Survey, which surveyed 675 employees and employers, more than 35 percent of employers said that a thank you note "always helps" a candidate, and and additional 42 percent said that it helps when deciding between two qualified candidates. Said one employer: "I have gone out of my way to hire/refer to my network candidates who have the grace to send a thank you note."

Letters or e-mails of appreciation, especially after a job interview, are as necessary as ever in our increasingly casual culture. This is your chance to remind your potential boss of your qualifications, how you would fit in with company culture and to makeover any mistakes you made in the interview.

"You want to stay on their radar screen and out of the garbage can," says Bob Rosner, author of *Working Wounded: Advice that Adds Insight to Injury*, explaining why you should consider thank you notes another chance to prove yourself.

If you really want an offer, send not only words of thanks but added-value attachments, including compelling news articles about the industry, the company or the competition, suggests Rosner, who is also a career columnist.

"Information is the ultimate currency because it helps people do their job," he says. The attitude you will be conveying is "I have my ear to the ground and am investing energy into [the job search] beyond what I did in the interview."

What? Me send a thank you note?

We know. You don't do thank you notes. Only 35 percent of workers surveyed by Vault last year said they always send thank you notes following interviews. Nearly 15 percent of people never, or almost never, follow up with a letter or e-mail even though 43 percent of them say such notes could be very important in getting a job.

Rosner's *Working Wounded* readers have similar habits. In his poll, 37 percent of his respondents say they always write thank you notes or letters. Twenty-two percent never do it and 41 percent say they do only when they really want to impress their interviewers.

Among Vault's thank you note rejectionists, 63 percent agreed with the statement "There's no need. If they want me, they will hire me." (Keep in mind, the poll was done in November 2000, back in the days when the job market still favored workers.)

Most people don't exactly reject the concept of thank you notes. They simply were never taught the importance of them, says Barbara Pachter, author of *When The Little Things Count...And They Always Count: 601 Essential Things That Everyone In Business Needs to Know.*

"Once people realize how crucial it is, they do it," Pachter says.

A business-training consultant, Pachter advises employees to send notes for almost any occasion calling for an express of gratitude, even after a round of golf with a more senior partner.

"If you're ever in doubt, do it," says Pachter, of Cherry Hill, N.J.

She recalls telling this to a group of accountants during a training session and getting groans from the crowd. The discussion ended when one of the founding partners stood up and said he always hand writes thank you notes.

"If the head of the company does it, there was no point in arguing," she says.

Visit Vault at **www.vault.com** for insider company profiles, expert advice, career message boards, expert resume reviews, the Vault Job Board and more.

VAULT CAREER LIBRARY

23

Perhaps more job hunters would send notes if they knew this: 36 percent of hiring managers polled by Vault say thank you notes always help a candidate's job prospects while another 42 percent say it could help when deciding between two or more qualified candidates. Only 22 percent said, in so many words, not to bother.

"It comes down to relationship building," one manager tells Vault. "The candidate who sends a thank you note extends a courtesy that encourages relationship building, in which it is always appropriate to show gratitude. The best leaders are quick to say thank you."

Another manager sees notes as a sign of good "follow-up." "Someone who takes the time to send a thank you note would probably use courtesy in other areas of their employment, i.e., co-workers, managers," the manager wrote.

As helpful as thank you notes are, experts point out, a bad thank you note could sink your chances of getting the job. Pachter recalls a story about a young man who was selected for the managerial fast-track program at a Fortune 100 company. The man sent a letter so filled with typos and misspellings that he was kicked out of the prestigious program.

Thank You Notes for Dummies

So obviously, it's not just the gesture. You have to get things right. Here are the basics, according to the experts.

Make sure you gather business cards during the interviews in order to spell everybody's name correctly and get their titles right. E-mail, in many cases, is as acceptable as a written letter. Then again, electronic messages can't replace the personal touch of a handwritten letter, says Pachter. You need to evaluate the situation to figure out what's appropriate.

E-mails are appropriate and even preferred if you know the company needs to make a decision fast. And if you're going for a dot-com job, a letter may seem downright antiquated. Then again, if the person lets on in an interview that she never checks her e-mail, buy stamps.

The best way to solve this conundrum is to ask during the interviews how best to follow up with them.

Timeliness

Rosner suggest sending your notes within three or four days after the interview. Pachtner recommends writing the day after the interview. If you forget, she says, it's better to send a letter late than not at all.

The perfect thank you

Keep your writing crisp, businesslike and focused. Use titles such as Mr. or Ms. unless you have a prior relationship or feel it would introduce a false note of formality.

Worried about sounding like a suck up? Then remove anything that sounds like gush—including statements like "I love your company."

Whom do you thank?

If you've met with six or so people during a whirlwind super Saturday-type interview, write to everyone. But save your best, most personalized follow-ups for the highest-ranking person in the room and the one who brought you in for the interview in the first place, Rosner says.

Among the points of writing, you want to prove to the bosses that you really listened to them during the interview. Therefore you should sum up the key aspects of the job.

"You really want to say to them that you've got the energy, that you listened attentively and that you connected [with them]," he says.

Be your own Mr. Fix-it

Did you screw up at any time during the job interview? It's rare to totally nail an interview, Rosner says. A thank you note is the perfect vehicle for making first impressions all over again.

"The attempt to do revisionist history is an art," Rosner says. "If one of their concerns [was] that you're job hopping a lot, you might want to revise their memory by reinforcing the long-term relationships you've had with your past bosses or other people."

Making yourself memorable is where Rosner's value-added plan—to send your potential employers compelling information along with the note—comes into play.

This takes pre-planning. During the hours you'll already be spending researching the company before the interview, make sure to save compelling news articles or other sources of information about the company.

Then, during the meeting, ask your interviewer what publications and web sites he or she reads. This way you can gauge if this manager has already seen your research, if he or she knows of other sources of information about the industry and, this is important, to save yourself embarrassment if he or she disagrees violently with the article you were planning on sending. "If there was a job I really wanted, I would have three or four possible things to send them before ever going in for the interview," he says. "If I really wanted the job, I would probably have a whole plan to stay on their radar for up to six weeks."

Visit Vault at **www.vault.com** for insider company profiles, expert advice, career message boards, expert resume reviews, the Vault Job Board and more.

VAULT CAREER LIBRARY

25

College

Why Go to College?

In 2007, more students applied to college than ever before, with many college admissions offices reporting double-digit percent increases in applications. Top colleges, including those in the Ivy League, broke records in 2008 when they reported acceptance rates of less than 10 percent. And the number of graduating high school students hasn't even peaked! (According to the U.S. Census Bureau, it won't peak until 2009.) Although there are many reasons for the surge in applications, the bottom line is that college is more accessible than ever to more students and families. Schools are increasing their financial aid efforts, making online applications easier and amplifying their recruiting efforts.

No matter what you want to do, you will need to learn about it. Every job, from waiting tables at a local restaurant to finding a cure for cancer, requires training. For most careers, college is the best place to start.

The school part

Whether you go to a liberal arts college or pre-professional school, college is a lot of work. Most colleges require students to take four classes a semester, minimum. You will read more, test more and write more than you did in high school. And most colleges expect you to do so on your own time—no more study hall—so time management is another important skill learned in college.

Traditionally, college is designed to expand your mind. Most colleges will require you to take classes both in and out of your major or concentration. At some schools, you will take general requirement classes, often called a core, in addition to classes within your major. Others will have "distribution requirements," meaning you will have to take classes across a number of fields and subjects.

Ultimately, college will teach you to express yourself clearly on a variety of subjects. It will also enable you to better understand the world and community around you, making you a better candidate for your dream job.

Job opportunities

Moreover, after several years of layoffs and hiring freezes, the U.S. job market began picking up in 2004 and continued to add jobs in 2005 and 2006. The market for more recent grads is even better. According to a November 2007 survey conducted by NACE, 2008 graduates are entering one of the most promising job market in years. Respondents to the NACE's Job Outlook 2008 reported that over 62 percent of employers call the 2008 job market "very good" to "excellent" and expect their college hiring in 2007-2008 to be 16 percent higher than in 2006-2007.

In addition, NACE reports that more and more employers will be coming to you, the student. In its 2007 Recruiting Benchmarks Survey, almost 90 percent of employers said that they participate actively in on-campus recruiting. Employers' biggest worry this year is competition for qualified applicants, and they plan to fight for the students they want. In Job Outlook, 78.5 percent said they will increase their salary offers and 53.6 percent plan to offer signing bonuses.

Still, for most first-time job seekers, finding that first gig is never easy. This Vault guide will help you get a leg up on the competitive job search, and will assist you in narrowing your search by giving you an overview of popular careers.

The fun part

College isn't just about work. It is also about building relationships, learning about yourself and the world, and having fun! For many, being at college is like being a kid in a candy store: there are so many wonderful options of things to do and see

Visit Vault at **www.vault.com** for insider company profiles, expert advice, career message boards, expert resume reviews, the Vault Job Board and more.

VAULT CAREER LIBRARY   27

that you couldn't possibly do them all. From theater to engineering, Greek life to study abroad, colleges are offering the world to their students.

In her historic address *Why Go to College*, Alice Freeman Palmer says about the college years: "We who are in it all the time feel that we live at the fountain of perpetual youth, and those who take but a four years' bath in it become more cheerful, strong, and full of promise than they are ever likely to find themselves again; for a college is a kind of compendium of the things that most men long for."

How to Choose a College

There is no one way to choose a college. Location, price, size, programs offered and more go into the decision to choose one college over another. Luckily, there are many resources available to help you make the decision.

Talk to your high school guidance counselor—he/she will have the most information about schools that fit your interests. There are also lots of guides, magazines and web sites out there to help you learn about what different schools offer, including Vault's. Once you've created a list of schools that interest you, check out their web sites and schedule a campus visit. It's not just the college admissions office's job to see if you're right for the school, it's also their job to see if the school is right for you.

SAT 101

The SAT, or Scholastic Aptitude Test, was originally created to test aptitude, or innate intelligence and capacity for learning. It was meant as an equalizer—a way to see how students from all over the country, in schools of different sizes and focus, public or private, compare to each other. In the words of the College Board (the company that creates the test), "The SAT was designed so you can demonstrate your reasoning and problem-solving abilities, not just the amount of information you've accumulated during school." In other words, it is designed to test not what you know, but how you use what you know.

The SAT is administered seven times a year across the country. The test lasts about three hours and 45 minutes, though test takers should plan to be at the test center for roughly five hours. The SAT has three basic sections, which we describe below:

- **Mathematics (Three sections, 70 minutes total)** The mathematics section breaks down into three sections (two 25-minute sections and one 20-minute section). Not all questions on the mathematics are multiple choice, some will ask you to "grid in" your answers. The section tests your math and logic skills, based on subjects you've studied through your third year in high school. It focuses on topics learned in algebra and geometry, such as linear functions and tangential lines, as well as statistics, probability and basic numbers and operations. If you're not a math whiz, don't worry: you can use a calculator.

- **Critical reading (Three sections, 70 minutes total)** Formerly known as the verbal section, critical reading is divided into two multiple-choice parts: reading passages and sentence completion (two 25-minute sections and one 20-minute section). The reading passages section asks you to read short and long passages and answer questions based on information in the passage. In short, it tests your ability to read critically. The sentence completion portion tests your ability to understand the nuts and bolts of sentences, including word definitions and how the parts of the sentence fit together.

- **Writing (Two sections, 60 minutes total)** The writing section tests your ability to express your ideas clearly, not only in style but also in word choice and grammar. It breaks down into two sections: multiple choice (35 minutes) and a short essay (25 minutes). The multiple choice section focuses on the fundamentals of writing: grammar, sentence completion, word usage, etc. The short essay focuses on how you use those fundamentals to express bind and support your ideas. According to the College Board, "The essay question will ask you to develop a point of view on an issue and support it with examples from your studies and experience." Remember, there is no wrong answer to the essay question, as long as you back it up!

Each of the three major sections of the SAT is graded on a scale from 200 to 800 (the highest possible score is a 2400). According to College Board, the average SAT score (of all test takers from across the country) is 1511 (502 in critical reading, 515 in mathematics and 494 in writing). The writing section has two sub-scores that do not affect your total score: multiple choice sub-score of 20 to 80 and essay sub-score of 2 to 12. Since the essay is not multiple choice, it is scored differently than the other sections. It is read by two high school or college teachers, each of whom give the essay a score from 1 to 6. Those scores are combined for your total essay score.

Like all standardized tests, there is one un-scored 25-minute section on the SAT. The College Board uses this section to test out new questions. You will never know which section it is, so it's in your best interest to try your hardest on all sections.

Preparing for the SAT can seem scary. In fact, there are movies about just how scary can be—in *The Perfect Score*, students are so overwhelmed, they plot to steal the answers! First: relax. There are many ways to prepare for the SAT that don't include theft. Companies, such as the Princeton Review and Kaplan, publish books and offer courses and tutors to help you prepare for the test. Private tutors and college counselors are also available to help you achieve your best score. Your high school guidance and/or college counselor will know the options available in your area. The most important part of preparing for the SAT is to be familiar with the test, the questions it asks and the time it takes. The College Board even publishes complete tests for you to use when preparing.

Visit Vault at **www.vault.com** for insider company profiles, expert advice, career message boards, expert resume reviews, the Vault Job Board and more.

VAULT CAREER LIBRARY

29

OCCUPATION PROFILES

Advertising Account Executive

UPPERS	DOWNERS
• Dynamic workplace	• Long hours
• Responsibilities and advancement opportunities	• Frequent travel
• Growing industry	• Low starting salary
• Young colleagues	• Potentially brutal office politics
	• Pressure to live/dress glamorously on an unglamourous paycheck
	• Need to kowtow to clients, deal with unpleasant people

Overview

An account executive (AE) handles the operational side of the advertising sector. The AE brings business clients to his advertising agency and then acts as a liaison between the two parties. He keeps track of what rival ad houses hold which clients, which firms are merging or working on new products, which are growing, and which are considering new agencies. After the AE finds a lead, he or she contacts that company to try to pitch an account. If the AE makes a good impression, the firm may ask for a formal pitch, in which the AE explains how the agency would present the company and its product. After securing the client, the AE is responsible for servicing and maintaining the account. The AE finds out what his or her client wants in an ad campaign and brings that information to the agency account team, which develops marketing strategy and creative concepts.

Perhaps the AE's most important job, however, lies in keeping the client satisfied while making sure everything falls within budget and the agency maintains its credibility. On the other side of the fence, negotiations with the creative department frequently require a great deal of diplomacy. Creatives and clients live in a perpetual state of mutual suspicion, and it's up to the AE to balance the tension between the creative department's integrity and the client's goals.

These days, potential hires with experience in Internet advertising or e-commerce are highly sought after. AEs live in a fast-paced and intense world of frequent travel, 50-hour work weeks and encroaching deadlines.

PERSONALITY MATCH	PERSONALITY MISS
• Good schmoozer	• Dependent on structure
• Creative	• Sensitive
• Persistent	
• Diplomatic	
• Detail-oriented	

Visit Vault at **www.vault.com** for insider company profiles, expert advice, career message boards, expert resume reviews, the Vault Job Board and more.

VAULT CAREER LIBRARY 33

Career Path

Most account executives start off as assistant AEs (at some agencies, this position is called an account coordinator). Just as the title suggests, an assistant account executive assists the primary AE, keeping tabs on all account activities. Assistant AEs have to be very detail-oriented and are often the ones who catch problems that have slipped by other team members. These assistants work closely with traffic and production coordinators, updating them on the status of projects and alerting them when an account is about to become active. They are also responsible for reminding co-workers about schedules and deadlines. Assistant AEs maintain a research file on each company account, which includes information on its competitors, press releases and past advertisements. Assistants spend a year or two in this position before moving up to the account executive position. (If an assistant spends more than two years at the junior level without being promoted, it's generally a signal that he/she will not advance within the agency.) After some years at an agency, AEs can move to the account supervisor level. Supervisors monitor several client accounts and the AEs who work on them. This is largely a managerial position, and supervisors are ultimately accountable for each AE's performance.

Advertising people frequently move from the creative side to account executive positions that feature a lot of client contact and networking/relationship-building possibilities. Turnover is especially high in the ad world—every day, accounts are lost, companies merge, and advertising budgets are slashed. The outlook for advertising is best in the ad capitals of the U.S.— New York, Los Angeles and San Francisco—where the median salary can be more than $10,000 higher than in other cities.

HOURS	SALARY
• Average about 50+ per week	• Median salary with less than one year experience: $34,785 • Median salary after 10 years experience: $48,455

Our Survey Says

One advertising executive describes his job as "a transfer of enthusiasm." Account executives are basically salespeople, and "they must be excited by the product" in order to create a convincing ad. AEs "make their own perks," as landing a big account benefits the agency as a whole and, subsequently, the individual in charge of the account. The job can be "unbelievably stressful" when it comes time to meet a deadline.

Account executives must be dressed to meet with (generally conservative) clients. Also, the challenges of keeping clients happy while not "irking creatives and stepping on their creative pride" is "a Herculean task." When the client is happy, one respondent explains, "everyone is happy, and when the client balks, it's my head." AEs consider their work a combination of "a science and an art." One AE says: "Clients can be unreasonable, demanding, horrible communicators and even demeaning at times. It is an absolute necessity to have exceptional people skills."

SKILLS TO ACQUIRE
• Bachelor's degree in advertising or related field
• Research skills

Accountant

UPPERS	DOWNERS
• Potentially high salaries	• Long hours
• Partnership opportunities	• High stress level
• Multiple career options	• Possibility of burdensome travel
• Wide variety of clients	

Overview

Accountants are usually depicted as bookish, anal-retentive social outcasts with few interpersonal skills. That image is changing, though, as accounting becomes an increasingly lucrative field. Public accountants are more than mere bean counters; they must interface with clients and handle sensitive financial information. During tax time, personal accountants are even occasionally thrust into the role of psychiatrist, as stressed-out clients unburden both business and personal concerns.

Public vs. private accounting

The accounting industry is typically divided into two segments: public accounting and private accounting. Public accountants mainly deal with financial accounting (the preparation of financial statements for external parties such as investors) and involves working for an accounting firm that provides accounting and tax advisory services to client companies. Depending on the accounting firm, these clients may be large corporations, regional businesses, small companies or individuals.

Private accounting refers to work for a non-accounting company as a staff accountant. Private accountants deal with both financial and management accounting. Because accounting staff work in many areas within a company (such as treasury and corporate finance, financial reporting, cost accounting, internal audit and business development), the potential job responsibilities for a private accountant vary, especially when compared to a public accountant's role.

There is also the chance of moving from public to private accounting or within the many sectors of public accounting. But it is rare to find someone who has actually made the switch between the two. Many accounting jobs are also available within all levels of government. Regardless of whether one chooses to be a public or private accountant, one thing is certain—come tax time (between January and April 15), you can kiss your spouse and kids goodbye and shack up at your job.

The Big Four

In the public accounting world, many accountants work for large professional service firms which, in addition to accounting, offer services such as management and IT consulting, financial advisory services and even legal advice. Those with a true familiarity with the modern accountant think of young, driven individuals with a working knowledge of many key business functions. The large international accounting firms (the Big Four) are now dubbed "key business advisors," and do more than file regulatory documents and double-check the arithmetic on company financial sheets.

For the modern professional, the changing face of accounting means the chance to analyze and influence corporate strategies, evaluate new business opportunities and develop a wide set of business skills. The robust economy of the 1990s and early 2000s led to the development of many new businesses; all requiring accountants to keep track of their books and their treasure troves of VC funds. Even though most businesses are now feeling the pinch of recession, accountants will always be in demand.

Visit Vault at www.vault.com for insider company profiles, expert advice, career message boards, expert resume reviews, the Vault Job Board and more.

VAULT CAREER LIBRARY   35

The CPA

While completing a four-year degree will garner you an entry-level job, advancing your career will most likely require becoming a certified public accountant, or CPA. The federal government regulates who can submit financial statements to the Securities and Exchange Commission (SEC), and any company that offers securities to the public or is listed on a stock exchange must submit an annual audited financial statement to the SEC. However, only a CPA can submit such an audit or sign an audit opinion. Therefore, becoming a CPA means the difference between an auditor and a senior associate, and is a very important step in any accounting career.

Becoming a CPA is no easy task, though many accountants think of it as a rite of passage. The American Institute of Certified Public Accountants (AICPA) is the national organization of CPAs and determines the requirements for admission, which include educational requirements (150 hours) and passing the CPA exam (think of it as the bar exam for accountants). It is a four-part exam administered over two days by the AICPA; each of the four parts must be passed. The four parts are: business environment and concepts; auditing and attestation; regulation; and financial accounting and reporting.

PERSONALITY MATCH	PERSONALITY MISS
• Anal	• Creative
• Analytical	• Disorganized
• Meticulous	

Career Path

The first place to start an accounting career is on campus. A bachelor's degree in accounting will lead to internships and entry-level jobs, as most of the big firms (especially the Big Four) recruit on college campuses. Master's degrees will also boost your employability.

Most major firms will not promote an accountant above a certain level unless he or she becomes a CPA. CPA certification carries with it authority and credibility, as well as a fat paycheck. Although you can be a successful accountant without becoming a CPA (e.g., as a public tax accountant), being a CPA widens your horizons considerably.

The traditional title groupings that most public accounting firms use are as follows:

• *Staff accountant* Usually, staff accountants have one to three years of professional experience. They perform the meat of an audit or tax work. Under the supervision of senior accountants, they work with the client to obtain information and determine the validity and accuracy of the accounting records.

• *Senior accountant* Usually, senior accountants have three to six years of professional experience. They are the glue that holds each project together, from planning to problem solving. They supervise the audit fieldwork of staff accountants and review their work products to ensure everything is thorough and properly documented. They are responsible for resolving any accounting issues as they arise. As the primary "workhorses" of an audit, many long-term public accountants describe working more hours at this level of responsibility than at any other.

• *Manager* The manager is ultimately responsible for managing client relationships. He or she performs a high-level review of all the audit work after the senior accountant is satisfied with the thoroughness and resolution of all issues. The manager also supervises, trains and evaluates senior accountants and staff.

• *Partner or senior partner* The main role of the partners is to maintain relationships with clients and oversee the business, in general. Younger partners are also on the lookout for new clients.

HOURS	SALARY
• Average about 50+ per week	• Average starting salary with a bachelor's degree: $46,718 • Master's degree: $49,277

Our Survey Says

Accounting is "not your standard 8-to-5 job." "Sometimes you can work 14 hours and then a week later, you can leave early," says one Big Four senior associate. While the job requires "monster hours," many employees are offered "flexible hours policies" in exchange for outstanding performance." And many accountants enjoy what they do, especially how expenses can tell a story, which makes the long hours not so bad. One tax associate says: "The best parts of my job are getting to see what some people make as far as salary and what they do, how much they give, etc. It's pretty interesting. It's also nice to see more detail about the companies you're doing work for as far as what they do." The job can be a "pressure cooker," and one auditor cites "being welcomed as warmly as a dental surgeon" as a still-prevalent attitude towards accountants.

The Big Four firms are becoming "less stuffy and hierarchical" than they used to be, "given the high turnover" and the "infusion of new blood" into the industry. Still, as one Big Four senior manager says, "I found public accounting to be a rigid and appearance-focused environment with many unwritten rules regarding mannerisms and work styles. However, I found this to be similar to many of the large corporate clients which I worked with during my tenure."

The accounting industry is a "dynamic" and "evolving" one, and the typical accountant is an "achiever" who is prepared for "hard work and long days." The training at the entry level is "fantastic," "intense but effective," and many accountants cite their "grueling beginnings" as "invaluable" learning experiences. "People joke about accountants," one quips," and we laugh—all the way to the bank."

SKILLS TO ACQUIRE

• Bachelor's degree in accounting
• Master's degree
• 150 hours of coursework for CPA certificate
• CPA exam

Visit Vault at **www.vault.com** for insider company profiles, expert advice, career message boards, expert resume reviews, the Vault Job Board and more.

VAULT CAREER LIBRARY   **37**

A Day in the Life: Staff Auditor

9:00 a.m.: I get into the office around the same time that everybody else does. From previous experience, I don't expect to hear from my superiors (i.e., senior auditor and/or manager) until at least 10 a.m. Based on my workload, I anticipate having two hours of availability today. Consequently, in accordance with the firm's policy, I e-mail the HR representative and inform her of my schedule. She e-mails me back, stating that one of the senior managers might need my help in the afternoon. For the next hour I read my e-mails, tie up loose ends from the day before and come up with the plan for the day. When working in the office, I usually sit with the other staff auditors, as the cubicles can only be used by the senior auditors and managers.

10:00 a.m.: Still have not heard back from my superiors. So I e-mail them the status of my work. Half an hour later the senior auditor calls me inquiring whether I have any questions and wondering how soon I will be done.

11:00 a.m.: The senior auditor stops by and asks me to put aside my current project. For the next 30 minutes, he wants me to make photocopies and deliver envelopes to the mailroom. Once these tasks are completed I continue the original project, which entails tying the quantity amounts on the holdings report to those found on the broker statement. I also have to foot (i.e., total) the holdings report and ensure that all the numbers in this report add up to the total holdings amount shown at the bottom of this statement.

12:00 p.m.: I e-mail other staff auditors wondering what they are doing for lunch. Most of us know each other from the summer internship (which took place between our junior and senior years in college). Turns out that half of my friends are at clients' sites and others are swamped with work. However, two of my buddies are heading to the local diner at 1 p.m. and I agree to join them. The work is monotonous, but the time is flying by. Once I finish working on the holdings report, I start working on the cash statement. For some reason, the total amount on the cash statement does not tie to the total on the bank statement, differing by $3 million. I call the senior auditor about this issue. He explains that the difference is due to timing. In other words, the bank statement does not reflect the $3 million deposit made at month end.

1:00 p.m.: Lunch.

2:00 p.m.: I check my voice messages and e-mails. One of the e-mails is from the client and is addressed to the entire team. Two weeks after requesting the documents, the client finally provided us with the necessary reports. This means that my workload is about to get heavier. Sure enough, 10 minutes later, I receive a call from the manager. He wants to meet with the entire team in order to come up with the plan of action and allocate the work. The meeting is scheduled to take place tomorrow at 10:30 a.m. I program it into my calendar and resume my activities from the morning.

3:00 p.m.: Receive a call from the HR representative. She wants to find out my availability for the rest of the day. I should be done with the current project by 4 p.m. and tell her so. She provides me with the name and phone number of a manager who is in need of assistance. I promptly call him. Turns out there is an Excel file that needs to be modified. The manager provides me with detailed instructions on what to do. This is an urgent project that needs to be completed by the end of the day. Once I get off the phone, I wrap up the morning project and commence work on the new assignment.

5:00 p.m.: I run into difficulty with the Excel file. The assignment requires me to use the "vlookup" function in Excel but I am not sure how to properly use this feature. I call the manager and he guides me through this issue.

6:30 p.m.: I finish the Excel project and e-mail it to the manager. I also e-mail the completed project from the morning to my senior for review and final sign-off. Before heading home I still need to update my hours in the system. Since I worked on two different projects today, I carefully allocate the proper number of hours worked to each of these projects. I organize my desk, turn off my laptop and start to head out. Glancing at my watch, the time reads 7. I am fortunate that this is not the busy season, when my departure time might be as late as 11.

Actor

UPPERS	DOWNERS
• Potential for fame and fortune • Creativity	• Job instability • Unpredictable hours • Low pay for most • Stiff competition

Overview

The working actor

While for many, thoughts of acting evoke images of the big screen and schmoozing with Hollywood stars or Broadway performances in front of packed theaters, for working actors the professional role is often much less glamorous. In addition to cultivating their acting techniques, aspiring actors must also hone their bartending, waiter/waitressing or secretarial skills because most actors' meager salaries will not keep the creditors at bay. In fact, fewer than 5 percent of all actors actually make a living at their trade alone, according to the U.S. Bureau of Labor Statistics.

The non-working actor

Far more common than the "working actor" is the actor who finds himself unemployed for long stretches of time and often working menial jobs. Throughout their careers, many actors subsist on part-time or night jobs so that they can have their days free to audition. They work as extras in films or on television shows or even nab small ("bit") speaking parts ("Would you like fries with that?"). Extras or bit part actors are usually paid between $40 and $100 a day, sometimes more if they belong to a trade union. If they are listed by a casting agency—such as Central Casting, a no-fee agency that supplies extras to all the major studios in Hollywood—some actors can rely on regular work. Stage actors often work with small repertory companies and off-off-off Broadway theaters while they wait to be cast in larger, more high-profile productions. For the non-working actor, the "open audition" becomes a way of life.

Agents and unions

The greatest opportunities for actors are in the nation's theater and film centers, New York City and Hollywood. Most agents are in these cities, and any actor who expects to get anywhere in the industry will eventually require an agent's representation.

Most working actors belong to union groups; in fact, actors just starting out complain that they have to belong to a union to get work. The Actors' Equity Association represents stage actors, and the Screen Actors Guild and Screen Extras Guild cover actors in motion pictures, television and commercials. The American Federation of Television and Radio Artists (AFTRA) represents television and radio performers. Some auditions are union-only; you have to belong to SAG, AEA or AFTRA to earn a chance at the part. Many actors who work more than a set number of weeks per year are covered by one of these unions, which provide health, welfare and pension funds, including hospitalization insurance. Under some employment agreements, Actors' Equity and AFTRA members have paid vacations and sick leave. Minimum salaries, work hours and other conditions are contingent upon varying agreements between employers and the unions that represent the actor.

Visit Vault at **www.vault.com** for insider company profiles, expert advice, career message boards, expert resume reviews, the Vault Job Board and more.

VAULT CAREER LIBRARY   39

PERSONALITY MATCH	PERSONALITY MISS
• Creative	• Analytical
• Sensitive	• Conservative
• Outgoing	• Shy
• Self-promoting	
• Discdiplined	

Career Path

Aspiring actors should build a strong repertoire of different roles and productions throughout their high school and college careers. Formal dramatic training is not a prerequisite, although the techniques and background education offered in college drama programs and dramatic arts schools in New York and Los Angeles can add to an actor's versatility and credibility.

The best way to start is in local and community theaters. Learning to sing and dance (or at least keep rhythm) is essential for stage actors. Sometimes modeling experience is helpful, as it teaches stage presence and movement, and assures the potential actor is at least photogenic. Agents are essential in an actor's search for work and contract negotiations; since the agent earns a percentage of an actor's earnings, they have a vested interest in the actor's success. As actors' reputations grow, they work on larger productions or in more prestigious theaters. Assuming a certain amount of talent or luck, actors also advance to lead or key character roles. A few actors move into acting-related jobs as drama coaches or directors of stage, television, radio or motion picture productions. An actor's career depends on training, skill, versatility, determination and luck. Some actors continue acting throughout their lives, though many leave the business because they cannot make a living.

HOURS	SALARY
• Average about 45 + per week	• Median hourly wage: $11.61
	• Average SAG member yearly earnings: less than $5,000
	• Top-level actor: $20 million per film

Our Survey Says

One respondent stresses "serious training" as a must for anyone pursuing an acting career, since "reputable teachers can properly prepare you for what you're going to be getting into." Beware of strangers trying to persuade you to sign or work with them, "particularly if they have never seen you act." For every nine auditions, you may get one job. This leads to another issue, that of finding an agent. The process can be "disheartening," but agents lend actors street value and credibility. When you do land an agent, "remember you are hiring them, only it won't feel like it."

Auditions are grueling: "Other auditionees will try to make you feel little and ugly and try to intimidate you." The best way to deal with such adversity? "Laugh it off," advises one respondent. According to another actor, landing a role is a Catch-22, since "you have to have had jobs to find jobs." Membership with SAG, the Screen Actors Guild, can cost upwards of

$2,500, and to get in you must show "past professional work." However, getting that professional work can be difficult without membership—another Catch-22. A seasoned actor gives the following admonition to those pursuing an acting career: "You must: (1) be exceptionally good and know it deep down; (2) have played outstandingly in a very good play, under expert direction, and gotten very good press; (3) be able to afford a long wait while earning a living at other pursuits; and (4) stuff anyone's advice and forge ahead on your own."

SKILLS TO ACQUIRE

• Drama degree is helpful

Visit Vault at **www.vault.com** for insider company profiles, expert advice, career message boards, expert resume reviews, the Vault Job Board and more.

V\ULT CAREER LIBRARY   **41**

Administration

UPPERS	DOWNERS
• Wide variety of career options	• Bosses can be difficult
• Promotion potential	• Sometimes uninspiring work

Overview

Office administrators are the linchpins of any office. They are the glue that allows the office to run. Managers, executives and virtually everyone in an office rely on administrative assistants and office managers to keep operations under control. Their responsibilities include scheduling appointments, acting as liaisons between executives or an entire company and clients, organizing and maintaining databases, and making social and travel arrangements. Administrative assistants also handle clerical duties like faxing, copying and answering phones; although depending on the size of the office, this may be left to a lower-level secretary.

But while administrative assistants, also called executive assistants, perform clerical tasks, their essential function is to serve as an executive's "right hand"—a trusty employee ready to fill in and add value wherever necessary. This function often means conducting research, preparing reports, writing speeches and answering correspondence.

Assistants who work in the medical or legal fields can expect to do work that is particular to their field. A medical assistant may help with a doctor's patients by taking their medical histories or making appointments for patients in addition to helping the doctor with materials for writing articles, attending conferences, and giving speeches. A legal assistant, likewise, assists the attorney with his or her professional needs, such as the many different types of legal papers they deal with—everything from complaints to motions, to subpoenas. And virtually all office assistants must be proficient in office software such as Microsoft Word and Excel, database programs like ACT, and financial software like Quicken. Ever-evolving software applications require that administrative assistants be efficient, skilled and open to change.

Administrative careers lend themselves to flexible hours and special arrangements, such as telecommuting and part-time work. Job-sharing arrangements, in which two people divide responsibility for a single job, have also become more popular.

Not all administrative assistants are lifers—many view their positions as prime opportunities to learn a business or to advance to positions with more responsibility in a company, especially in hard-to-crack industries like publishing and high tech.

PERSONALITY MATCH	PERSONALITY MISS
• Efficient	• Easily stressed
• Organized	• Sensitive

Career Path

A bachelor's degree isn't always required to become an administrative assistant; however, a love of education is vital. As office technology continues to evolve, retraining and continuing education remains an integral part of administrative jobs. Continuing changes in the office environment have increased the demand for administrative assistants who are adaptable and versatile. Testing and certification for entry-level office skills is available through the Office Proficiency Assessment and Certification program offered by Professional Secretaries International (PSI).

Visit Vault at **www.vault.com** for insider company profiles, expert advice, career message boards, expert resume reviews, the Vault Job Board and more.

VAULT CAREER LIBRARY 43

Qualified administrators who broaden their knowledge of the company's operations and enhance their skills may be promoted to executive assistant or office manager. Administrators with word processing experience can advance to positions as word processing trainers, supervisors or managers within their own firms. Their experience in administration can lead to jobs as software instructors or paralegals.

Breaking into the profession is not difficult, although starting out as an administrative assistant is unlikely, as many of the skills required are gained only through experience. As offices consolidate responsibilities, administrative assistants find themselves acquiring skills that might lead to a better job outside of their current company, where they may be overlooked for a promotion.

HOURS	SALARY
• Average about 40 per week	• Median salary for administrative and executive assistants: $37,240 • Median salary for administrative services managers: $67,690 • Top-level executive assistants can earn $100,000+

Our Survey Says

One administrative assistant describes the position as "the boss's confidant, office manager, supply and equipment purchasing manager, 'jack of all trades,' and master of office mysteries." There is real "diversity" to the position, adds another. While communication is "the most important tool in your portfolio" as an administrative assistant, you must at the same time maintain an "air of confidentiality" and, depending on for whom you work, you "may have to retain a great deal of information without speaking of it to anyone."

Many administrators enjoy the challenge of "being able to keep all the balls bouncing in the air and still get everything done at ground level." However, this position at the front lines of office activity means that assistants occasionally deal with the pressure of "being assigned something today and handling it yesterday." Also, our contacts say they are often expected to "know everything or at least know where to find the answers to everything." And the job can be thankless; assistants must be ready to correct problems without expecting "a pat on the back." Other downers include "problem people, cliques, gossips and backstabbers," although most assistants go into the job with the knowledge that office politics can be brutal.

SKILLS TO ACQUIRE
• High school diploma • Typing • Proficiency with office software

Anthropologist

UPPERS	DOWNERS
• Exposure to different cultures • Wide variety of career options	• Competition for teaching jobs • Difficulty getting funding for projects • Remote locations

Overview

Everything can be studied

That gesture a truck driver makes when you cut him off on the freeway has a complex linguistic and cultural history. Anthropologists make it their business to trace the history of language, customs, and how people interact with each other. The study of other cultures and how people have lived in the past has a great deal to do with how we behave today. Anthropology is an interesting and exciting profession.

Anthropologists do much of their fieldwork in other countries and often live for many years abroad, but some remain stateside and research American culture—everything from colonial customs to modern urban life. Anthropologists are academics and most are employed by universities, researching their areas of specialization and reviewing the work of their peers. Becoming an expert on a particular culture or region can require many years of study in a particular, often remote, location. This necessitates an extreme resolve, as one may be shut off from any and all communication with the outside world for extended periods of time. Cultural anthropology requires a broad base of knowledge, a strong command of foreign languages, excellent writing and research skills, and a passion for the subject. Formulating and understanding cultural theories requires a solid grasp of history, sociology, science and linguistics, which means that it takes many years of study, both in the classroom and outside, for an anthropologist to become an expert in his/her field.

A close community

Almost all of an anthropologist's professional time is spent with colleagues as they edit and critique each other's work. Anthropologists also spend a great deal of time writing grant proposals to get research funding. A necessary evil of the profession is that great discoveries require money, and a researcher must become a professional schmoozer in order to sell the federal government, universities and private grant-giving organizations on the value of their research. No anthropologist enjoys this process, which takes time away from the part of the job that they love. The adage "publish or perish" applies particularly to anthropology; anthropologists must publish articles in scholarly journals to foster awareness about their work and to build strong reputations among their colleagues. There is cutthroat competition among researchers for grant money.

Aspiring anthropologists must develop a specialty early on. One way of doing this is to spend time as a research assistant for professors. At the graduate level, students either decide to pursue their PhD or to leave academia to work at museums, travel abroad or enter a non-research related field. Cutting-edge anthropological fields of study deal with economics, such as emerging markets and race and gender studies. Some large corporations hire anthropologists to study their corporate structure. Teaching positions are very limited, so anthropologists specializing in newer and less-researched areas may have a better chance at being appointed to fledgling departments.

Visit Vault at **www.vault.com** for insider company profiles, expert advice, career message boards, expert resume reviews, the Vault Job Board and more.

VAULT CAREER LIBRARY 45

PERSONALITY MATCH	PERSONALITY MISS
• Conceptual • Empathetic • Inquisitive	• Closed-minded • Introverted

Career Path

Many anthropologists cite an early research assistant position with a favorite professor or mentor as their first real "job" in anthropology. Research assistants read and summarize articles, grade papers and transcribe interviews. After graduate school, many anthropology students travel or join the Peace Corps to gain practical experience with cultural observation. They continue to assist established anthropologists and acquire more responsibility; they actually get to write reports and conduct interviews.

After acquiring a PhD, most anthropologists seek out professorships at universities, where they derive their primary income from teaching and grants. The most renowned anthropologists are often asked to advise government agencies and companies on domestic and foreign endeavors. For successful anthropologists, pay after 10 years on the job is not astronomical, but is definitely comfortable.

HOURS	SALARY
• Average about 40 per week	• Median salary: $49,930

Our Survey Says

Anthropology is "more a field of study than a type of job." Preparation for the field consists of "sitting and talking with people," "living in their communities, bouncing their babies, putting Band-Aids on their cuts, sharing food and stories," and, as another respondent says, "sometimes unintentionally being an annoyance to them." The academic market for anthropologists is "limited," so some find it "more profitable" to become consultants to businesses examining "corporate social structures" or on development projects overseas, "including health care development." The knowledge and perspective that anthropology provides can be used "in a great many ways." One anthropologist says he went into the field because he had been a Peace Corps volunteer for two years after college, "teaching school in Africa." Other people work for "organizations like Oxfam or Teach For America—anything that will give you a perspective on other cultures." The initial pay is "low and the work is often demoralizing," and "you feel like you're wasting your time" until "you get into the field and start doing your own work." Then, anthropologists say, "there is no more rewarding life."

SKILLS TO ACQUIRE
• Master's degree or PhD • PhD required for most university teaching positions • Statistics and quantitative reasoning

Architect

UPPERS	DOWNERS
• Partnership opportunities	• Long hours
• Wide variety of career options	• Slow advancement
• Tangible results	• Grueling training process
• High job satisfaction	

Overview

Look around you. Whether you're sitting at your desk in your home or outside in a park surrounded office buildings, chances are you can see architecture. While glamorous skyscrapers and revolutionary structures make up a large part of architecture, there is much more to the field. Architects are involved in the construction process—from site selection to the project's completion.

Building from the ground up

In addition to years of technical training and an extensive licensing process, architects must also possess well-developed communication skills. On any given project, architects will work with clients, engineers, urban planners, interior designers, landscape architects and construction crews, among others. They must be able to understand and coordinate the information they receive from all those different people and teams, and then turn around and communicate their own vision (incorporating the new info) to those people. It is a compromise of creative designs, client demands, governing codes and rules and regulations.

Pre-design services include feasibility and environmental impact studies on possible sites. During the design process, an architect can draw inspiration from many sources, including art, philosophy, nature, and the practical purpose the buildings will serve. Once the client approves the design, it is developed to integrate heating, cooling, electrical and plumbing systems. Structural design also shapes the final version of the project. Since they assume legal responsibility for all projects under their name, architects must also incorporate all the laws and regulations that apply to a project. For this reason, the architect must visit the building site often during construction to ensure that the project is being built according to the plans and other construction documents.

Architects can specialize in building types (offices, hospitals, airports or housing) or different phases of the process (planning, construction management or design). The many years of training expose prospective architects to all parts of the industry and allow for participation in the wide range of architectural services.

The importance of intern-architects

Entry-level workers are called intern-architects. While preparing for the Architect Registration Examination (ARE), they are provided with practical work experience; this training period follows the completion of a bachelor's or master's of architecture degree. Duties of an intern-architect center on the use of CAD, or computer-aided design technology. They also research building codes and materials, and write specifications for new building materials, installation criteria and similar details.

Visit Vault at **www.vault.com** for insider company profiles, expert advice, career message boards, expert resume reviews, the Vault Job Board and more.

VAULT CAREER LIBRARY 47

An intern needs to be exposed to all aspects of the profession. To make sure the young architect is fully trained, in almost every state, interns must participate in IDP, the intern development program organized by the National Council of Architectural Registration Boards (NCARB). This program pairs an intern with professionals who help provide opportunities to accrue required credits in 17 different categories (including building cost analysis, design development, code research and project management). Once this program is complete, generally in about three years, an intern-architect can sit for the ARE.

PERSONALITY MATCH	PERSONALITY MISS
• Creative	• Unfocused
• Good with numbers	• Impatient
• Conceptual	• Rigid
• Patient	
• Problem solver	

Career Path

Before becoming an architect, all 50 states and the District of Columbia require the completion of licensing requirements: a professional degree in architecture (bachelor's or master's degree), a period of practical training (internship), and a passing score on the ARE. Most states require an accredited degree to be from one of the 114 schools certified by the National Architectural Accrediting Board (NAAB); however, a handful of states will consider other certified degrees or assess eligibility based on work experience.

The traditional degree is from a five-year bachelor of architecture program, but for students with an undergraduate degree in architecture or a related area, many schools offer a two-year master's program. Students with no previous architecture training and a degree in another field must enter a three- or four-year master of architecture program. Regardless of educational background, anyone interested in a career in architecture should pursue hand drawing and sketching. This is one of the most important stills that an architect will continue to use throughout his career. Additionally, several states currently require continuing education to maintain a license, and many more are adopting similar educational programs.

Advancement for architects follows a slow schedule based on years of experience. Architects without a degree from a NAAB program have a limited shelf life in the industry, and little chance of promotion. However, the talented and persistent can be well rewarded. Successful architects eventually become partners with a firm and can earn up to $100,000 a year. And then there are the handful of celebrity architects who are regularly commissioned to build new and exciting buildings and whose buildings are recognized as art, such as Frank Gehry, Renzo Piana, Zaha Hadid and Steven Holl.

Still, many architects prefer to circumvent the glacier-slow advancement process and open their own firms. Solo practitioners make up one third of all architecture firms, and another third are small firms of two to four employees.

HOURS	SALARY
• Average about 40 per week	• Median salary: $49,930
• Cyclical periods of 50+ per week	

Our Survey Says

Many architects bemoan the "tedious and dry" work they have to do when they are starting out in the field and "it can be a very demanding job, meeting deadlines, producing drawings, building models, etc.," but those with "enough faith in what they will one day be able to do" persevere in hopes of landing a position with an established firm. Architects also recognize the stiffness of the competition in the industry, and feel "an intense pride" to be doing the work they are doing, "even when the day is filled with paperwork." Luckily, once they reach that coveted position, architects enjoy room to be creative and the responsibility for different projects. Says an architect at a consulting firm, "Architecture offers great diversity in what one does from day to day. It's one of the things I truly love about my job."

Architects are not in the profession for the money. As one contact explains about the compensation in the industry, "the pay has to be superseded by the joy of the work itself," and no architect is planning to "get rich." In fact, architects are the worst paid of the licensed professions (including lawyers and doctors) and are the most likely to be affected by an economic downturn. Luckily, architects look forward to "a comfortable life surrounded by interesting people." And the profession can be "flashy" and "people are impressed when they hear you're an architect," contacts report.

SKILLS TO ACQUIRE

- Professional degree in architecture (bachelor's or master's)
- Practical training or internship
- Passing score on all sections of Architect Registration Examination (ARE)

A Day in the Life: Principal at Architecture Firm

9:00 a.m.: Arrive at the office. Check with the administrative staff for messages and the day's schedule. Return e-mails and phone calls, particularly regarding East Coast projects, so they get any information they need before the close of business (considering the three-hour time difference). Deal with any pressing administrative issues and make task lists for the day.

10:00 a.m.: Since it's Monday, conduct a project meeting with all the managers to review pending and upcoming issues on all projects. Afterwards, have meeting with administrative staff to review the coming week and all scheduling and administrative issues. On other weekday mornings, attend construction meetings at project sites with the clients, contractor, decorator and any necessary subcontractors. These meetings can last several hours or consume the majority of the day.

12:00 p.m.: Break for lunch with Brian. We usually go "off campus" and discuss any urgent issues, calendar issues or projects, potential clients, etc.

1:00 p.m.: Address project issues. Conduct client meetings.

3:00 p.m.: Deal with paperwork of various kinds: memos, project correspondence, billing. Read all mail, review accounts payable. Spend time directing staff on both administrative and design issues. Deal with contracts and proposal packages for new clients. Some days, have to pick up daughter from school and spend the afternoon with her; when this occurs, work from the home office, which is connected electronically with the office server.

Visit Vault at **www.vault.com** for insider company profiles, expert advice, career message boards, expert resume reviews, the Vault Job Board and more.

VAULT CAREER LIBRARY   **49**

A Day in the Life: Architect at a Consulting Firm

Vault spoke with an architect at a consulting firm specializing in building envelope design. Here is a general day in the life for him.

Each morning I usually arrive around 9 a.m. I check my e-mail and review what is still to be completed on the number of ongoing projects.

Around 10 a.m., if need be, I head out to one of the construction sites in the city to review the progress of installation. I speak with several people on site about the current conditions and monitor the installation to see that it conforms to the agreed upon specifications.

At 12:30 p.m., I will have returned to the office and start putting together a report of today's progress for the design team to review. Any issues or problems that come up will be in these reports and they are a way to assure that the installation is properly conducted.

After lunch, depending on the day, I:

- Work with colleagues on new projects
- Review shop drawings
- Attend design meetings both in and outside of the office

Each day, I leave around 6 or 7 p.m.

Architecture offers great diversity in what one does from day to day. It's one of the things I truly love about my job. With great diversity comes great uncertainty in the day-to-day happenings.

Art Dealer

UPPERS	DOWNERS
• Possible proximity to masterpieces • Sophisticated work environment • Interesting people • Travel	• Long hours • Pay by commission • Difficulty building a client base

Overview

Not your standard job

On television series *Sex and the City*, Kirstin Davis plays an intelligent art dealer named Charlotte York. Unique access to top art collections from around the world and sophisticated social and professional circles give art dealers a certain shine—enough to be idealized on television, anyway. The Charlotte Yorks of the world must have an eye for what's hot and keep their fingers on the pulse of trends in the art world. They must also anticipate what will appeal to their current and prospective clients and which artists will make or break their galleries. Success at the job also entails playing to people's personalities to build a base of clients. In the art business, much of a dealer's success depends on her network, which includes artists, critics and collectors.

Concentration

Most dealers concentrate on a specific genre of art, such as expressionist, pop, folk (outsider) or contemporary art. Many art dealers who are starting their collections and galleries have a safety net of savings, trust funds or loans to sustain them while they go through the difficult process of acquiring clients and building a reputation. The business isn't for wallflowers, as meetings between dealers and prospective clients and artists take place at parties, auctions and gallery openings. It also helps to be a bit of a risk taker because the profession is anything but stable. The art market depends on the health of the economy, and one dip in the market can force a small gallery owner or independent art dealer out of business. Most dealers have degrees in art history and start out in the industry as assistants. Others have extensive collections themselves and then decide to get into the business.

PERSONALITY MATCH	PERSONALITY MISS
• Creative • Sophisticated • Outgoing • Penny-pinching	• Risk-averse • Poor money manager

Visit Vault at **www.vault.com** for insider company profiles, expert advice, career message boards, expert resume reviews, the Vault Job Board and more.

VAULT CAREER LIBRARY 51

Career Path

After obtaining undergraduate and/or graduate degrees in art history, or after having cultivated a specialization, individuals who want to become art dealers get in on the ground floor at galleries or auction houses such as Christie's or Sotheby's as assistants. It's at this point that they learn how to develop the business and interpersonal skills that will allow them to establish their own businesses. Would-be art dealers also work in art museums as curators or even docents as they decide what to specialize in. After a few years, an aspiring dealer should be confident that he or she can spot the artists that will be successful. People who are able to withstand market shifts and build their clientele after 10 years should have a strong reputation and count museum curators among their clients.

HOURS	SALARY
• Average about 40 per week	• Average entry-level salary: $20,000

Our Survey Says

The art dealership field "is not easy to earn a living in by any means." It's expensive to run a gallery and to "run it right." Those who succeed usually do so because they know how to "pinch pennies where it counts." Unfortunately, "staffing falls into this [penny-pinching] area," so don't expect to make much and "you won't be disappointed." One insider notes that many "gallery people" could "very easily earn more waiting tables in a restaurant." As dealers' sales abilities and expertise grow, they experience "slight income increases," and it "doesn't hurt to build a client base." As far as the perks go, "there are few if any." The job consists of "long hours, hard work, tough negotiations, possibly a great deal of travel and very little time to yourself."

One art dealer says that some days he "feels like a babysitter to the rich and famous who treat you like the favorite house pet of the moment." Art dealers "grow tired" of telling "would-be artists that they just don't have what you're looking for and possibly permanently destroy the hopes someone may have had about making art their life." On the upside, they do "see lots of wonderful art" and meet "high-profile, fascinating people," some of whom "will actually become friends." The art world is "fun and trendy," and galleries are "pretty chi-chi." Also, the art field seems to be "one of those few vocations where what you do and who you know matters more than what the color of your skin or your gender is." In sum, insiders say, "the job is not all bad, but it's hardly a glamorous life." If you survive "with sanity intact," you "might be able to look back on your life and say it was all worth it."

SKILLS TO ACQUIRE
• Bachelor's and/or master's degree in art history
• Knowledge of art
• Business and accounting skills
• Foreign languages
• Research abilities

Attorney

UPPERS	DOWNERS
• High salaries • Large-firm perks such as firm retreats and free meals	• Long hours • High stress level • High level of dissatisfaction

Overview

No respect

Question: "What do you call 5,000 lawyers on the bottom of the ocean?" Answer: "A good start."

So the joke goes—one of thousands of wisecracks about a profession that just doesn't get much respect these days. Lawyers are blamed for many of society's problems, particularly of thwarting business growth with an ever-increasing flood of litigation.

I want my lawyer

Despite their sometimes dismal reputation, lawyers are an essential force in virtually every aspect of modern society. Many lawyers work as associates in large firms, where they engage in corporate transactional work (including mergers & acquisitions) or litigation (typically commercial disputes, with some "white collar" criminal defense). Other lawyers work in smaller firms and may specialize in such areas as divorce or tax law. Many lawyers spend a few years at large firms and move on to work as in-house counsel at corporations, where the pace is slower. Some law school grads elect to work directly in criminal law, where they help defend or prosecute accused criminals. Finally, a sizable contingent of lawyers work at public interest organizations, where the pay is comparatively low but the satisfaction can be high.

Long hours, high pay

Whatever their focus, most lawyers's careers are arduous. While some big firm lawyers may have sleek offices with beautiful views, they must labor in those offices for an average of 12 to 14 hours a day. Attorneys must also put up with intense stress, a formal dress code (although this is beginning to change in some legal circles), and a culture that values workaholism. Add to this the fact that few young lawyers will make partner, and you have a profession that some view as tedious and disillusioning.

Nevertheless, some lawyers are delighted with their chosen field. The financial rewards can be substantial, as partners at top firms make millions of dollars. Even first-year associates at the largest firms enjoy starting salaries of $160,000. Lawyers at the top of the industry also have the opportunity to work on headline-making deals and cases with global implications. For those willing to endure long hours and high stress, law can be a lucrative and intellectually rewarding career choice.

PERSONALITY MATCH	PERSONALITY MISS
• Detail-oriented • Driven • Tenacious	• Unassertive

Visit Vault at **www.vault.com** for insider company profiles, expert advice, career message boards, expert resume reviews, the Vault Job Board and more.

VAULT CAREER LIBRARY 53

Career Path

Upon graduating from college, an aspiring lawyer must take the law school entrance exam (the LSAT) and then go through three years of law school, with summers spent in internships or clerkships at law firms. After passing the bar exam, an associate at a law firm might spend up to eight years at a firm, with the ultimate goal of becoming a partner. There are also many legal jobs within government at in the federal, state and local levels. Alternately, a lawyer could aspire to become a judge or law school professor—positions with lower pay but high amounts of prestige.

With over one million lawyers in the United States alone, there are many different options for those fresh out of law school. Fierce competition for legal talent continues to escalate the starting salary for top firms in major cities. The reality, though, is that those searching for—and getting—the big bucks straight out of law school are usually educated at the elite institutions, i.e., the top 20 or 25 of the 190 accredited U.S. law schools.

HOURS	SALARY
• Average about 55 per week (more for first- and second-year associates)	• Median salary: $88,280 • Starting compensation at top New York, San Francisco, Los Angeles, Boston and D.C. law firms: $160,000+

Our Survey Says

The law profession may be the ultimate example of the "golden handcuffs" dilemma. On one hand, law school graduates who work in large firms generally "rake in the cash" and enjoy status "that is second only to physicians." As one contact puts it, "there's a reason why your mom wants you to marry a lawyer." If you want "easy admission to the local country club" and "plenty of expense account dinners," this is the field worth considering.

But big bucks, exalted status and plentiful perks come at a high price. More than a few respondents warn of the "stultifying lifestyle" that involves "endless hours," "monotonous work" and "sinking morale." A few complain about "overweening" partners "who will remind you that you are beneath them" and "who will make sure that you don't leave the office before 10 p.m." Says one respondent, "At my firm, they want you to get your work done—and done perfectly. If you don't, they get angry." All of this translates into a profession in which "many of us would be doing something else if we had the chance." Despite this low morale, however, law schools have no shortage of applicants who see law as a means of "doing some good in the world" or at least "making some fast loot while impressing your neighbors." For those who are "analytical," "willing to take orders," and "anal or at least willing to work with anal people," law may be a good choice. Just "know what you're getting into."

SKILLS TO ACQUIRE
• Law degree (JD) from an institution accredited by the American Bar Association • Passing the state bar exam

A Day in the Life: Assistant District Attorney

9:00 a.m.: Arrive at office, check e-mails and get files and paperwork for court.

10:00 a.m.: Arrive at court for multiple issues, including an arraignment for a burglary case, hearings for drug possession cases, money laundering case and attempted murder case. Speak with court clerks while clients arrive and judge hears various issues.

12:15 p.m.: Meet opposing counsel for plea bargain agreement for drug possession case.

1:00 p.m.: Quick lunch at desk, looking over e-mails and phone calls. Wait for witness to show up at 2 p.m.

2:00 p.m.: Witness doesn't show. Work on research for motion on attempted murder case involving Fourth Amendment right of seizure.

3:00 p.m.: Brief interview with police officers on felony assault case.

3:30 p.m.: Witness for 2 p.m. finally shows up with father and sister. Conduct fact-finding issue on domestic violence case. Witness recants some testimony and father pressures her not to testify against her husband, leaving ADA uncertain as to strength of case.

4:45 p.m.: Contact court clerks regarding hearing status of various cases.

5:10 p.m.: Review documents for money laundering and call witnesses and corporate officers for interviews in the next few days.

6:15 p.m.: Head home.

A Day in the Life: Employment Litigator

Theresa Whitman

Associate, Employment Law Department

Paul, Hastings, Janofsky & Walker LLP

7:45 a.m.: Arrive at office; checked e-mail, voicemail and a few faxes.

8:00 a.m.: Edit an outline prepared within the firm that summarizes recent significant California employment law cases.

8:15 a.m.: Prepare to attend ex-parte hearing regarding an application by plaintiff to shorten time to file and have the court hear a motion to compel further response to interrogatories.

9:30 a.m.: Attend a hearing with a partner regarding cross-motions for summary judgment. The plaintiff's motion was denied and our client's motion was granted, resulting in a judgment against plaintiff on his entire complaint.

11:00 a.m.: Meet with senior associate to discuss preparing opposition to a motion to compel further responses to interrogatories to be heard the next day (the same matter on which I was in court earlier in the day for the ex-parte hearing).

11:30 a.m.: Prepare opposition to motion to compel further interrogatory responses.

12:30 p.m.: Review documents and deposition transcripts to prepare to attend expert witness deposition.

1:00 p.m.: Eat lunch on the way to expert witness deposition.

1:30 p.m.: Attend expert witness deposition.

Visit Vault at **www.vault.com** for insider company profiles, expert advice, career message boards, expert resume reviews, the Vault Job Board and more.

VAULT CAREER LIBRARY

55

4:00 p.m.: Continue to prepare opposition to motion to compel further interrogatory responses and supporting documentation.

7:00 p.m.: Meet with senior associate to receive feedback on opposition to motion to compel.

7:30 p.m.: Leave office and head home.

A Day in the Life: Corporate Law Partner

This day in the life is a snapshot of the life of a relatively young New York corporate partner who is also the mother of a young child.

6:15 a.m.: Wake up.

6:30 a.m.: Forty minutes on StairMaster with *The Wall Street Journal* and walkman; read front page, op-ed pages and "Money & Investing."

7:10 a.m.: Play with daughter (15 months old)—read books, play with toys, watch dogs, buses and taxi cabs from window.

7:30 a.m.: Make coffee and daughter's breakfast; drink coffee.

8:00 a.m.: Play with daughter.

8:30 a.m.: Nanny arrives. Discuss day and play with nanny and daughter.

8:45 a.m.: Check voicemail and e-mail; four new voicemail messages including voicemail from colleague regarding transaction for Client A—Client A wants to accelerate closing for end of month (two weeks away!)—proposed call at 4 p.m. on revised documents; get ready for work.

8:55 a.m.: Drink more coffee; get ready for work.

9:30 a.m.: Cab to office with newspaper; call assistant—no new messages; call associate re: transaction for Client A and get update on status; associate believes new proposed closing date is very aggressive particularly in light of annoying opposing counsel.

10:00 a.m.: Arrive at office; check voicemail and e-mail; receive call from Client B regarding an agreement that needs to be drafted relating to a deal that was recently closed; Client B needs letter agreement by following day.

10:15 a.m.: Call from Client C regarding new deal—wants to invest $25 million in company with publicly traded debt—Client C has worked with lead investor on transaction and wants to review, provide comments and sign off on documents by end of day; discuss transaction with Client C.

10:45 a.m.: Conduct conflicts search with respect to new target company for Client C.

10:50 a.m.: Receive call from associate regarding questions related to preparation of organizational documents for a start-up company (Client D); refer associate to examples of charter and bylaws we have prepared for similar clients and we discuss some of the key points in the documents and making sure that the start-up company will have the flexibility it needs.

11:00 a.m.: Review draft of investment agreement for Client C.

1:15 p.m.: Contact senior and mid-level associates to staff transaction for Client C; brief associates on background, timing and key points of deal.

1:30 p.m.: Order lunch and eat at desk while continuing to review investment agreement.

1:45 p.m.: Receive call from Client C; discuss significant deal points on new transaction with Client C.

2:30 p.m.: Conduct Internet research on potential new client in preparation for a lunch meeting with a potential new client the following day. Contact business development department to request relevant materials and press articles on our firm's practice and recent transactions.

2:45 p.m.: Meeting with associates regarding investment document related to new transaction for Client C.

3:00 p.m.: Begin to review revised equity documents (shareholders agreement, stock purchase agreement, registration rights agreement, charter and bylaws) regarding transaction for Client A in preparation for 4 p.m. call.

4:00 p.m.: Receive call from opposing counsel on matter for Client A—4 p.m. call has been pushed to 5 p.m. (thankfully).

4:10 p.m.: Client D (start-up company) calls with two of its founders. They have several questions on corporate governance issues and matters that need to be addressed in organizational documents. I propose call for following day at 10:30 a.m.

4:15 p.m.: E-mail associate working with me on organizational documents for Client D to confirm her availability for the 10:30 a.m. call.

4:16 p.m.: Continue to review documents on matter for Client A in preparation for 5 p.m. call.

4:45 p.m.: Call from Client B regarding changes in required letter agreement. Client needs revised letter by 7 p.m.

4:50 p.m.: Call associate on matter for Client B to confirm that associate is drafting agreement and discuss points raised by client. Continue reviewing documents for Client A.

5:10 p.m.: Meet with associate working on matter for Client A and discuss revised documents.

5:15 p.m.: Conference call begins with opposing counsel on matter for Client A; discuss remaining open points in stockholders agreement, stock purchase agreement, registration rights agreement, charter and bylaws. Develop list of open points to be discussed with our respective clients.

6:25 p.m.: Call ends. Associate and I call Client A to discuss open points in equity documents.

6:30 p.m.: Client C calls (and interrupts call with Client A) and would like me to join him in a meeting with the lead investor and lead investor's counsel on new matter. Meeting to begin at 7 p.m. Client would like us to first address the significant business issues with the lead investor and opposing counsel, then both clients will leave and he hopes that I can continue to work through the legal and contract drafting points with opposing counsel. The goal is to have a document ready to sign by later in the evening or the following day.

6:33 p.m.: Rejoin call with Client A; summarize significant open points based on 5 p.m. call and propose 9:30 a.m. call the following morning to review all open issues.

6:40 p.m.: Call senior associate on matter for Client C regarding impending meeting.

6:45 p.m.: Review draft letter agreement for Client B.

7:00 p.m.: Prepare for meeting and leave office with colleague to go to opposing counsel's office on matter for Client C.

7:05 p.m.: Meeting with client, lead investor and lead investor's counsel. Discuss and resolve several of the significant business issues.

8:30 p.m.: Client C leaves and my colleague and I continue to negotiate with lead investor's counsel regarding the remaining business and legal issues in the document. Together we develop a list of open business issues for our respective clients.

Visit Vault at **www.vault.com** for insider company profiles, expert advice, career message boards, expert resume reviews, the Vault Job Board and more.

VAULT CAREER LIBRARY

57

9:50 p.m.: Client C calls the conference room. He is transferred to another conference room where my colleague and I discuss the remaining open issues with Client C. I advise him of their proposals and suggest counter proposals. We discuss risks and benefits of deal and typical provisions for comparable transactions.

10:10 p.m.: We rejoin the main conference room with counsel for lead investor. The lead investor returns and Client C calls in. We discuss open points and resolve significant open points. Certain points will continue to be discussed following revised draft. Lead investor's counsel will revise document and circulate document overnight. We agree to review document and call opposing counsel midday after discussing revised document with Client C.

10:30 p.m.: Car home. Check voicemail. Five messages including two calls from junior associates on matter for Client C. I call associate and update him based on meeting. We discuss various issues in the meeting that will need to be confirmed in our due diligence.

10:45 p.m.: Arrive home. Check e-mail. Send responses to e-mail messages.

11:15 p.m.: Go to bed.

Outside New York, partners at top firms work a similar number of hours, but they tend to work them earlier in the day. Rich Gale, a partner at the Washington, D.C., office of Arent Fox, for example, gets in the office around 7:45 a.m. and stays until 7:30 p.m., usually five days a week, with an occasional weekend. These partners report that their schedules do not generally decrease as they advance at a large firm because the pressure to bill and record time to measure production doesn't go away.

Biologist

UPPERS	DOWNERS
• Flexible hours • Relaxed dress code	• Low starting pay

Overview

It takes all types

Biologists study the world around us—how living things work, change and affect each other and their environment. It seems that there are almost as many types of biologist as there are fauna and flora. Biologists are classified by the type of organism or by the life processes they study. For example, biochemists unravel the relationships between physiology and chemistry and the way living organisms metabolize, grow and reproduce. Microbiologists, on the other hand, study bacteria, algae and fungi; medical microbiologists study the cause of diseases and develop antibiotics. Other types of biologists include marine biologists, botanists, physiologists, zoologists, agricultural scientists and biomedical scientists.

Research

The essence of biology is research—both in the laboratory and out in the field. Some of the research is pursued simply to expand the knowledge of living organisms. Other researchers work on immediately applicable research, geared toward different goals such as developing new medicines, improving farming techniques or cleaning up the environment. Not only do biologists often work toward different ends, but they also have a variety of work environments to choose from. Some work at colleges and universities or for the federal government. Still others work for private companies, where the pay is high, but research opportunities relatively restricted (controlled by the employer). Often, private sector biologists work as consultants to businesses or in testing development for biomedical companies.

Working for the Man

One out of every three biological scientists is employed by federal, state or local government. Federal biologists work mainly for the Food and Drug Administration, the U.S. Department of Agriculture, the Departments of the Interior and even for the Department of Defense. Increasing interest in genetic mapping and biological terrorism, and the resulting flood of books and movies dealing with biological subjects has shone a spotlight on the work of biologists.

With this focus on their area of expertise, biologists are sometimes viewed as the crusaders, tackling the blights of the last century: global warming, depletion of the rainforests and AIDS. The majority of PhD-holding biologists work in colleges and universities, sharing their research with their colleagues and students. In general, career biologists work long hours, particularly those working in the public sector or doing independent research, because they are driven by a love for their subject.

PERSONALITY MATCH	PERSONALITY MISS
• Inquisitive • Open-minded • Aptitude for science	• Rigid • Conformist

Visit Vault at **www.vault.com** for insider company profiles, expert advice, career message boards, expert resume reviews, the Vault Job Board and more.

VAULT CAREER LIBRARY 59

Career Path

With a bachelor of science degree, aspiring biologists can start out in testing and inspection work or find positions as technical sales or service representatives for biomedical and pharmaceutical companies. However, those without advanced degrees have difficulty finding work in a lab or doing original research; most career biologists have a master's or PhD degree.

Master's holders work as research assistants for post-doctorate biologists or as managers and inspectors. Doctoral candidates engage in classroom and fieldwork, and lab research and must also write their thesis or dissertation. After earning their PhDs, new biologists often take temporary post-doctoral research positions, which provide specialized research experience. A PhD is a prerequisite for college teaching, independent research and advancement to administrative positions. For those interested in applied research, secondary school teaching, working for the government as inspectors, or in the business side of biology, a master's degree is sufficient.

Medical scientists who administer drug or gene therapy to humans, or who have any medical contact with patients, must have a medical degree in addition to the PhD.

HOURS	SALARY
• Average about 40 per week	• Median salary: $60,940 • Median entry-level salary (with a bachelor's degree): $34,953 • Average Federal Government biological scientist salary: $72,146

Our Survey Says

The hours of a biologist are "among the most flexible of any job." "Research is not a 9-to-5 job," says one biologist. "You may find yourself going to work in the middle of the night or on weekends." Some biologists at universities and colleges can feel a "publish or perish" mentality that will affect how much biologists are expected to work. But, "due to the level of independence in research jobs, this schedule doesn't seem to be too bothersome." Co-workers, who have committed their lives to science, are reportedly "dedicated and warm." And that high opinion goes beyond the laboratory; says one biologist, "another plus is the respect and image that most people give you when you tell them that you are a scientist."

Biologists' "corporate culture," so to speak, is dictated by their specialization and workplace. For many lab and research positions, "T-shirts and jeans are quite fine," and suits are seldom required. Biologist contacts we spoke to are satisfied professionals, "just happy to be doing something (they) care about and believe in."

SKILLS TO ACQUIRE
• Bachelor of science, master's or PhD degree

Brand Manager

UPPERS	DOWNERS
• Strong advancement opportunities	• Long hours
• Wide variety of career options	• Can be political and bureaucratic
• Travel	• Extensive travel

Overview

Brand fascination

Are you captivated by the variety of products you pass on your trips down supermarket aisles? Do you like to scrutinize particularly eye-catching cereal boxes or shampoo bottles? Do you watch TV commercials and wonder what type of consumers they're targeting, and how they're accomplishing those goals? Do you see spin-offs of existing products and think you can come up with better versions?

With an overflow of advertising emanating from mass media, and with an economy that lets the masses indulge in status symbols, we all live on a planet filled with brands such as Coca-Cola, Mercedes-Benz, Starbucks and the Gap. Furthermore, there are people who make a handsome living for creating and manipulating this branded world. These cognoscenti are marketers and brand managers. These are the people who devise new products. They also decide how to package them, how to price them and—most importantly—how to market them. Wall Street yanks on our purse strings, and Hollywood shapes our dreams and fantasies. But it's the brand managers who guide what we eat and wear, and they influence how we think about consumption in our society.

What is marketing?

Marketing encompasses a wide variety of activities. Some marketing positions are very close to sales, whereas others set overarching strategy. What marketing jobs have in common is the sense of ownership over the product or service, understanding customer needs and desires, and translating those needs into some kind of marketing communication, advertising campaign or sales effort. The manager of product or service marketing is called the brand manager, and he or she is the ruler of that marketing universe.

Careers within the marketing/branding arena are high profile. The business world has realized that strong brands and solid marketing programs drive shareholder value, and that companies can no longer make fundamental strategy decisions without truly understanding how to market a product. Today's business challenges—industry consolidation and deregulation, the quest for company growth and the emergence of new technologies—make marketers even more valuable. As a result of interactive media such as blogs, consumers have started to play a larger role in shaping brands and developing new products. Some brand managers focus specifically on how to brand products through the Internet.

The titles of brand manager and marketing manager are basically interchangeable. Some companies use one title, and some use the other. Brand management, however, implies more complete supervision of a product. The typical brand management framework gives a brand "group" or "team"—generally comprised of several assistant brand or assistant marketing managers and one supervising brand manager—responsibility for all matters relevant to its product or products. In actuality, the level of responsibility depends on the size of the company compared to the number of brands it has, the location of the brand group, and the company's attitude toward marketing.

Visit Vault at **www.vault.com** for insider company profiles, expert advice, career message boards, expert resume reviews, the Vault Job Board and more.

VAULT CAREER LIBRARY   61

PERSONALITY MATCH	PERSONALITY MISS
• Creative	• Sensitive
• Aggressive	• Easily stressed
• Multi-tasker	
• Flexible	
• Decisive	
• Tactful	

Career Path

Branding yourself

For marketing management positions, some employers prefer a bachelor's or MBA with an emphasis on marketing, though a wide variety of backgrounds is acceptable and common. Courses in business law, economics, accounting, finance, mathematics and statistics are also helpful. In highly technical industries, a BS in engineering or science combined with business savvy is essential.

Many companies fill jobs such as product or brand specialists by promoting experienced staff into the roles. However, firms such as Procter & Gamble and General Mills hire marketing and brand managers almost exclusively out of top MBA programs. At these top companies, a career in marketing management is the ticket to upper-level general management. MBAs start as assistant brand or assistant marketing managers, where they stay for 18 to 24 months. From there, they move to a brand manager position, first managing a small brand for a year or two, and then shifting to a larger one. Successful brand managers move on to manage a "category," such as detergents or cat food, and eventually to general management.

The marketing industry is very tight-knit, and the job market for brand managers is becoming increasingly competitive. There's also a significant amount of turnover, which means that marketers have numerous contacts in companies throughout the industry. This strong community creates an excellent networking environment. Headhunters will call you with job openings. It's also common for friends within the industry to tell a headhunter to contact you and see if you're interested in a position.

While certification for marketing managers is scarce in the industry right now, it is becoming increasingly popular and beneficial for prospectives to obtain one. Certification merely indicates competence in the field, but with growing competition in the market, this designation of professionalism will be useful. The Sales and Marketing Executives International program awards certification based on education and job performance; applicants must also pass a four-hour examination.

HOURS	SALARY
• Average about 50 per week	• Average starting salary: $40,161
	• Median salary: $98,720

Our Survey Says

Insiders say being a brand manager is "lots of fun." One associate brand manager explains, "Every day is different, and you're the hub of the wheel." The contact mentions that "perks like free products, trips, etc. don't hurt, either." Another marketing manager enjoys the "flexibility in work environment" as well as "networking with Fortune 500 clients." On the downside, hours can be long and "corporate bureaucracy is rampant."

Brand managers say it's helpful to be good with numbers. One insider explains that marketing "requires creativity," but "it still ultimately comes down to how much profit the ideas can make for the company." The brand manager adds that a big portion of the job "revolves around numbers (sales data analysis, income statement, consumer research data analysis, etc.)." Another insider advises, "You need to have a skill set across many disciplines." Although you don't need an MBA to go into the field, one branding consultant says, "if you want to move to upper management it will be critical."

When it comes to hours, brand managers generally enjoy more balanced lifestyles than people in other world-conquering industries such as investment banking, venture capital, media and consulting. For one thing, brand managers generally have consistent hours; they don't get calls at 3 a.m. telling them that the Indonesian rupiah is crashing, or that the mayor was just arrested for driving while intoxicated. Although brand managers travel for consumer research, commercial shoots and sales meetings, these gatherings are planned well in advance. Deadlines loom, but you usually have a good idea when you'll be able to leave the office.

Brand managers' hours vary from 9 a.m. to 5 p.m. during the off season, to 7 a.m. to 10 p.m. during planning season (planning season is usually a three-month period in the middle of the fiscal year when each product team is trying to develop marketing plans and recommendations for the following year). Hours can intensify during budget-preparing season, and one assistant brand manager reports working more than 60 hours a week for two or three weeks while preparing an annual plan. "It's usually not that bad, but there are long hours during peak periods," says a marketing manager at a major packaged foods company.

Because many major consumer goods companies are expanding overseas, international assignments often present themselves. According to one insider at a major company, "You must be willing to work overseas for five to eight years minimum." And although brand employees generally don't have to work ultra-long hours, "they want to know you'll stay in the office 24-7 if you have to."

People who work in brand marketing say the field offers excellent opportunities for women. "Half of my brand manager counterparts are women, with about the same proportion in junior marketing roles," reports one insider at a company that focuses on cleaning products. Says a marketing insider at another consumer goods company, "A lot of women do part time when they have families. You see a lot of families here, and women with kids. They do promote family in every way, which is great for women, as you are free to leave and take care of matters when you have to."

SKILLS TO ACQUIRE

- Bachelor's degree
- MBA for positions in top companies and senior-level jobs
- Certification from Sales and Marketing Executives International

Visit Vault at **www.vault.com** for insider company profiles, expert advice, career message boards, expert resume reviews, the Vault Job Board and more.

VAULT CAREER LIBRARY 63

A Day in the Life: Assistant Brand Manager

8:30 a.m.: Get into work. Listen to voicemails. Check e-mails. Print out calendar of today's events. Skim the Markets section of *The Wall Street Journal* to find out what's happening "on the street." Go to the cafeteria and grab breakfast. (Of course, you're only eating products that your company produces or has some relationship with!)

9:00 a.m.: Meet with market research department to discuss specifics of your latest round of quantitative research. You are trying to understand why people are not repurchasing your product, but you don't feel that the data presented actually answers your questions. You decide that you'll need to design another round of research—but where's the money going to come from?

10:00 a.m.: Budget meeting to determine how you will be spending second quarter funds. Given the decision to spend more money on research, you might need to cancel an instant redeemable coupon or a local promotion in a poorly performing market.

10:30 a.m.: You head to the long-awaited product development meeting. Your team has recently discussed reformulating your product to take advantage of new technology. This new technology may raise your product's performance levels, but it will cost more to manufacture and will take some advertising effort (and more money) to explain the changes to the consumer. The group must decide whether these changes are strategically and financially justified. As always, very few people agree. You decide to summarize all the costs and benefits to the project and present the issues to your brand manager at the status meeting you have scheduled for the end of the day.

12:00 p.m.: A fancy lunch with a *People* magazine salesperson. For months the magazine has tried to convince you that your product should be advertised in *People*. During lunch the represenative explains to you how the publication can effectively reach a healthy percentage of your target audience and how it can provide you with the extended reach you need to communicate with potential new users. You leave lunch with a fancy *People* backpack and a headache. Where can you find the money to add *People* to your media plan? Let's ask the media department.

1:30 p.m.: Media planning meeting. Because sales of your product have come in slightly under budget, you have been forced to give up 10 percent of your media budget. You now must meet with the media department to determine how to cut media funds without sacrificing your goals.

2:30 p.m.: Time to review changes to the latest advertising campaign. Your ad agency presented a new concept about three weeks ago that was a diamond in the rough. You and your brand manager made comments to the storyboard (drawing/copy that explains a commercial) and now you are anxious to see what the agency comes back with. You review the changes with the agency via conference call and promise to present the new work to your brand manager at your status meeting later in the day.

3:15 p.m.: Keep the ad agency on the phone and bring in the in-house promotions department. This ad campaign will be blown out into a promotional campaign in the top-20 performing markets in the country. You want to make sure that before you get the promotions people working on a concept, they agree with the agency on the strategy going forward. The following 45 minutes is a creative brainstorming session that offers wonderful possibilities. You promise to type all ideas up and distribute them to the group later in the week.

4:00 p.m.: Strategy development with sales manager. Your category manager is insisting that all brands work to gain a better presence in supermarkets. You meet with the regional sales manager to understand what types of strategies might work to get better shelf space and more consistent in-store promotions. Once you hear his/her ideas, you start to cost out options and see if this is possible within the current budget.

5:00 p.m.: Status meeting with brand manager. You present the proposal for new research as well as the implications of the new product development issue. You also review the latest advertising changes and the changes to the media plan. You aggressively present your data and your opinion and discuss these with your boss. The two of you decide on next steps.

6:00 p.m.: Back in the office you wrap up for the day. You spend an hour checking the 20+ e-mail/voicemail messages you received during the day but failed to return. You go through your inbox to read any documents relevant to your product. You start to attack all of the work you have to do and promise that tomorrow you'll block out some private time to make some progress.

Chef

UPPERS	DOWNERS
• Prestige	• Long hours
• Constantly surrounded by food	• High stress level
• Camaraderie	• Potential for career burnout

Overview

Hard, hot work in the kitchen

Want to be the next Rachael Ray or Emeril Lagasse? It takes a lot of work to get that cool white hat. Chefs work long and sometimes unconventional hours, oftentimes between 4 p.m. and 2 a.m.—and almost always on weekends and holidays. Their social lives are significantly altered as a result. Pay is relatively low, though executive chefs and culinary wizards at large city restaurants earn tasty salaries. Becoming a chef takes about 10 years of study, beginning with culinary school. Aspiring chefs usually work as unpaid apprentices while they're still in school to decide on a specialty of their own. Some people labor for years as prep chefs or sous chefs, looking for any opportunity to demonstrate their prowess to the head chef.

The years working toward chefdom aren't spent poring through cookbooks, either. The physical strain is enormous, as chefs must stay on their feet constantly. Cooking involves kneading, chopping and stirring, as well as lift heavy pots. Besides the stress associated with preparing food for hungry, critical customers, chefs also order food, create menus and manage large kitchen staffs.

In addition to the head (or executive) chef, the kitchen of a large restaurant is crowded with other chefs and cooks, including the sous chef, pastry chef and short-order cooks. A garde manger focuses on preparing cold foods. The sous chef, who is just underneath the executive chef, manages the logistics and staff of the kitchen. Some individuals, known as a chef de partie, or station chef, specialize in preparing certain types of foods or techiques—such as pastry or sauces. All positions in a kitchen are building blocks towards a career as a head chef.

Aspiring chefs gravitate to large urban centers, where there is an abundance of restaurants and chefs who can serve as mentors and exchange ideas and food innovations. Executive chefs often partner with financial restaurateurs to open their own restaurants. One chef who has done this successfully is David Bouley of the world-famous and exclusive Bouley in New York. Chef Kevin Rathbun also worked with financial partners to open his first restaurant in Atlanta in 2004, and he now runs several of the city's best eateries. These top chefs spend more time associating with patrons and investors and away from the kitchen. Some well-known chefs also earn recognition and added income by writing cookbooks or becoming stars on the Food Network.

PERSONALITY MATCH	PERSONALITY MISS
• Organized	• Emotional
• Opportunistic	• Pessimistic
• Creative	

Visit Vault at **www.vault.com** for insider company profiles, expert advice, career message boards, expert resume reviews, the Vault Job Board and more.

VAULT CAREER LIBRARY 65

Career Path

An aspiring chef must spend either two or four years at an accredited cooking school, followed by at least five years of working under head chefs at different restaurants as an apprentice. Most chefs start out as support staff in the kitchen, with a special task to perform, such as preparing vegetables. Young chefs aim to be sous chefs under the top brass at the best restaurants, particularly in large cities. They often work at several restaurants, acquiring experience under different mentors before they decide on a specialty.

People who are able to withstand the high stress and pressure of the job will probably find themselves at the helm of a kitchen as head chef within 10 years. A head chef will direct a kitchen staff, in addition to preparing meals, or strike out to start his or her own restaurant.

The outlook for would-be chefs is good. The Bureau of Labor Statistics expects that job openings for cooks, chefs and other food preparation employees will be ample through 2016. But, as always, competition will be steep for the top jobs in the kitchens of fancier, trendier restaurants.

HOURS	SALARY
• Average about 50 per week	• Median salary for head cooks and chefs: $34,370 • Median salary for restaurant cooks: $20,340

Our Survey Says

Chefs view themselves as "bringing quality to life," and treat the profession as seriously as any corporate job. Professional cooks love the creativity of their careers. One insider explains, "I like spending my time at the kitchen and experimenting with new recipes."

Being surrounded by the "beauty and the sensuality" of the food is "what every chef lives for" and why most of them would not dream of another profession. "For most of us, we have no other choice in life," explains one chef. "It is grueling and heartbreaking," but the rise up the ladder can be exhilarating, says another.

Aspiring chefs train under mentors they have "patterned their whole careers after." The training process is "so grueling, you think you can do anything when you come out—even major surgery." The dinner rush, between 6:30 p.m. and 9:30 p.m., turns the kitchen into an "intensive care unit"—high stress, high precision. If everything is working—and even sometimes when it's not—this is the time all cooks feel a head rush. One chef describes the routine as "exploration" because "you can truly forge your own route."

One source says that chefs are currently in great demand. The insider says that, as a result, there are lots of opportunities "all over the world" and in a variety of settings. The chef adds, "I can work on a cruise liner or in a five-star hotel."

SKILLS TO ACQUIRE
• Certification from two- or four-year cooking school (preferably one certified by the American Culinary Federation) • On-the-job training in kitchens

Chemical Engineer

UPPERS	DOWNERS
• Good pay • Wide variety of career options	• Some initial grunt work • Weird smells

Overview

The work of chemical engineers can be seen in virtually every aspect of our lives. For example, chemical engineers create toothpastes designed to whiten your whites, and work to ensure that your glasses are shatterproof. In short, chemical engineers apply the principles of chemistry to engineering, seeking to develop ways of producing and using chemicals for practical purposes.

Chemical engineers are the "jacks of all trades" in the engineering profession; their knowledge is broad enough to cover an expansive range of fields, such as physics, mathematics, and mechanical and electrical engineering. For example, one chemical engineer may work on creating a new chemical, another may find ways to maximize the chemical's production, and another may discover the optimal ways to use the new chemical. As they continue their work, chemical engineers will focus on one chemical process or a specific area that becomes the center of their career. Chemical engineers generally work in teams, which fosters an environment at once competitive and cooperative.

About 70 percent of the chemical engineers in the U.S. work in the manufacturing industry. Others work for research and testing firms, engineering consulting firms or as independent consultants. Consulting firms and consultants work on a contract basis on projects such as designing chemical plants.

PERSONALITY MATCH	PERSONALITY MISS
• Detail-oriented • Perceptive • Cooperative	• Impatient • Scatter-brained

Career Path

Most entry-level engineering jobs require at least a bachelor's degree in engineering. A master's degree or PhD in chemical engineering is encouraged. Furthermore, earning that graduate degree will require you to do research, which will translate to hands-on experience when you're looking for your first job.

Entry-level chemical engineers do a lot of number-crunching, tests and experiments. Within a year or two, engineers graduate to projects with greater responsibility. After gaining experience with a corporation or the government, some engineers choose to strike out on their own, establishing engineering consulting firms or starting their own engineering companies, where they pull down six-figure salaries.

Visit Vault at **www.vault.com** for insider company profiles, expert advice, career message boards, expert resume reviews, the Vault Job Board and more.

VAULT CAREER LIBRARY 67

HOURS
• Average about 45 per week

SALARY
• Median salary: $78,860
• Average starting salary with a bachelor's: $51,356
• Master's: $59,240

Our Survey Says

If you enjoy "fixing things, improving things, and creating new and innovative processes," then you might just want to be a chemical engineer. The hours vary depending on the employer and position. Says one chemical engineer, "There's a lot of work to get done and it can be done in a variety of settings, including occasionally working from the home office or a coffee shop." Some chemical engineers who work for corporations handle "swing shifts," while others work the regular 9-to-5 schedule. Chemical engineers who work in the field generally have more flexible hours and have to wear "clothes that can get dirty." Engineers who meet with clients must dress in "business fatigues," says one engineer, dryly referring to suits.

From chemical engineering, one can "go into almost any field," as chemical engineers work with all types of other engineers. However, be prepared to log long hours in developing this wide expertise; many chemical engineers log "40 to 100 hours a week in classes to learn new skills." Having a "good mentor" in college or graduate school "makes for more successful engineers." Once you're done and have that PhD, "you do get a lot of instant respect due to the academic rigor inherent in the achievement."

SKILLS TO ACQUIRE
• BS, MS or PhD
• General computer and statistical skills

Chemist

UPPERS	DOWNERS
• Good pay	• Exposure to potentially harmful chemicals
• Wide variety of career options	

Overview

We make it, you use it

Chemicals are all around us—they make up everything we see and use. Nowadays, if you eat it, clean with it, put it in your car or feed it to your plants, it probably came from a chemist's lab. Chemists are in the business of researching the properties, composition and principles of elements and compounds—and they apply basic chemical principles (like polymerization) to developing new products and processes. Chemists work in every sector, including academia, the private sector and the government.

Most chemists work in research and development—they learn about different chemicals and develop ways to use them—and there are many new products made every day. In the private sector, for example, it is the chemist who instructs plant workers on manufacturing techniques, monitors automated processes to ensure proper product yield and tests samples for quality. Chemists with business savvy and a taste for schmoozing apply their expertise to sales and information distribution at manufacturing companies.

Specialization

Since chemistry is a broad discipline, most chemists specialize in a subfield. For example, analytical chemists are theorists who identify the structure and composition of substances and can break down the concentration of certain compounds in air, water and soil. Organic chemists focus on carbon-based compounds used in prescription drugs and fertilizers. Physical chemists work on what one might call "big reactions," studying atomic and molecular reactions. More than half of all chemists spend their time analyzing data and constructing models; the remainder are in the field, collecting samples of pollutants or working in chemical plants. Regardless of a chemist's chosen specialization, it is desirable to have skills in other areas, including economics and marketing, as chemists are increasingly more involved in the full development of a new product.

PERSONALITY MATCH	PERSONALITY MISS
• Analytical	• Unfocused
• Meticulous	• Undisciplined
• Inquisitive	

Visit Vault at **www.vault.com** for insider company profiles, expert advice, career message boards, expert resume reviews, the Vault Job Board and more.

VAULT CAREER LIBRARY   69

Career Path

People with bachelor of science degrees in chemistry are particularly marketable if they have a strong liberal arts background. Most undergraduates do not focus on a specific field of chemistry to avoid limiting their job prospects. In government and industry positions, entry-level chemists with bachelor's degrees assist senior chemists in research and development laboratories. Sometimes they undertake product testing and analysis in research positions, but these are technical niches with limited advancement possibilities.

Research chemists, particularly in the pharmaceutical industry, require a PhD and several years of post-doctoral experience. A PhD is preferred not only for research positions but for administrative ones, as well. Chemists who work in sales, marketing or professional research positions often move into management after a few years. And for academic teaching positions, that PhD is a must.

HOURS	SALARY
• Average about 40 per week	• Median salary: $ 59,870
	• Average entry-level salary, bachelor's:$41,506
	• Average entry-level salary, master's: $ 44,500
	• Average entry-level salary, PhD: $63,250

Our Survey Says

Chemists are among the few professionals who "apply almost all [they] learned in school." Lab work, particularly in the environmental industry, is "pressure-inducing and stressful." Starting out with a strong idea of what field most interests you is "imperative," as many chemists report that their first few years were spent "floundering, trying to find a niche." One chemist advises that a beginning chemist work in the area that stimulates him or her, "even if the money is not that great to begin with." Mentors "are instrumental" in learning the ropes and offering career guidance.

The workplace for chemists is "perpetually evolving," and the knowledge to "function successfully" changes every few years, which makes it necessary for chemists to keep up by taking continuing education courses and reading the latest trade journals.

SKILLS TO ACQUIRE
• BS, MS, PhD in chemistry
• Some liberal arts classes

Child Care Professional

UPPERS	DOWNERS
• Flexible schedules	• Low starting pay
• Working with children	• Enormous responsibility
• High levels of personal satisfaction	• Constant exposure to illness
	• High stress level
	• Physical exertion
	• Nagging parents

Overview

The toughest boss

Children are among the toughest of bosses: their demands are unreasonable, they cry or scream when you show up late, and early on they have little or no control over their bodily functions. It takes a special kind of person to be a child care provider.

More than babysitting

Most everyone has babysat at one time or another, whether watching a younger sibling while one's parents are out or being paid to take care of the neighbor's kids after school. But moving from babysitting for extra cash and pursuing child care as a career is a big leap.

Being a child care provider means more than just making sure a child is clean and out of harm's way. Child care, which generally takes place at day care centers, nursery schools, preschools and in private homes (40 percent of child care providers are self-employed), involves the nurturing and teaching of children aged five and younger. In addition to preventing children from eating crayons and sticking their fingers in light sockets, child care professionals look after the emotional, intellectual and creative well-being of children. This means that they organize stimulating and interesting activities, manage creative play time, and supervise interaction with other children. Preschool teachers and day care personnel must be open-minded and learn to think like small children in order to keep them engaged—reason and traditional discipline techniques have a short shelf life with toddlers.

Caretakers also keep records of each child's progress and discuss the child's development and needs with the parents, who often feel left out of their children's day-to-day lives. It is a huge responsibility, as early childhood caregivers prepare children for the rigors of elementary school and, in most cases, help to shape a child's first memories. In addition, child care providers can often spot developmental problems or learning disabilities, which helps the parents adjust their child's schooling needs. Recent research continues to show that the early childhood years are the most crucial in a person's intellectual and emotional development.

A draining position

Child care also has a physical element that can be demanding. Those who care for children must be prepared to lift small children constantly, pick up toys and equipment, and engage in a number of physical activities ranging from singing and clapping hands to helping children clean and feed themselves. There is little or no time to sit down and rest. Preschool teachers and caretakers must be enthusiastic and alert, and they must be firm but caring. Their days can be long, especially at day care facilities that stay open later for working parents. The hours can extend from 7:30 a.m. to 6:30 p.m., with few or

Visit Vault at www.vault.com for insider company profiles, expert advice, career message boards, expert resume reviews, the Vault Job Board and more.

VAULT CAREER LIBRARY

71

no breaks. Dedicated child care workers will also work unpaid hours planning curricula, open houses and fund-raisers. Turnover in the field tends to be high because of the long hours, low pay and poor benefits. However, people who work with children do so because they love them and enjoy being integral to their development.

PERSONALITY MATCH	PERSONALITY MISS
• Sensitive • Compassionate • Creative • Patient	• Misanthropic • Rigid • Afraid of children

Career Path

Get that certification

Many states prefer that preschool teachers and child care workers have Child Development Associate (CDA) accreditation, which is offered by the Council for Early Childhood Professional Recognition. The CDA credential is recognized as a qualification for teachers and directors in 46 states and the District of Columbia. There are two ways to become CDA certified: either by direct application or by completing the Council's one-year training program. Direct application may be the best option for people who already have some background and experience in early childhood education, since the training program is intended for people with little or no childhood development education or experience. Some employers may not require the CDA credential, but may require secondary or postsecondary courses in child development and early childhood education.

Certain employers may require further certification. For example, Montessori preschool teachers must complete an additional year of training after receiving their bachelor's degree in early childhood education or a related field. Public schools require a bachelor's degree and state teacher certification.

Moving up

Many people start in child care at a relatively young age, usually at a day care center. With experience, preschool teachers and child care workers may advance to supervisory or administrative positions in large child care centers or preschools. These positions often require bachelor's or master's degrees. Many people choose to open their own day care centers, often working out of their homes. Other workers move on to work in resource and referral agencies, consulting with parents on available child services. Some workers become involved in policy or advocacy work related to child care and early childhood education. With a bachelor's degree, preschool teachers may become certified to teach in public schools at the kindergarten, elementary and secondary school levels.

HOURS	SALARY
• Average about 45 per week	• Median salary for child care workers: $16,320 • Median salary for preschool teachers: $20,920 • Potential for high-earnings with self-owned centers

Our Survey Says

Being a child care provider requires one to "see things differently every day, through the eyes of a child." The work is "never really a downer," those in the field tell us, as "children have a way of making your life look brighter and they can really make you laugh when you are down." "Working with the kids is so rewarding," says one assistant teacher. "You will learn so much." Children are "quick to let you know if you are doing your job well. I think it's the best feedback you can get."

On the other hand, child care is a very stressful job that "should not be taken lightly." Says one day care aide, "there are always variables that can throw your day into chaos." Small children "like to test the waters" to see "how far they can push you." That fact, combined with their "fearlessness of dangerous things like climbing or sticking their fingers in places they don't belong," often fill days with anxiety. The stress of child care is "definitely worth it," but the job is certainly "no bed of roses" and "patience is a must." Child care givers advise finding a hobby to help relieve stress, "such as running or karate." One caretaker offers the following advice: "Learn not to take life so seriously—kids don't and look at how much fun they have."

SKILLS TO ACQUIRE

- High school diploma
- Child Development Associate (CDA) accreditation

Visit Vault at **www.vault.com** for insider company profiles, expert advice, career message boards, expert resume reviews, the Vault Job Board and more.

VAULT CAREER LIBRARY   73

Civil Engineer

UPPERS	DOWNERS
• Possibility for travel	• Potentially long hours
• Wide variety of career options	• Uninteresting work

Overview

The oldest (engineering) profession

Civil engineers can trace their occupation back to the designers of Ancient Roman aqueducts (some of which are standing to this day) and the Great Pyramid at Giza. In modern times, civil engineers are responsible for the systems that make life in modern towns and cities civilized and bearable for the rest of us. The road or bridges that your car or bus travels along, the building you work in, and the water you drink and even flush away are all the products of civil engineering. Specialties in civil engineering include: geotechnical engineering, transportation, water resources, structural, environmental and construction

Specialties

For the most part, civil engineers work either inside an office or in the field, depending on whether they choose to concentrate on design or construction. Engineers who focus on design work for up to eight hours a day at a computer, designing on CAD (computer-aided design) applications. Those in the field supervise construction.

Over 40 percent of the civil engineers in the U.S. are government employees, working largely as municipal employees for state and local governments. The other 60 percent work in construction, public utilities, transportation and manufacturing. Civil engineers generally work near major industrial and commercial centers. Some projects, however, take civil engineers, especially those who work in architectural and engineering firms, to remote areas or foreign countries.

Civil engineers work an average of eight hours a day but are often called in when disasters strike; emergency flood relief projects keep civil engineers working seven days a weeks. Starting out, civil engineers can earn up to $40,000 or $50,000 a year if they do not mind relocating frequently. (Engineers in the water or sewer treatment field who are adept at designing treatment systems command the highest salaries in the field.) There are more lucrative segments in engineering, but civil engineers choose the field because of the vast challenges it affords; following projects from "cradle to grave" provides satisfyingly tangible results of their work.

PERSONALITY MATCH	PERSONALITY MISS
• Conceptual	• Undisciplined
• Logical	• Indiscrimate
• Deductive	• Scattered
• Detail-oriented	

Visit Vault at **www.vault.com** for insider company profiles, expert advice, career message boards, expert resume reviews, the Vault Job Board and more.

VAULT CAREER LIBRARY   75

Career Path

At the very least, civil engineers starting out need a bachelor's of science in civil engineering. More and more, employers are expecting their engineers to have obtained a master's degree.

Civil engineers must obtain professional engineer licenses. In their first year on the job, civil engineers complete their licensing exams and work for senior engineers. For example, a field position as a staffer for a resident engineer at a highway company can provide valuable experience in civil engineering, especially for those who are interested in becoming designers. Work availability varies by region and fluctuates with the economy—good times see more projects. After about five years, many civil engineers design or direct projects of their own. After 10 to 15 years, many civil engineers go into private consulting.

HOURS	SALARY
• Average about 45 per week	• Median salary: $68,600 • Average starting salary, bachelor's: $43,679 • Master's: $48,050 • PhD: $59,625

Our Survey Says

To see a project they have designed being built is a source of "immense pride" to civil engineers. In addition, civil engineering is a field that continues to develop and change, with "interesting technical challenges that require ability to be innovative." However, most civil engineers will tell you that working for non-engineering management can be frustrating. One Canadian civil engineer says that some of his/her management "does not understand technology," describing them as "glad-hands," "all hat no cattle" and "highly directive."

Although compensation is "variable" and can include benefits, such as stock options, bonuses and savings plans, most civil engineers "have never heard of a civil engineer striking it rich," unless he or she owns his or her own company. The work is "not necessarily physically demanding, but it can be stressful, with a great deal of responsibility." A recent graduate reports that he "is dying to get some hands-on field work," which is what keeps many civil engineers in the business despite initially long hours and lower pay than their friends in other engineering fields.

SKILLS TO ACQUIRE
• Bachelor's, master's and PhD degree in civil engineering

College Professor

UPPERS	DOWNERS
• Flexible hours	• University bureaucracy
• Wide variety of career options	• Ungrateful students
• Tenure provides security	• Extremely difficult to achieve tenure
• High pay once full professorship is achieved	• Competitive

Overview

Inclined toward academia?

Have an intellectual bent and thinking about becoming a professor? Do you entertain notions of one day ambling through gothic arches, smoking a pipe and crunching over piles of autumn leaves while contemplating the phenomenology of Hegel? With good reason, the life of the professional academician is often romanticized. College professors (at least those with tenure) enjoy flexible hours spent in research, writing, teaching and meeting with students and colleagues.

Beyond the classroom

At four-year universities, professors who have achieved senior status also have administrative duties: serving on academic and administrative advisory committees that deal with issues such as curriculum, hiring, budgets and university politics. Some also serve as mentors, thesis advisors, fellows and department chairs.

The amount of time professors actually spend teaching in a classroom setting is about 12 to 16 hours a week. They also meet with students during their three to six weekly hours of office consultation time. At very large universities, professors usually teach both graduate and undergraduate courses. For the undergraduate classes, they frequently have teaching assistants to help grade papers and exams and lead recitation sections. The student-to-professor ratio at smaller universities affords professors more one-on-one contact with students, allowing them to grade papers themselves. Most large universities also have honors programs where professors and students can interact in smaller classroom settings, much like at liberal arts colleges. Professors can also work one-on-one with students as thesis advisors and academic mentors.

Off campus

College professors are also professional researchers; their work does not end with their dissertations. In order to be considered for tenured positions, professors and assistant professors must consistently write articles for scholarly journals and publish books. Professors in engineering and the sciences conduct laboratory or field research. Depending on the size, budget and mission of the college or university, professors may feel pressured to focus most of their time on research and publishing during the academic year, while others are afforded frequent sabbaticals so that they may give undivided attention to both teaching and research. Professors tend to give exceptional and interested students the opportunity to assist them with their academic research.

Experts are in high demand for lecturing tours and speaking engagements, so travel plays a large part in their jobs. These lectures and engagements can sometimes yield significant supplementary income. Even though professors work during the summer, their hours while students are on vacation tend to be shorter, and this is when they do the bulk of their traveling. Sometimes professors have the opportunity to be guest professors at universities around the world, requiring them to live in foreign cities for a semester or two.

Visit Vault at **www.vault.com** for insider company profiles, expert advice, career message boards, expert resume reviews, the Vault Job Board and more.

VAULT CAREER LIBRARY   77

Grades aren't just for students anymore

The days of academic superiority (and even job stability) are numbered for professors who think the importance of their research outweighs molding the impressionable minds that make up a freshman class. With the launching and increasing popularity of teacher-rating web sites like www.ratemyprofessor.com, professors' teaching abilities are coming under heavy scrutiny. Comments such as "speeds his lectures a bit too quickly" and "spends an inordinate amount of time talking about things that have no relevance to the subject" blur the academic prestige of a published professor. The modern college student (paying modern college tuition rates) expects a professor who is as dedicated to teaching the material as the student is to learning the material.

College and university administrators are also taking note of professors' dedication to the classroom and students' learning with institutional surveys and evaluations asking students to rank their professors' performance in a variety of categories, ranging from availability to lecture style. While a growing number of universities use these evaluations to review professors and even influence tenure offers, a few have decided to "expel" professors based on poor "report cards." Many states are adapting post-tenure review (PTR) policies for their state universities, which set procedures for how to revoke tenure, to encourage ongoing evaluation of tenured faculty members.

While on the tenure track

Full-time professorships are becoming harder to land, particularly in the liberal arts, because there is little demand for literature and history experts in the private sector. Young faculty members are often employed on a part-time (adjunct) basis and feel pressure to spend the majority of their time researching and writing in order to advance. In order to support themselves, they often work at more than one college or university and sometimes divide their time between four-year universities and community colleges. The low pay and uncertainty of an assistant professorship leaves little time for the pursuit of the research they want to be doing.

PERSONALITY MATCH	PERSONALITY MISS
• Intellectual • Creative • Studious • Inquisitive	• Impatient • Scattered

Career Path

College and university faculty appointments adhere to a strict hierarchy: professor, associate professor, assistant professor, instructor and lecturer. Most faculty members are initially hired as instructors or assistant professors. Four-year colleges and universities generally consider only doctoral degree holders who are published for full-time, tenure-track positions but may hire master's degree holders or doctoral candidates in certain disciplines, such as the arts, or for part-time and temporary jobs. At two-year colleges, master's degree holders can qualify for full-time positions. However, with increasing competition for available jobs, institutions are becoming more selective in their hiring practices. Master's degree holders may find it increasingly difficult to get hired as they are passed over in favor of candidates with PhDs.

Newly-hired tenure-track faculty members serve a period of usually seven years under term contracts. Their record of teaching, research and overall value to the institution is reviewed; tenure is granted if the review is favorable. With tenure, a professor cannot be fired without just cause and due process, which is seldom followed through. Those denied tenure must usually leave the institution. Tenure protects the faculty's academic freedom to teach and research without jeopardizing their jobs for championing unpopular ideas. It also gives faculty and institutions the financial stability they need to continue researching and teaching. Six out of 10 full-time faculty members at universities in the U.S. are tenured, and others are in the probationary period.

HOURS	SALARY
• Average about 40 per week	• Average salary, professor: $98,974 • Associate professor: $69,911 • Assistant professor: $58,662 • Instructor: $42,609 • Lecturer: $48,289

Our Survey Says

One contact in academia explains that, "getting someone to understand, if not love, a subject, is a great feeling." Another adds that he loves being able to "help people understand themselves and grow." For professors, their "love and enthusiasm" for their subjects keep them "constantly engaged in the job" at a level that excites them. "I love my life!" says one communications professor. Professors who are engaged with their fields are "never bored teaching or talking shop" and rarely feel "burned-out."

The biggest perks, according to many professors, is "interaction with students," (while one humorously adds "getting the good parking spaces" to the list). Another perk: Every day is potentially "dress down day" and there is the potential for "lots of autonomy" and "freedom" to research. Professors "hang around interesting people" from whom they can "learn neat stuff" for the rest of their lives, although one contact notes that his colleagues "run the gamut from academic snobs to true free-spirits."

The main problem with pursuing college professorship as a profession is, of course, "difficulty in getting a tenure-track job." Other downsides are that "educational institutions are driven by profit like any other big business;" the result is that schools are filled with a "tremendous amount of bureaucratic and political garbage." Advancement can be based on "a lot of petty administrative politics." These politics, our contacts say, are what drives many people out of the profession.

SKILLS TO ACQUIRE
• PhD

Visit Vault at **www.vault.com** for insider company profiles, expert advice, career message boards, expert resume reviews, the Vault Job Board and more.

VAULT CAREER LIBRARY

79

Court Reporter

UPPERS	DOWNERS
• Exposure to high-profile cases	• Physical strain
• Opportunities for self-employment	• Long hours

Overview

Court reporters are as much a fixture in a trial as the judge and jury. Court reporters record on their stenotype machines all statements made in an official proceeding. Many reporters freelance their skills outside of the courtroom, recording out-of-court depositions for attorneys or proceedings of meetings and conventions. Court reporters are also hired by government agencies (such as the U.S. Congress) to take notes for the record.

Because the court reporter's transcript is often the only record of testimony given in a trial, accuracy and speed are essential. Court reporters use stenotype machines that print shorthand symbols on paper and record them on computer disks. The disks are then loaded into a computer that translates and displays the symbols in English, a process known as computer-aided transcription. Highly-skilled court reporters can work from home and an increasing number of them are choosing to set up their offices as subcontractors for law firms, hospitals and transcription services. Nearly one-fifth of the more than 100,000 court reporters in the U.S. are self-employed freelancers or work part-time. Of those who are salaried, one-third work for federal and state governments.

On the inside

Stenographers are privy to privileged information in their day-to-day activities. Because of this, court reporters must be scrupulous as well as hyper-efficient. Court reporters are the proverbial "flies on the wall," especially when they are assigned to high-profile cases (like the O.J. Simpson trials). The press relies on their hundred-page-a-day reports to fill them in on the latest courtroom dramas from which they are barred. This kind of privileged access is given to the best in the field—court reporters whose typing exceeds 225 words a minute with nary a typo. Court reporters and other stenographers must also be well-versed in legal jargon and other technical terms of any other fields they are working for. The pay can be quite rewarding to reporters who build strong reputations, and the benefits of flexible schedules keep people in the profession.

Not all fun and games

There are downsides to the position, though. So much importance is placed on the word-for-word accuracy of legal transcripts that the pressure and stress can take its toll on a court reporter. He or she must be able to work consistently for up to 10 hours straight without letting his or her concentration lapse. Other hazards of the position include work-related physical strains, the worst of which is carpal tunnel syndrome, an often debilitating inflammation of the tendons. Also, court reporters work alone, so camaraderie among colleagues is rarely an option.

PERSONALITY MATCH	PERSONALITY MISS
• Focused	• Creative
• Disciplined	• Restless
• Perceptive	• Easily distracted
• Efficient	

Visit Vault at **www.vault.com** for insider company profiles, expert advice, career message boards, expert resume reviews, the Vault Job Board and more.

VAULT CAREER LIBRARY

81

Career Path

Stenography skills are taught in high schools, vocational schools and community colleges, so a college degree is not required to become a court reporter. For stenographer jobs, employers prefer to hire high school graduates and seldom have a preference among the many different shorthand methods. Although requirements vary in private firms, applicants with the best speed and accuracy usually receive first consideration in hiring. For those who aspire to a court reporter position in the federal government, stenographers must be able to take diction at a minimum of 80 words per minute and type at least 40 words per minute.

For court reporter jobs, most employers require knowledge of stenotype, not because it increases reporters' writing speed but because it facilitates a computer's ability to read notes for high-speed transcription. Over 300 schools offer two- to four-year training programs in court reporting, but only 110 of them are accredited. Most court reporters complete one of these programs before they begin their careers. Some states require court reporters who stenotype depositions to be notary publics and 18 states require each court reporter to be a Certified Court Reporter (CCR). A certification test is administered by a board of examiners in each state that has CCR laws. The National Court Reporters Association confers the designation Registered Professional Reporter (RPR) upon those who pass a two-part examination and participate in continuing education programs. Although voluntary, the RPR designation is recognized as a mark of distinction in the profession.

HOURS	SALARY
• Average about 40 per week	• Median salary: $45,610 • Median salary, local government: $45,080

Our Survey Says

Contacts tell us that a court reporter's hours are "long;" the days sometimes seem to "never end." Court reporters in the litigation field spend "lots of time on the job and little else." One reporter says that his travel keeps him on the road "300 days a year." Dress for court reporters is "business-like," while transcribers are "as casual as you can get." One reporter complains that "people are being replaced with machines," which break down often. In those cases, reporters are made to "run around like crazy" when they are on break to "cover the machine's duties." "Except when they are in court," reporters' "typing time" is "their own," and they are not "tied down to a 9-to-5 schedule."

One contact explains that court reporting is a field that "a person with a good liberal arts background would find challenging and rewarding." Because reporters take testimony of "people from all walks of life," reporters "had better be versed in popular culture, medical terminology and technical terms." Practice is the key to advancement, "just like a musician."

Respondents confirm that "going behind the scenes" is a major perk of the job, since they "hear what few get to hear, and schmooze a bit with notable people, if they're chatty." And, as one contact put it, they are "there when history is being made."

SKILLS TO ACQUIRE
• Knowledge of stenotype
• Minimum typing speed of 175 words per minute
• Successful completion of the Court Reporting Exam

Dentist

UPPERS	DOWNERS
• Good pay	• Long hours
• Flexible hours	• Patient fear and hostility
	• Intense education

Overview

The hated helpers

Dentists have feelings, too. Though dentists are dedicated to preventing and treating their patients' tooth and mouth ailments, few professionals, including other physicians, are as dreaded as the dentist. In reality, dentists do a great deal of good. Besides the general practitioner most of us are familiar with, there are also specialists who enable even the ugliest of mouths to shine like the sun. These include orthodontists, who straighten children's and teenagers' teeth and repair chips and fractured molars; periodontists, on the other hand, perform corrective surgery on gums and bones to treat diseases. Oral and maxillofacial surgeons operate on the mouth and jaws, correcting disfigurements from accidents and removing abscessed teeth. Unpleasant as these procedures are, new techniques and anesthetics can minimize the pain and discomfort. Furthermore, if we visited dentists more regularly than most of us do, we could avoid the painful, tooth-drilling experiences that give them a bad rap.

Tough work keeping your teeth clean

Roughly one out of every five health care practices is a dentist's office. Most dentists are solo practitioners and work with a small staff in private practice, although a few have partners, and some are employed by large employers, such as universities or corporations. Dentists with their own businesses have fairly flexible schedules, as they make their own appointments. However, this doesn't mean they're out on the golf course every day. Most dentists work four or five days a week, while some work evenings and on Saturdays to accommodate their patients' schedules.

Being a good dentist requires more than just hard work, though. Dentistry requires keen diagnostic abilities and manual dexterity. Newly minted dentists should also enter the profession armed with a sense of humor, both to put patients at ease and to deflect the poor morale that can stem from patients' uneasiness. And then there are the official prerequisites. Requirements for certification by the American Dental Association (ADA) are strict; candidates must graduate from an ADA-accredited school and pass written and practical examinations after completing four years of dental school.

PERSONALITY MATCH	PERSONALITY MISS
• Compassionate	• Hypersensitive
• Patient	• Squeamish
• Comforting	

Visit Vault at **www.vault.com** for insider company profiles, expert advice, career message boards, expert resume reviews, the Vault Job Board and more.

VAULT CAREER LIBRARY   83

Career Path

Aspiring dentists spend four years in dental school, the last two years of which are spent treating patients, usually in clinics under the supervision of licensed dentists. Most dental schools award the Doctor of Dental Surgery (DDS) or the Doctor of Dental Medicine degree (DMD). Each year about one-fourth to one-third of new graduates enroll in postgraduate training programs to prepare for a dental specialty such as orthodontics.

All 50 states and the District of Columbia require dentists to be licensed by the American Dental Association in order to practice dentistry. Although a dentist can open up a private practice as soon as this certification is gained, many recent dental school graduates work for established dentists as associates for a year or two in order to gain experience and save money to start their own practices or buy an existing one.

HOURS	SALARY
• Average about 35 to 40 per week	• Median salary for general practitioner: $136,960 • Self-employed dentists generally earn more than salaried dentists

Our Survey Says

Dentists report that they are "often drained" from a week's work, especially if they are still trying to get established. The pay, however, is well worth it "after about seven years." Even though they are feared by the general public, they "maintain a sense of humor;" one dentist cites actually cites this strange relationship with patients as one of the positives of the job. "I wish I had written down all the funny things that were either done or said in my 20 years of work," says that contact. "We've been in stitches many times."

SKILLS TO ACQUIRE
• DDS or DMD • American Dental Association certification

Ecologist

UPPERS	DOWNERS
• Travel	• Long hours
• Flexible schedules	• Low starting pay
	• Intense competition for grant money

Overview

Not just nature lovers

Ecologists have acquired an image as tree-hugging crusaders who chain themselves to redwoods, lest they be felled by money-grubbing capitalists to be made into picnic tables. In fact, ecologists are serious scientists who spend most of their time collecting and interpreting data to assess the effects of environmental change. Most ecologists approach their work with an ardent interest in their specific environments, but this love for nature is tempered by keen analytical thinking. An ecologist studies the way organisms are affected by their environment and vice versa, which includes looking at everything from population size to pollution and how they impact a biological system. In order to study these systems, ecologists conduct extensive lab work and can spend months doing field research.

Public or private

Ecologists can work for a variety of employers. Some research for federal, state and local government agencies. For example, one of the most compelling current ecology issues is the conservation of wetlands, which are valued for their filtration capabilities in treating all sorts of water pollutants. Wetland plant species are being studied for the various ways in which they purify commercial runoff, from heavy metal uptake to neutralizing acidity.

Ecologists can also work in the private sector as eco-consultants with major corporations, such as refineries and pharmaceutical companies. In this (more lucrative) capacity, ecologists advise companies on their waste and disposal policies to ensure accordance with EPA regulations. Employment in a university teaching or corporate position is an attractive option as competition for research grant money is intense. Many ecologists (and other scientists) must spend inordinate amounts of time completing grant applications. The federal government has slowed its grant programs for scientific research, so competition is expected to increase in the coming years.

PERSONALITY MATCH	PERSONALITY MISS
• Patient	• Money-grubbing
• Detail-oriented	
• Open-minded	

Career Path

A bachelor's degree in a scientific discipline is adequate for some non-research jobs and laboratory positions in ecology. A master's degree is sufficient for some jobs in applied research and for jobs in management and consulting. A PhD in

Visit Vault at **www.vault.com** for insider company profiles, expert advice, career message boards, expert resume reviews, the Vault Job Board and more.

VAULT CAREER LIBRARY 85

chemistry, environmental science, geology or biology is generally required for college teaching, independent research, and for advancement to many managerial positions.

In academia, ecologists are usually expected to spend several years in a post-graduate position before they are offered permanent jobs. Post-doctoral work provides valuable laboratory experience, including experience in specific processes and techniques that are transferable to other research projects.

HOURS	SALARY
• Average about 45 per week	• Average salary (federal government): $58,250

Our Survey Says

Ecology is "a great field to work in, but very competitive," our contacts report. The pay is "not great," but the work is "incredibly rewarding and fun." One ecologist says that she is in the field because she believes in "the importance of the work and preservation of wildlife and nature—not to get rich!" Although consulting jobs pay more, they are not necessarily the most rewarding. According to one respondent, the job requires that ecological consultants "bust their asses to help employers do as much damage to the environment as possible without getting into trouble." A 20-year veteran of the ecological profession concurs by stating his motto: "Even a bad day in the field is better than a good day at the office."

SKILLS TO ACQUIRE
• MS or PhD

Editor

UPPERS	DOWNERS
• Proximity to interesting people	• Low starting salary
• Abundance of career options	• Long hours
• Free books	• High stress level
	• High level of dissatisfaction

Overview

The long road

The pay is low to start, the hours are long, the competition is stiff, and there is no guarantee you will make it all the way to executive editor. Why try to make it as an editor? Those entering the magazine, book or newspaper publishing industries know the pitfalls of the job but recognize them as necessary evils of a labor of love.

Working from the bottom up

The bottom rung of the publishing ladder is the editorial assistant, a glorified secretary to an editor. An assistant takes care of all of the editor's clerical tasks, setting appointments, writing letters, reading and assessing manuscripts, and most of all soaking up the mechanics of the editor's job. Assuming they don't burn out, assistants spend about two years at this level before becoming promoted to assistant editor. Many editors are former writers who have demonstrated an ability to "be the boss" and encourage and motivate people.

Why stick it out? Editors at major book publishing houses get to make stars out of new writers. At the highest level, editors command six-figure salaries and rub elbows with the most famous people in the literary world.

Magazine editors enjoy similar benefits. They dictate the creative direction of a magazine and work with art directors, photographers and writers to execute their vision. The editor-in-chief of a magazine is a full-fledged member of the jet set, with a salary to match.

Newspaper editors, especially those at large dailies like *The New York Times*, enjoy much of the same prestige as famous magazine editors. Section and managing editors are also treated well, as they are in charge of large amounts of content and employees.

Editors are bibliophiles and workaholics and though they find little time to rest their eyes, they claim to be among the happiest professionals in the world.

PERSONALITY MATCH	PERSONALITY MISS
• Creative	• Disorganized
• Detail-oriented	• Rigid
• Assertive	• Outdoorsy
• Honest	
• Bibliophile	

Visit Vault at **www.vault.com** for insider company profiles, expert advice, career message boards, expert resume reviews, the Vault Job Board and more.

VAULT CAREER LIBRARY   87

Career Path

An editor's career often begins with an internship at a magazine or a publishing company to establish contacts. Although college interns are not always guaranteed a job upon graduation, the knowledge and contacts they glean from working in the industry can give them a leg up during the job. Finding an "in" is essential in book and magazine publishing, and many employees in the industry recommend placement and temp agencies as a way of getting a foot in the door. A crack editorial assistant will have sharp reading and comprehension skills and be able to write clearly, as part of the job entails summarizing manuscripts for an editor. Other entry-level positions include fact-checkers, researchers and copyeditors, all of which can be pit stops on the track to editor.

After making assistant editor, the next level is associate editor, followed by senior editor and then a top editorial position, such as editor-in-chief or executive editor. The road to the top is long and hard, and the competition in both magazines and publishing companies is cutthroat. Promotion comes with dedication, which comes with a love of reading—lots of reading. In book publishing, editors take home five to 10 manuscripts a week, and usually work on weekends. There is no getting out of "homework," since an editor's day is taken up by paperwork and deal making.

Slightly different is the path taken to a job as a newspaper editor. Many writers are promoted to editor after demonstrating leadership and organizational abilities. The newspaper editor is often in charge of a stable of writers and assigns, edits and occasionally writes stories.

HOURS	SALARY
• Average about 50 per week	• Median income: $46,990

Our Survey Says

"This is not a field to dabble in, really," says an assistant editor. "The first couple years are devoted to learning the business, and it's not until a few years in that an editor can really begin to work on his or her own projects." Editorial assistants are "secretaries, let's face it," sources say. The work is "grueling," and editors can be tough on their assistants. One editor says that as an editorial assistant, she used to "cry a few times a week." This bleak world can sometimes be attributed to the harshness of editors; the attitude in publishing that "time is of the essence" means there is little time to "explain and explain again." But, as one editor explains, "once you have paid your dues and suffered through years of eating TV dinners, the rewards are so much sweeter." But life as an editorial assistant isn't entirely dim. Assistants in both book and magazine publishing "catch the leavings" of their editors in the form of "invitations and free books."

Becoming an editor requires that you "spend a lot of time schmoozing" and, in addition to being able to spot new talent, "be a manager of people and their egos." Magazine editors, particularly at fashion magazines, are "rarely in the office." An intern at a high-profile fashion magazine remarks that she "had never even seen the editor-in-chief until she had been working there three months." Magazine editors attend conferences, gallery and restaurant openings, and photo shoots to spot trends and ensure that the magazine is keeping up with "what's hot and what's not." Book publishing is more intimate, and editors spend much of their time reading and working with authors. Says an editor at Random House, "the best part of being an editor is discovering manuscripts and bringing them to life as books. It's a very personal, educational and rewarding process."

SKILLS TO ACQUIRE

- Bachelor's degree
- Good writing and communication skills

A Day in the Life: Editorial Assistant

Editorial assistant at Redbook *magazine.*

I have to stress that some days are different. We have long editorial meetings once a week.

9:00 to 9:30 a.m.: Arrive in the office.

9:30 to 10:00 a.m.: I return phone calls, check e-mail, open up my boss's office (the executive editor), check her inter-office mailbox and distribute all copy (stories, articles). Open up mail (and there is a lot of it!).

10:00 a.m.: I meet with my boss to discuss who has called, what needs to be done for the day. Run around the office handing back things to other editors from her.

10:30 to 11:00 a.m.: I read all of the daily newspapers for the day so I can let my boss know what's important in the news.

11:00 a.m. to 1:00 p.m.: I research, write and report for the columns I work on: Red in the Face Page (our readers' most embarrassing moments), RedLetters (the letters to the editor page), and the Saving Time page (ways that our readers can cut down their time in different ways). Maintain a running and up-to-date list of the status of all of our current articles and columns.

1:00 to 2:00 p.m.: I generally eat lunch, run errands and read current magazines to stay ahead of trends.

2:00 to 5:30 p.m.: I work on projects the executive editor assigns to me, continue to work on articles, route copy to different departments and editors, and answer all of the letters from readers that *Redbook* receives, deal with requests from public relations organizations. Read through unsolicited queries to see if I should pass them along to an editor.

Note: While I am doing everything else, I am also answering the phone for my boss, as well as covering the phones and helping the editor-in-chief. A large part of my job is clerical based, but in magazine publishing, that is how you break into the business. In addition to performing administrative work, I am able to participate in the editorial side by suggesting story ideas in our biweekly ideas meetings, and writing, researching and reporting for the columns I work on.

A Day in the Life: Book Editor

Russell Davis

Editor

Five Star Authors (Waterville, ME) [a division of International Thomson]

Education

BA in English from University of Wisconsin at Green Bay, with an emphasis in creative writing, and minors in humanistic studies and American Indian studies. I also worked with the student literary magazine in the roles of fiction editor, business manager and managing editor and was also heavily involved in the writing community as a whole—organizing public readings, working with established authors to have them come in for guest lectures, etc.

Visit Vault at **www.vault.com** for insider company profiles, expert advice, career message boards, expert resume reviews, the Vault Job Board and more.

VAULT CAREER LIBRARY 89

Professional history

By the time I finished college, I'd already begun selling my short fiction and working as a freelance editor. I co-edited anthology titles for Cumberland House and DAW Books, and continued to write and sell my short fiction. I co-wrote a young adult novel. Shortly after, I was asked to come to Maine and start a publishing company for a private investor. This turned out to be a double-edged sword: The job only lasted a year, but I learned a great deal about how to run a publishing company—and what it's like to edit novels every day. When that job ended, I landed at Five Star Publishing (an imprint of Gale). I now oversee the romance and women's fiction line, as well as the speculative fiction lines. Additionally, I've continued to write and publish my own work, as well as do the occasional bit of freelance editing.

Job description

Basically, it's my job to review both solicited and unsolicited manuscripts and acquire those that meet the needs of the house. After that, I work with the author to edit the book, and this includes both story editing as well as line editing. I also shepherd the book throughout the production process. Beyond that, I promote the house by making public appearances at conferences and conventions, writing articles, etc.

Describe your day today

Usually, I arrive at the office around 9 a.m. and stay until 6 p.m., sometimes later. Throughout the course of the day, I'll receive (on average) more than 100 e-mails, and get between 15 and 25 phone calls. I'll review production proofs, answer correspondence from writers and draft editorial letters. I may write cover or catalog copy, work with an artist on the cover art, a designer on the cover design and negotiate a book contract. I rarely read at the office, especially full manuscripts. Usually, I read at home, a few hours on a weeknight, quite a bit more on the weekend.

Favorite part of job

The best part of the job is seeing an idea develop into a manuscript, then into a polished manuscript, and finally into an actual book. It's a huge rush to see what was once words on paper in a finished format. Also, calling a new writer, who's never been published before, and saying you'd like to make an offer on their book. That's a very cool thing.

Least favorite part of job

I rarely read for pleasure anymore—when you edit books all the time, it's difficult to turn that side of yourself off and just enjoy it. I miss sitting down with a good book for company. I still read an average of a book a week, just for myself, but it's not the same.

Advice

Read anything and everything—in all sorts of genres, in fiction or non-fiction, in newspapers, books or magazines—as often as you can. Get an education from a good school in English or literature or a related field. Ask questions of people in the field: writers, editors, journalists, whomever. You'd be surprised how happy they'll be to talk about their work. Go to conferences and conventions in the field of your interest—meet people, talk with them about what and how they do what they do. Always be willing to learn about the business side as well as the art side of publishing; explore the craft of the field at the same time as you experience the art of it.

And, above all things, you must love the well-written word.

Firefighter

UPPERS	DOWNERS
• Camaraderie	• Danger
• Flexible schedules	• Long, irregular hours
• Respect in neighborhoods	• Work on holidays

Overview

Long hours? That's the easy part

Many jobs require 60-hour workweeks. Many companies require their employees to work on holidays. However, very few employers ask their employees to run headfirst into flaming buildings to rescue children and pets.

Firefighters respond to medical emergencies like car accidents as well as to fires. They rescue cats from trees, and when your little brother gets his head stuck in between the iron bars of the front gate, the fire department is usually called to pry him out. Because they are often the first to arrive at the scene of accidents, many firefighters hold additional certification as emergency medical technicians (EMTs).

Firefighters also specialize, by department or by company, within the department. Most metropolitan departments have different companies within their ranks, each with a specific task. Engine and ladder companies are examples of companies you'll find at almost any fire station. Firefighters can also specialize by incident type. Hazardous materials firefighters deal with incidents involved hazardous materials. Wildland firefighters battle wildfires, jumping out of helicopters into the middle of a burning forest. The most elite and highly trained wildland firefighters are appropriately called "hotshots."

In addition, fire departments must be prepared to coordinate with other authorities, including fire departments in other jurisdictions or with other specialties and non-fire departments, such as the police or government. The Federal Emergency Management Agency (FEMA) created a standardized system, the National Incident Management System (NIMS), for how to respond to larger incidents, like natural disasters and emergencies.

Get in shape

Being in tip-top shape is a must for firefighters. For starters, the protective gear that firefighters wear weighs about 40 pounds (the equipment that they use has become increasingly sophisticated in recent years). Next, consider the physical activity involved in firefighting. In the few seconds that they have when they arrive at a fire, fighters set up ladders, connect their hose lines to hydrants, operate a pump and, in some cases, climb many flights of stairs before reaching trapped victims. While they are testing their limits of physical exertion, firefighters must contend with toxic gases and smoke inhalation. Because of these physical demands, and also because of the responsibility they hold, firefighters undergo occasional polygraphs and periodic drug testing to ensure their enduring integrity and health.

At the station

Firefighters spend most of their workday at fire stations, where they eat and sleep when they are on 24-hour shifts. Between alarms, they have classroom training, and spend hours cleaning and maintaining equipment. This maintenance can take up to four hours and must be done after every call.

Visit Vault at **www.vault.com** for insider company profiles, expert advice, career message boards, expert resume reviews, the Vault Job Board and more.

VAULT CAREER LIBRARY   91

The hours of a firefighter vary. In some cities, firefighters are on 24-hour duty, then are off for 48 hours; in other cities, they work a day shift of 10 hours for three or four days, a night shift of 14 hours for three or four nights, have three or four days off, and then repeat the cycle. These irregular hours are an additional source of stress in a firefighter's life and often impacts family life. The fact that they work in close quarters for many hours a month means that firefighters tend to bond strongly. This camaraderie is more than just a convenience, as firefighters have to rely on their peers when they go into a fire, usually in teams.

PERSONALITY MATCH	PERSONALITY MISS
• Courageous • Confident • Compassionate • Diligent • Resourceful	• Squeamish • Unassertive • Introverted

Career Path

Once they have passed the required stamina, coordination, agility, medical and reading exams, firefighters are trained for several weeks at their department's training center. Through classroom instruction and practical training, the recruits study firefighting techniques, fire prevention, hazardous materials, local building codes and emergency medical procedures, including first aid and cardiopulmonary resuscitation. They learn how to use axes, saws, chemical extinguishers, ladders and rescue equipment. If they pass this training, they are put on a probation period, which can vary from six to 18 months. Many fire departments have apprentice programs where applicants can spend three or four months "shadowing" firefighters to gain on-the-job training, where they do everything except actually fight fires.

Firefighters are now encouraged, and in some cities required, to hold up to 45 hours of college credit or courses in fire engineering and fire science, as well as training as emergency medical technicians. Many fire departments offer firefighters incentives, such as tuition reimbursement or higher pay, for completing advanced training. As firefighters gain experience, they may advance to higher ranks, such as lieutenant, captain and chief. Advancement generally depends upon written examination scores, job performance and seniority. Some departments require chiefs to have a master's degree. Firefighters can also become part of a department's fire prevention team, which includes a fire marshall and fire inspectors who visit buildings to make sure they are fire code-compliant.

Firefighters are almost exclusively male, although women are seen more and more often riding the big red trucks. Competition for jobs is intense; the civic duty aspect of being a firefighter attracts many applicants and nepotism runs rampant in many towns.

HOURS	SALARY
• Average about 50 per week	• Median annual salary for firefighter: $62,900 • Mean average salary for fire chief and other managers/supervisors: $65,030

Our Survey Says

There are many benefits to being a firefighter, such as "working three days and being off for four" and "relaxation at the firehouse." As one firefighter puts it, "If you can handle going into a structure where the temperature is in excess of 3,000 degrees and looking at people who have been severely injured in a car wreck that could have been prevented, then this is the job for you."

Firefighters are immensely proud of the work they do and cite "professionalism, camaraderie, love for people, compassion and emotion" as the primary qualities of their peers and themselves. The camaraderie that develops among firefighters stems from the fact that their lives "are in each other's hands." Firefighters are "constantly faced with death." Though this is "emotionally exhausting," to "save a person or an animal is a huge payback for the hardship." One firefighter says that he has seen enough death to "last two lifetimes and saved enough lives to last four lifetimes." Firefighters are also invariably well-liked by communities. As one contact explains, "people call for firefighters because they want them there," and there is "rarely any hostility" directed towards them.

SKILLS TO ACQUIRE

- Academic qualifications vary between cities: some require only a GED, others require at least two years of college
- Successful completion of civil service exam
- Physical aptitude test
- Drug test
- Polygraph test

Visit Vault at **www.vault.com** for insider company profiles, expert advice, career message boards, expert resume reviews, the Vault Job Board and more.

VAULT CAREER LIBRARY 93

Flight Attendant

UPPERS	DOWNERS
• Great travel perks • Flexible schedules	• Long hours • Irregular schedules • Low pay

Overview

Like you and me

They are not all pneumatic babes, they're not called stewardesses any more and, no, they don't want to hear about your cockpit. Flight attendants are both male and female, they vary in appearance, age (age restrictions were recently abolished) and ethnicity, and they can make the difference between a comfortable flight and a nightmarish one. And while you may think that getting your bag of pretzels is of paramount importance, the primary responsibility of a flight attendant is the safety of the passengers.

Tested and trained

Flight attendants are trained and tested professionals: they undergo weeks of (often unpaid) training; most large airline companies require them to pass a grueling exam that tests them on every nut and bolt of the aircraft on which they serve. In the wake of the September 11 hijackings, many flight attendants have also undergone training in self-defense.

Flight attendant training lasts about four to six weeks, during which trainees learn emergency procedures, such as how to operate an oxygen system and give first aid. Trainees for international routes get additional instruction in passport and customs regulations and terrorism coping techniques. The training is rigorous and not all trainees pass their examinations. The lure of free travel to exotic locales attracts applicants, but the often unglamorous process of being cloistered with a hundred other trainees at a budget hotel in Houston or Cleveland weeds many would-be flight attendants out of the group.

At home and away

The hours for flight attendants vary widely, and many flight attendants work at night, on weekends and on holidays. They spend about 75 to 80 hours a month on the ground preparing planes for flights, writing reports following completed flights, and waiting (just like passengers) for planes that arrive late. In-flight work can be strenuous because of demanding passengers and crowded flights. Attendants are on their feet during much of the flight and must remain helpful and friendly regardless of how they feel or how obnoxious their passengers are. As a result of scheduling variations and limitations on flying time, many flight attendants have 11 or more days off a month. Attendants can be away from their home base—often the hub city of the airline they work for—a great deal of the time, and are compensated by the airlines with hotel accommodations, meal allowances and, of course, discounted or free tickets for both themselves and their immediate families.

Visit Vault at **www.vault.com** for insider company profiles, expert advice, career message boards, expert resume reviews, the Vault Job Board and more.

VAULT CAREER LIBRARY 95

Save yourself

It takes a patient, extroverted personality to become a flight attendant. It also takes nerves and a sense of duty. In the event of an emergency, they must take into account the passengers' safety before their own. This can entail anything from simple reassurance to directing passengers during evacuation following an emergency landing. Though the chances of a plane crash are small, flight attendants must be undaunted by the prospect of disaster.

PERSONALITY MATCH	PERSONALITY MISS
• Friendly • Outgoing • Fastidious • Cool under pressure	• Aggressive • Impatient • Shy

Career Path

After they complete initial training, flight attendants are assigned to one of their airlines' bases. New attendants are placed on "reserve status" and are called on to staff extra flights or fill in for attendants who are sick or on vacation. Reserve attendants on duty must be available on a moment's notice. Flight attendants usually remain on reserve for at least a year; in some cities, it may take five years or longer to advance from reserve status.

After time spent as a reserve, attendants graduate and bid for regular assignments. When bidding for assignments, attendants are staffed based on seniority. Because of this system, usually only the most experienced attendants get their choice of base and flights. Advancement as a flight attendant has become slower because attendants are staying in the profession longer. Because of the long career path, some attendants transfer within the company to become flight service instructors, customer service directors, recruiting representatives, or one of many other administrative positions.

HOURS	SALARY
• Average about 150 per month including 65 to 75 hours of flight time	• Median salary: $53,780 • Median starting salary: $15,849 • Compensation for overtime as well as night and international flights

Our Survey Says

Although flight attendants for national airlines get to fly around the world, they often only stay overnight "and hardly leave their hotels." Entry-level flight attendants "get all the red-eye assignments" and the "pogo stick assignments—short hop flights." As one contact puts it, "It is damned hard work." However, this all-travel, no-fun lifestyle is not always the case: attendants occasionally enjoy day trips and shopping excursions, on which "sometimes even the pilots come along."

Of the pilots, insiders say that they are "generally terrific," but that "there are plenty of egos in the cockpit." There are also complaints of the occasional unruly clientele—the "Friday afternoon businessman crowd going home after a tough week." Explains one contact, "They all think they are exactly the kind of guy that a young woman like me really needs."

Flight attendants are "constantly worried about economic hardships and layoffs." However, for those with senior status, job security is not so much a concern; those attendants with hard-earned tenure also have "first pick at the Bahamas trips."

SKILLS TO ACQUIRE

- High school diploma
- Flight attendant training

A Day in the Life: Commuter Working at a Regional Airline at LAX

My first flight out of LAX is at 10 a.m., but since I live in Reno, I first have to get myself to LAX. The first flight out is at 6:30 a.m., so I need to be to the airport by 5:45 a.m. I don't normally cut it so close, but I wasn't able to hold a schedule with later sign-ins this month. Sometimes I'll fly in the night before and get a cheap hotel room near the airport, but my daughter had a dance recital last night, and there was no way I was going to miss it. But since I couldn't get a babysitter, I had to take her to my folks' place last night, which is just as well since I was up at 4 a.m. today.

From LAX, I do a double Vegas turn before heading to Phoenix for the night. That means L.A. to Las Vegas and back twice, and five legs altogether. And after the second Vegas turn, I have about three hours' sit time at the airport before heading on to Arizona. I go to one of the hotels nearby, and from all the times I've gotten a room there, they let me use the gym there for free. My layover is really short, so I won't have a chance to do anything later. When I get back from the gym, I still have over an hour, so I crack open the books. To earn some extra money on the side, I'm taking classes on massage therapy, and it's tougher than you'd think. There are all kinds of anatomy and physiology exams, and I hate tests! I'll study a little bit just before going to bed, after talking to my little sugarpie.

The second day is a little odd because it doesn't fly through my base city. From Phoenix, I go to Albuquerque and then do a really long flight to San Francisco (I guess it's all relative when you're used to doing these short hops). Luckily, I have a longer layover the second night, although I'd really rather be at home. Once we get into the city, the pilots offer to take me out for dinner and drinks. It's really good to get out of the house and have some time for friends. The guys are really sweet and we get crazy and decide to get last-minute tickets to see a play near Fisherman's Wharf. It's kind of a cabaret, and before you know it, we're doing shots. I'll regret this tomorrow, but I'm having so much fun. Before I get too bombed, I check in with my parents and daughter to make sure everything's going all right.

Our relatively short day and early arrival in SFO means an even earlier start the third day. We're doing a 5:30 a.m. flight down to LAX before doing another double Vegas turn. Why did I bid this trip again? Since it's the first flight of the day, I'm kind of in charge of stocking my galley and setting up supplies in the plane. I get bulk packs of soda, ice, sugar, beer and wine and juice that I have to separate into two different carts and into various galley compartments. These smaller regional jets have so little room, it's always a challenge to figure out where to put everything. And since the ice cubes have sort of melted and refrozen in one huge block, I have to break up the ice so it fits in the cups.

They start boarding the plane, but because the plane sits so low to the ground, few of the airports have jetbridges that can connect and the passengers have to walk across the tarmac. I'm so glad it's not raining today because rain puts everyone in a bad mood right off the bat. I greet everyone, and luckily since the overhead bins are so small, there's a crew of two guys taking the passengers' bags and loading them into the cargo hold behind the passenger cabin during boarding. It's kind of a light load, with only 15 people for 38 seats, so I have to make sure that the plane's passenger cabin is balanced for weight reasons. To do this, the cabin is broken up into three zones of four rows each. I count the passengers sitting in each zone and move a few people to balance out the plane a little better. Then I let the captain know the cabin is ready for taxi-out. Once that's done, I press play on the CD player with the recorded safety announcement. There are no screens on the plane, so I

Visit Vault at www.vault.com for insider company profiles, expert advice, career message boards, expert resume reviews, the Vault Job Board and more.

VAULT CAREER LIBRARY   97

demonstrate the seat belt and oxygen mask while the announcement plays on. During the flight, I take my little cart out to deliver drinks and a little granola bar.

Once that's done, I go through and pick up any garbage, and by that time, it's usually time to prepare for landing—"Please raise your seat back all the way up." "Can you please stow your briefcase under the seat next to you?" It does get a little lonely, but I have the passengers, and the pilots are always cracking jokes between flights to make up for it. I do appreciate the independence that I have, and not having someone always looking over my shoulder. After two more flights, I check in for my commuter flight back to Reno later that night before going on the second Vegas turn. They usually let me check in about four hours before departure, which is just enough time to get to Vegas and back. In five more hours I'll be done with another trip and have three days off to spend with my daughter, help her with her dance routines and her homework, get some gardening done and go to class. The pay could be better (OK, a lot better), but the time off is so great and lets me focus on other things. Sometimes my daughter and parents wish I were around more often, but they seem to understand—especially when we fly for free out to Disney World every year!

Geologist

UPPERS	DOWNERS
• Travel	• Long hours
• Flexible schedules	• Physical strain

Overview

Global office

The study of the Earth, its history and evolution, is called geology. Geoscientists (geological scientists) study the Earth and its terrain for many purposes. Some use their research to locate water, mineral and energy resources; protect the environment; predict geological hazards; and offer advice for construction and land use.

Geologists, specifically, examine the composition, processes and history of the Earth to learn how rocks were formed and what has happened since formation. Using animal and plant fossils, geologists also study evolution. Much of their time is spent in the field collecting samples and analyzing satellite data to take back to the lab where they can look at the chemical and physical properties of specimens.

The rocky road to specialization

In the oil or gas industry, geologists incorporate cleaning and preserving the environment with searching for resources. Geologists design waste disposal sites, monitor water supplies, and locate safe areas for hazardous waste and landfills. The federal government employs geologists through the Department of the Interior, mostly within the U.S. Geological Survey (USGS). Geologists also apply their studies to solving structural engineering problems and work for consulting and engineering firms in this capacity.

Still other geologists are professors of geology, oceanography and geophysics and supplement their teaching with research excursions and consulting. During their education and in their career, geologists can specialize in areas such as seismology, the detection of earthquakes; hydrology, the study of underground and surface waters; and volcanology, the study of volcanoes and volcanic phenomenon.

PERSONALITY MATCH	PERSONALITY MISS
• Intellectual	• Artistic
• Curious	• Non-critical
• Outdoorsy	• Timid
• Methodical	
• Circumspect	

Career Path

Most employers require a master's degree in geology or geophysics. Advancement will also require a strong academic and practical background in physics, chemistry, mathematics or computer science. Research positions at colleges and universities,

Visit Vault at **www.vault.com** for insider company profiles, expert advice, career message boards, expert resume reviews, the Vault Job Board and more.

VAULT CAREER LIBRARY

99

as well as jobs with Federal Government agencies, require PhDs. When working in the public sector (e.g., for the government), most states also require a license.

Many employers require field experience from their applicants in the form of internships or summer employment in an environmental field. Geologists and geophysicists often begin their careers in field exploration or as research assistants in labs. They may be eventually promoted to project leader, program manager or another management and research position.

HOURS	SALARY
• Average about 45 per week	• Median salary of geoscientists: $72,660
	• Average starting salary, bachelor's: $40,786
	• Doctoral degree: $61,050.
	• Average salary, Federal Government: $87,392

Our Survey Says

Geologists wouldn't trade their careers "for anything in the world." This isn't to say that the jobs are cushy. While there are "many opportunities to travel," the hours are "long" and the jobs are "dirty." For example, one field geologist reports having to take an early retirement due to disability, saying the "job wore (her) down."

One environmental consultant says that while geology is a "pretty good field," there is a great deal of "back-stabbing and politics" in the non-academic side of geology, but the pay is higher than in academia or government research. The "real money, relatively speaking," is at the major oil and natural gas companies—"pay starts in the mid to upper $40s."

SKILLS TO ACQUIRE
• Master's degree or PhD in geology or geophysics

Graphic Designer

UPPERS	DOWNERS
• Diversity of tasks	• Long hours in front of a computer
• Wide variety of career options	• Strict deadlines
• Hot industry	

Overview

A dream life

Many people dream of turning something they love, such as an art form, into a living. Graphic designers are among the few professionals who manage to do just that. And because of the rapid ascent of the Internet into our day-to-day lives, designers who work with web sites are now among the hottest of commodities.

Traditional graphic artists create print products such as packaging, promotional displays, marketing brochures, magazines or books. Many graphic designers work on the visual designs of annual reports and other corporate publications. They also design logos and graphic identities for products and businesses. Increasingly, graphic designers are channeling their artistic talents into the lucrative and fast-evolving profession of web design. Web designers use a combination of technical know-how and a keen eye for design to create the snazzy sites on the Internet. Broadcast/motion designers create animated graphics for film and television, as well as for web sites and electronic devices, like iPods and cell phones.

Free to be

Because they often work on projects that eventually end—such as a seasonal catalog or redesign of a web site—graphic design jobs are often staffed on a freelance basis. About 25 percent of graphic designers are freelancers; they sell their skills and pitch their designs to advertising agencies, retailers, design firms, magazines, newspapers and Internet companies. While freelancing offers many advantages, such as the opportunity to take off large chunks of time and the chance to work in many different environments, working on a project-to-project basis is far from a breeze. Freelancers must be versatile enough to market their skills to a wide variety of businesses and must also be shrewd businesspeople. A freelance artist's ability to meet deadlines and work within a budget is important to a company. Artists who prove themselves earn repeat business and invaluable word-of-mouth advertisement.

In-house graphic designers, who work on salary from one company, often work in the creative departments of advertising agencies and design firms and often are assigned less glamorous tasks to start. After an "apprenticeship" period, they will be able to work on actual designs and layouts.

Although becoming an established graphic designer is difficult, successful freelance artists can make a comfortable living and tend to enjoy their freedom. In-house graphic designers, such as those who become art directors at magazines or ad agencies, can command high salaries.

PERSONALITY MATCH	PERSONALITY MISS
• Artistic	• Unassertive
• Creative	• Reserved
• Energetic	

Visit Vault at **www.vault.com** for insider company profiles, expert advice, career message boards, expert resume reviews, the Vault Job Board and more.

VAULT CAREER LIBRARY   101

Career Path

A strong portfolio is essential for any aspiring graphic designer. The portfolio is a collection of the artist's best work; some graphic artists include new takes on existing ads or logos to demonstrate their ability within a certain industry. In fact, many graphic designers freelance while still in school in order to develop experience and a portfolio of published work.

Although no formal education is required for graphic or web design, a bachelor's degree program in fine art, graphic design or visual communications is valuable training for both traditional graphic designers and web designers. (An associate's degree will also be serviceable for some positions.) For web design, courses in languages such as HTML, CSS and Java add highly sought-after skills. Internships are a good way to acquire hands-on experience and to gain contacts within the industry.

Designers hired into advertising agencies or graphic design studios often start with relatively routine work. While doing this work, however, they can hone their skills and learn all aspects of the business first-hand. Many graphic artists work full-time jobs in other industries while working part-time as freelancers to establish themselves.

HOURS	SALARY
• Average about 40 per week	• Entry-level: $35,000 • Staff-level (one to three years of experience): $45,000 • Senior designers with management responsibility: $65,000 • Design directors: $98,600 • Senior art directors at top magazines can command a salary of $200,000 to $300,000

Our Survey Says

Graphic designers "love their jobs" but complain of exhaustion as well. The strain of "constantly having to sell [themselves] and their work" "takes a toll on [their] confidence and sense of self-worth." The amount of work that they get is "proportionate to how hard" they pitch their designs. They are "happiest when working on a project." Many graphic designers realize that they "won't be raking in the cash" but seeing their work used in national campaigns and logos fills them with "tremendous pride." Constant rejection is part of the job also. "A lot of people lose faith in themselves or burn out early," according to one veteran designer. But those who "make a reputation for themselves" can look forward to a long career if they are versatile and diligent.

SKILLS TO ACQUIRE
• Familiarity with computer design applications: Quark, Adobe Photoshop and Illustrator • For web designers, knowledge of languages such as HTML, Java and Cold Fusion • For broadcast/motion design: Adobe Flash, Dreamweaver, After Effects and Premiere, as well as Autodesk Maya.

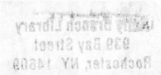

Hotel Manager

UPPERS	DOWNERS
• Employee hotel discounts • Free or discounted meals	• Long hours (holidays and weekends) • Low starting pay • Rude patrons

Overview

According to the Bureau of Labor Statistics (BLS), nearly 62,000 establishments—including upscale hotels, RV parks, motels, resorts, casino hotels, bed-and-breakfasts and boarding houses—provide overnight accommodation in America, with a staggering 4.4 million rooms on offer each night. Each of these establishments requires a managers or team of managers to make sure they accommodate each and every guest.

Not always hospitable

It isn't easy working in the hospitality industry—guests can be rude, the holiday rush is nightmarish and some employees work seven days a week. Hotel managers must oversee and synchronize the activities of all the different departments of a hotel, such as housekeeping, dining, recreation, security and maintenance, and make sure both their guests and employees are happy. Hotel managers are also responsible for the behind-the-scenes operations, including accounting, personnel and publicity. They often assume a financial role, overseeing the business side of things, such as budgeting and revenue management.

It takes a team

Every member of a hotel staff, from housekeeping to the hotel manager, is responsible for the seamless operation of the establishment. At smaller hotels and motels, the responsibility for overseeing rooms, food and beverage service, registration, and overall management can fall on the shoulders of a single manager.

Large hotels, such as The Plaza in New York, employ hundreds of workers, and have many different levels of managers. The general manager may be aided by a staff of assistant managers, each with his or her own department to supervise. The hotel manager sets the establishment's standards of operation (within the owners' or executives' guidelines); it is the job of the assistant managers to see that these are executed adroitly. The general manager sets room rates, allocates funds to departments, approves expenditures, and establishes standards for service that employees in housekeeping, decor, food quality, and banquet operations must offer to guests. Many hotels have resident managers, who live in the hotel and are on hand 24 hours a day for guests and staff (though they usually work a standard eight-hour day).

Leadership-in-training programs

Because hotel managers oversee so many different departments, even the most senior general manager must have an understanding of each one. Like orchestra conductors, they bring together a group of different departments and employees to perform in harmony. The best way to learn about each part of the hotel team is through hands-on experience. Most hotel chains, such as Hilton Hotels, have leadership development programs for their managers. For example, in Hilton's Leadership-in-Training (LIT) program a trainee rotates through about a dozen different hotel departments in a six- to eight-month period. The central goal of a rotational training program like LIT is to provide trainees with an overview of an organization's operations so that they can best coordinate them.

Visit Vault at **www.vault.com** for insider company profiles, expert advice, career message boards, expert resume reviews, the Vault Job Board and more.

VAULT CAREER LIBRARY 103

High School Career Bible • 2008 Edition
Hotel Manager

PERSONALITY MATCH	PERSONALITY MISS
• Friendly • Outgoing • Cooperative • Diligent	• Sensitive • Shy • Disorganized

Career Path

Although in the past, most hotel managers have been hired from food and beverage, front desk, housekeeping and sales positions without formal education, employers now give hiring preference to individuals with degrees in hotel and restaurant management. Internships and part-time jobs also give a step up when it comes to getting hired for a management-track position.

Graduates of hotel or restaurant management programs usually start as trainee assistant managers or at least advance to such positions quickly. Another in is the leadership training programs, which hire recent graduates to participate. New hotels without formal on-the-job training programs often prefer experienced personnel for higher-level positions.

HOURS	SALARY
• Average about 45 per week	• Median salary for hotel managers: $91,383

Our Survey Says

Most hotel managers agree that meeting "all kinds of people, from all over the world" and "the ability to make someone's day by fixing a problem" are some of the "best perks of this job." However, it's not all about mingling with the guests. Being a hotel manager means that the buck stops with you and you have to be "willing to do whatever needs to be done." Says one manager, "if someone doesn't show up for work, it is your responsibility to do the job yourself, even housekeeping or maintenance."

If you don't enjoy people, "please do not even attempt a career in this field," insiders warn. Low- to mid-level and resident managers also have to be on-call all the time. "Be prepared to work and work whatever hours necessary to make it work," says one general manager. "The hotel never closes so you could always get a phone call at any time. Being woken up at 4 a.m. for the night auditor to tell you the pool pump pipe burst is never fun," adds as assistant general manager. For those individuals who are truly cut out for the hotel business, however, it "gets in your blood." The diversity of experience in hotel management "is greater than in any other profession and the gratification can be tremendous."

SKILLS TO ACQUIRE
• Training in hotel or restaurant management • Bachelor's or master's in hotel management or business

Human Resources

UPPERS	DOWNERS
• Access to confidential information • Work with people	• Long hours • Low starting pay • Listening to constant complaining

Overview

From start to finish

If you've ever interviewed for a job, you've probably met with a human resources assistant or director. HR professionals are the "people people" at companies. They follow the careers of employees throughout their term of employment; they file the paperwork when someone is hired and file it when that person retires (or is "downsized"). In between the coming and going, they also track employee absences and job performance, process promotions, supervise benefits packages, and listen to employee grievances. If an employee has a query or a gripe regarding pay, retirement or benefits, he or she talks to someone in human resources. In addition, HR professionals organize any employee outings or community outreach programs—the fun stuff!

Growing the business

Human resources personnel are also instrumental in recruiting new employees. They post new job openings; review applications and resumes; interview and test applicants; and hire based on each department's needs. Part of a HR assistant's or director's job is to screen applicants, deciding who gets to the next level of the interview process. Human resources assistants also handle internal recruitment, notifying company employees of openings within the firm and matching qualified applicants to the position. And if that's not enough, HR personnel generally dish out the acceptance and rejection letters to candidates.

A kind ear

HR personnel listen to both employee complaints and concerns. They also work with management to institute policies designed to take into account the "people" aspect of the business, such as incentive compensation plans. As their goal is to create the most productive work environment possible, HR professionals must have expert people skills.

Different paths

Some companies have one HR manager or staff who handles all employee-related issues, from recruiting and training to safety and workplace issues, to health care and other benefits. Other companies, however, need different HR professionals for different areas and hire HR professionals who specialize in those areas. For example, a construction company will require a health and safety professional who focuses on workplace safety to make sure all their construction sites are safe. The health and safety professional works closely with compensation and benefits professional to make sure that, in the event of an on-site injury, the employee and employer are taken care of, and to ensure that the injury does not happen again. Another growing specialization is organization development (OD). OD professionals evaluate the overall organizational structure of a company and how its employees interact to create a system for the highest productivity and cohesion.

Visit Vault at **www.vault.com** for insider company profiles, expert advice, career message boards, expert resume reviews, the Vault Job Board and more.

VAULT CAREER LIBRARY 105

PERSONALITY MATCH	PERSONALITY MISS
• Affable • Good listener • Fair-minded • Resourceful	• Disorganized • Shy

Career Path

While there are academic programs that prepare candidates for careers in HR (generally master's programs), most human resources professionals do not come through these programs. Many have degrees in "people-related" fields such as psychology. Also, companies tend to hire candidates with experience dealing with people, such as those with a retail or service background. Employees in other areas of a company often transfer to the HR department for a change of pace.

Starting out in human resources, an assistant earns a salary in the mid- to high-$20,000s. Motivated HR professionals may advance to managerial positions or specializations within five years. A master's degree in human resources, labor relations or business administration may be useful for those seeking general or top management positions. The highest-ranking HR professionals can earn six figures or more. After seven to 10 years in the business, HR professionals often start their own consulting businesses or become trainers.

HOURS	SALARY
• Average about 40 per week	• Median salary: $50,230 • Average entry-level salary with an undergraduate degree: $41,680 • Median for HR managers: $88,510

Our Survey Says

Most HR professionals say that "being able to interact with many people each day and their changing needs/wants," giving employees "a sense of value inside the door and out" are their favorite parts of the job. Looking at the bigger picture of the workplace as a whole, they are the "real contributors" to culture. One New York HR manager says, "the real job in the end" is the "ability to affect culture," a place where employees can do their best and "make a company an employer of choice." In the words of a HR manager, HR professionals are "driven to help and see people be successful." An HR manager from California describes her colleagues as "creative" "good listeners," "highly sensitive and bright," "sometimes nosey" and very loyal to the company.

Human resources professionals enjoy being "at the pulse of an organization." However, the job can sometimes be thankless. Some HR professionals get too bogged down by the technical stuff, such as coordinating benefits packages, that they forget about the joy of "setting cultural tone." HR life can be "hectic" and it makes an assistant's day when "someone actually appreciates what" he or she does or gives him or her a "pat on the back." Human resources is a field where "you're damned if you do and damned if you don't," since it is hard to keep managers and employees happy, insiders confide. "Everyone has some sort of axe to grind and favor to demand," which makes "burnout" a common malady.

Those in the HR department generally have "access to top-secret information," such as "salaries, discipline problems and health problems." It is considered an HR asset to "keep one's mouth shut about sensitive, confidential information." It is important to HR professionals that they breed trust, not only with themselves but also with the company as a whole.

SKILLS TO ACQUIRE

- BA, BS or MS

A Day in the Life: HR Generalist

8:30 a.m.: Today I am in by 8:30 for a partner meeting. It's rare that I get to go to these, but my HR director is presenting to the partners on a new vacation policy based on some of the research I did. She's asked me to be there, since I did a lot of the work.

9:45 a.m.: At 9:45, I am back at my desk. I got to listen to the partners debate about the policy, and my director has asked me to do some additional research on a statistic they'd like before making a decision.

10:30 a.m.: I send the research off to my director and head off to the second meeting of the day. There are 15 HR staff members in our office, and we meet once a week to go over the tasks we're working on. There are three of us who are generalists, and we usually work on projects for the managers, so it's good to hear what my peers are working on.

12:00 p.m.: Today happens to be my performance review day, so my manager is taking me to lunch to talk about it. I have already seen the review, and was satisfied with it, but we're going to lunch to talk about what things I can do to work on some of my weaknesses.

1:30 p.m.: Back at my desk again, I get to work on the employee satisfaction survey. Our company is launching this survey nationally, and there is one generalist in each office responsible for the administration. It's a big project because I have to set the survey up for our office and get all of the communication ready for my manager to review.

4:00 p.m.: I have a quick afternoon status meeting with my manager and director on the survey. They have a lot of questions on how the survey will be administered and how we'll access the data. I have been the main point of contact with HQ on this so I update them.

5:00 p.m.: I finish answering a few e-mails before getting out the door pretty quickly. I am taking classes at night toward a master's degree in HR, so I have to make sure I leave on time to get to class on time.

What I didn't get to today: There are probably a thousand things I haven't done today. I have about 30 e-mails I haven't even read that I will get to first thing in the morning, and I also have to go through some resumes that were submitted for an HR generalist position that is becoming vacant.

Reflections on my typical day: Today was an overly busy day—more meetings than I usually have. I typically spend most of the day at my desk doing research, answering employee questions or laying the ground work for big projects. But I like the meetings, too. It's energizing to learn from my colleagues.

A Day in the Life: Associate VP, Human Resources

Maxine Klump Kent, Associate Vice President, Human Resources, Central Michigan University

7:00 a.m.: I generally arrive around 7:00 a.m. I organize my day, look at my calendar to make sure I am ready for any meetings I have today or for the week (if I know they will take longer prep than one day) and also at my pending list to see what the priorities are. I plan my day—what has to get done, etc. I also clear my e-mail (if I can) and go through mail from the prior day.

Visit Vault at **www.vault.com** for insider company profiles, expert advice,
career message boards, expert resume reviews, the Vault Job Board and more.

VAULT CAREER LIBRARY **107**

8:00 a.m.: I try to have 8 a.m. to 9 a.m. as hold time so I can continue with the items above, reading mail, responding, correspondence, etc. This is not always possible, as sometimes I have breakfast meetings. Since I have three directors reporting to me, I often have policies, proposals or other reports from them to read and respond to.

9:00 a.m. to 12:00 p.m.: This time is generally spent in meetings. The meetings can be for a variety of things. I meet weekly for an hour with each of my directors to get updated on what they are working on, answer questions and give feedback. I also meet weekly for an hour with the VP to keep him posted on what is happening in HR and on campus. Every two weeks, we have a department-wide staff meeting for two hours. The first hour is generally a presentation on a new process or new information someone has gotten from a conference, the second is a roundtable to keep everyone informed on what is happening. My meetings might also be to address special topics, like a proposed policy. It might be to deal with a pending personnel issue like a discipline, investigation, grievance/arbitration, termination or criminal history check. Currently, we are doing our annual analysis of market competitiveness, preparing for bargaining with two unions and doing our annual calculations to set our self-insured rates for medical, prescription drug and dental coverage—so I will be attending lots of meetings to discuss our findings and prepare our recommendations for the Board.

12:00 p.m.: If I do not have a lunch meeting, I generally network with a colleague over lunch or grab a salad while trying to catch up with professional reading.

1:00 to 6:00 p.m.: My afternoons vary from completely filled with meetings as noted above, or doing project work, such as making recommendations based on the analysis of my staff as to how much salary and benefit adjustments should be, how we should handle upcoming layoffs, what our strategy should be for retention of our star players, our strategy and goals for bargaining, etc., returning phone calls, answering e-mails and so on. I generally take a final look at the rest of the week to make sure I have my priorities accounted for.

6:00 p.m.: I generally work until about 5:30 p.m. doing any of the above that didn't get done for the day. I also sit on a nonprofit board, so I frequently have meetings in the evening for that or events associated with the university.

What I didn't get to today: There is never enough time to get it all done. Right now sitting on my desk is the editing of our self-study for accreditation, preparing mid-year evaluations for my directors, preparing a 5 percent budget reduction from our HR account, updating our strategic report and goals, a wellness proposal for my review and an issue dealing with benefit deductions for 18 pay faculty among other things. I also have a stack of professional reading that I am very interested in, but never seem to find the time to review.

Reflections on my typical day: I really enjoy what I do. I find it challenging, with lots of opportunities for creativity and opportunities to make the university a better place for people to work. I deal with people issues, benefit plan design, calculations for budget and bargaining, strategy—my work is never boring.

Insurance Agent

UPPERS	DOWNERS
• Independence	• Long hours
• Strong advancement opportunities	• High level of dissatisfaction
• High pay	

Overview

Most people would rather not think about insurance at all. But when the time comes to buy into a plan, an insurance agent can be a big help. Insurance agents, also called producers, sell one or more types of insurance, such as life, property, casualty, health, disability and long-term care, from one or more insurance company. Insurance policies provide protection to individuals and businesses against loss or catastrophe.

We'll help you plan

Insurance agents don't just hawk the same insurance plans to everyone they meet. They consider the financial status and life situation of their clients and assist them in selecting their optimal insurance policy. When selecting a policy, an agent helps tailor the value of the policy to the financial needs of the policyholder, whether that person needs to send a child to college or build up their nest egg for retirement. Increasingly, insurance agents and brokers offer comprehensive financial planning services to their clients, such as retirement planning counseling. Because of this, many insurance agents and brokers are licensed to sell mutual funds and other securities.

The work of an insurance professional includes such things as helping policyholders when they have a claim, generating reports and keeping records. Specialists in group policies may help employers provide their employees the opportunity to buy insurance through payroll deductions. Agents may work for one company or independently for several companies. Brokers do not sell for a particular company, but direct their clients to companies that offer the best rate and coverage.

The insurance industry is broadly split into two main categories: property and casualty, and health and life. Property and casualty insurance agents and brokers sell policies that protect individuals and businesses from financial loss as a result of automobile accidents, fire or theft, tornadoes and storms, and other events that can damage property. Health and life agents sell insurance that covers medical bills and provides compensation to a family in the event of a death.

People, people, people

An insurance agent's success is contingent upon his or her ability to seek out and retain clients and on the agent's reputation among colleagues. Difficulty in developing a client base drives many insurance agents from the field early. However, those who are able to withstand such adversity can look forward to high salaries and career autonomy.

PERSONALITY MATCH	PERSONALITY MISS
• Outgoing	• Sensitive
• Organized	• Creative
• Persistent	• Timid
• Independent	
• Confident	

Visit Vault at **www.vault.com** for insider company profiles, expert advice, career message boards, expert resume reviews, the Vault Job Board and more.

VAULT CAREER LIBRARY 109

Career Path

Insurance agents and brokers must obtain a license in the states where they plan to sell insurance. By law, licenses are issued only to applicants who complete specified courses and then pass written examinations covering insurance fundamentals and insurance laws. Agents who plan to sell mutual funds and other securities must also obtain a separate securities license. New agents typically receive training at pre-licensing schools conducted by state insurance agents' associations or at the home offices of the insurance company. Most states also have mandatory education requirements focusing on insurance laws, consumer protection, and the technical details of various insurance policies.

An insurance agent who shows sales ability and leadership may become a sales manager in a local office. Those who continue to advance move to executive positions. Agents with a strong client base, however, usually prefer to remain in sales because of the high pay. Often, these agents will use these relationships to go into business for themselves.

This high pay comes in various forms. Working on commission is the most common type of compensation. Independent agents normally receive commission only, while insurance agencies or carriers may pay their agents a salary only, a salary plus commission or a salary plus bonuses. Commissions are usually dependent upon the type and amount of insurance sold and whether the policy was new or a renewal.

HOURS	SALARY
• Average about 40 per week	• Median salary: $43,870

Our Survey Says

Insurance agents are, by and large, "proud" to be in the "business of helping people." One agent lauds the "exceptional pay" and perks such as scholarships for employees' children and on-site child development centers. Independent agents and brokers appreciate not having to deal with "restrictions on autonomy" and sometimes "inflexible" responses to change. Says one insurance agent, "The biggest benefit is that you have some flexibility in your work schedule." Agents cite the "peaks and valleys" of working on commission as unsettling at times, but the "earning potential is tremendous" for those who do so. Many appreciate the ability to determine their own income—"to control your own destiny." One California agent describes it as "freedom to make my own income level: the more I sell, the more I make. If I want or need a raise, I just have to sell more to earn more commission."

Those who have the drive, determination and talent to make it past the first years of learning to work independently report loving their jobs. Employers want their agents to "think outside of the box," have "time management skills," "discipline" and "the ability to accept rejection." Although some agents lament the formal dress code, most happily endure "dark suits or silk blouses" in exchange for the chance to make "sky-high commissions." One agent sums up the agent experience by saying that "the hours are long but this is the chance to run your own show and get paid handsomely for it."

SKILLS TO ACQUIRE
• For insurance agents selling financial products: certification from the National Association of Securities Dealers (NASD) or the Securities and Exchange Commission (SEC)

Interior Designer

UPPERS	DOWNERS
• Travel	• Low starting pay
• Exposure to high-profile clients/industries	• Difficult clients
• Creativity is encouraged	

Overview

Not just decoration

As their name implies, interior designers design interiors. It's not just about shopping for antiques and picking out curtains. They determine the functionality and safety of a space as well as its aesthetic, which all determine in how the space makes one feel. Their work encompasses a wide range of specialized knowledge, including structural engineering and basic architectural principles.

Interior design requires an eye for spatial relations, color, texture and fashion, as well as the intuition to know what a client will enjoy. In their assessments, interior designers consider size, safety, ease of use and cost, among other things. They must also be good listeners and visionaries, with the know-how to execute their clients' sometimes vague and fantastic requirements.

Interior designers engineer spaces for homes, hotels, offices, art galleries and fashion shows. Most specialize in a certain area, such as residential design, and some have more specific specialties, like kitchen or bathroom design. The main difference between interior designers and interior decorators is that designers are responsible for the internal operations of the spaces they design, including electrical wiring, stress levels and installation procedures. They have to think like architects, as clients often call in interior designers to begin working on sketches and models before a space is built, with only a blueprint to guide them. Designers aren't just concerned with whether the structures will hold up: all of their designs must be in accordance with federal, state and local laws, including building codes and accessibility standards for the elderly and disabled. Thus, a career in interior design requires a license in many states.

The tools of the interior design trade include CAD (computer-aided design) programs to create and visualize the final product. CAD tools also allow clients to see what changes can be made at any stage of design without affecting costs.

PERSONALITY MATCH	PERSONALITY MISS
• Creative	• Conservative
• Outgoing	• Disorganized
• Detail-oriented	
• Multi-tasker	
• Persistent	

Visit Vault at **www.vault.com** for insider company profiles, expert advice, career message boards, expert resume reviews, the Vault Job Board and more.

VAULT CAREER LIBRARY　　111

Career Path

Almost all interior designers have a bachelor of arts or a bachelor of applied arts, and additional formal interior design training and accreditation. Few clients, especially commercial clients, are willing to entrust responsibility for designing living and working spaces, not to mention huge budgets, to a designer with no formal credentials.

Formal training for interior designers is available in two- and three-year professional schools that award certificates or associate degrees in design. Graduates of two-year programs generally start as assistants to designers. The curriculum in four-year bachelor of fine arts degree programs includes art and art history, principles of design, designing and sketching, as well as specialized studies for individual design disciplines such as textiles, mechanical and architectural drawing, computerized design, sculpture, architecture and basic engineering. A liberal arts education, with courses in merchandising, business administration, marketing and psychology, along with training in art is also a good background for interior design. And those with training or experience in architecture have an advantage in interior design.

Beginning designers usually receive on-the-job training and normally need two to three years of training before they advance to higher-level positions. Experienced designers in large firms may advance to chief designer, design department head or other supervisory positions, while some experienced designers seek out the big money by opening their own businesses.

Licensing

Interior design is the only design field subject to government regulation; 21 states and the District of Columbia require licensure. Because licensing is not mandatory in all states, membership in a professional association is universally recognized as a mark of achievement for designers. Professional membership usually requires the completion of three or four years of postsecondary education in design, at least two years of practical experience in the field, and completion of the National Council for Interior Design qualification examination.

HOURS	SALARY
• Average about 45 per week	• Median salary: $42,260
	• Highest salaries are in engineering and architectural services
	• Lowest salaries are in furniture and home furnishings stores

Our Survey Says

A career in interior design "allows your creative juices to flow." Insiders describe it as a "highly competitive line of work," particularly in big cities like New York, Atlanta, Chicago and Los Angeles. Most designers who make "big bucks" are those with "exceptional talent, experience, backers, money to help them get started" and, of course, "clients who are willing to pay."

Clients and other designers can be "a joy" or "very difficult to work with;" regardless, interior designers have to "know a lot about people and public relations." Most designers agree that they derive the most enjoyment from "creating fantasy spaces." Assignments range from designing "the inside of a spaceship to designing cartoon landscapes for toy companies."

The hours in interior design are "never 9 to 5," especially for new graduates who have to learn on the job about detailing and space planning material. Dress code varies between firms, but the general rule is "funky but sophisticated." Often, "the perks are unreal, particularly if you're working for a big company," insiders say. One recent design school grad was "driven around in a limousine, taken to bars, and showered with champagne on the way back to the airport."

SKILLS TO ACQUIRE

- BA or BS
- Accreditation from National Council for Interior Design (NCID)

A Day in the Life: Design Assistant for Interior Design Firm

8:00 a.m.: Arrive at the office before the rest of the staff, brew coffee and ensure the office is in order. Wash dishes left over from yesterday's client meeting.

8:30 a.m.: Check voicemail and e-mail for messages. Review calendar for day's appointments and call for confirmations. Adjust schedule as necessary and print revised schedule for head designer.

9:00 a.m.: Other employees arrive. Operate switchboard for all incoming calls and take messages for staff who are unavailable. Field calls from sales representatives requesting appointments with designers. Interface with clients and vendors.

10:00 a.m.: Speak with the head designer. Receive instructions on several tasks, such as picking up fabric samples from design center, contacting dealers regarding memo items (pieces on loan for display only) for a client meeting, dictation of a letter for a potential client that must be messengered by noon.

11:00 a.m.: Work on projects assigned by head designer while continually operating switchboard. Letter is first priority; complete it and give to head designer to proof. Contact dealers regarding memo items and arrange shipment with local delivery service.

12:00 p.m.: Send revised letter to potential client. Once messenger arrives, escape for lunch. Pick up fabric samples while picking up lunch—a reprieve from the switchboard for at least an hour. Visit several fabric houses and leave design center loaded down with bags. Pick up lunch for yourself and other office mates at nearby café.

1:30 p.m.: Check voicemail and e-mail for messages while you were out. Open and sort mail. Address envelopes for bookkeeper. Prepare office for client meeting at 2:30. Run up the street to purchase a new orchid for entryway. Brew more coffee and tea. Ensure conference room is organized and clean. Gather any last-minute information head designer needs for meeting.

2:30 p.m.: Show clients to conference room, offer drinks and snacks. Work on additional projects other staff members have requested: errands, scheduling of appointments, shipments of furniture. Keep track of money in meters and ensure clients do not get parking tickets while in meeting.

4:00 p.m.: Clients leave. Clean conference room, wash dishes. Empty trash throughout office. Return calls on behalf of designer and schedule additional appointments for remainder of week.

5:00 p.m.: Since there is nothing urgent to complete, you get to leave on time!

Visit Vault at **www.vault.com** for insider company profiles, expert advice, career message boards, expert resume reviews, the Vault Job Board and more.

VAULT CAREER LIBRARY 113

A Day in the Life: Corporate Interior Designer

8:30 a.m.: Arrive at the office. Peruse e-mail and phone messages.

9:30 a.m.: Attend construction meeting for a current project, the law offices of a prestigious downtown law firm. Consult with architects and other team members of the project; answer design questions. Listen to progress report regarding status of building.

12:00 p.m.: Break for lunch. Grab a quick bite at the local deli, then head back to check e-mails and phone messages left during meeting. Return calls regarding orders and requests for meetings. Send correspondence to carpet supplier, checking on delivery date of order. The installation date is only a month away and the carpet still hasn't been shipped from overseas— very nerve-wracking!

2:00 p.m.: Spend time in the sample library, pulling together finish samples and product ideas for a new project—a doctor's office in Beverly Hills. Have to keep in mind that all the finishes and fabrics must be resilient since doctors' offices get a lot of traffic, wear and tear.

4:00 p.m.: Gather internal team members who will be working on the new project to discuss responsibilities and deadlines as well as the overall design scheme.

5:30 p.m.: Technically, time to go home, but there is still a stack of orders to be reviewed and e-mails to return. Since work usually requires four to six overtime hours a week, might as well try and catch up some tonight.

7:00 p.m.: E-mails returned, orders processed, time to head home!

Investment Banker

UPPERS	DOWNERS
• Through-the-roof salaries	• Back-breaking hours
• Perks like free meals and car service	• High stress level
• Power	

Overview

Masters of the Universe

Tom Wolfe called them "Masters of the Universe" in *The Bonfire of the Vanities*; Michael Lewis called them a few unprintable things in *Liar's Poker*. Who are they? Investment bankers, salespeople and traders. Investment banks aren't like your local branch office with ubiquitous ATMs (those are commercial banks, like Citibank or Bank of America); investment banks work with corporations, governments, institutional investors and extraordinarily wealthy individuals to raise capital and provide investment advice.

The different parts of the investment bank

There are dozens of specialized functions at an investment bank, ranging from private wealth management (essentially, brokers to the rich) to risk managers (those who make sure the bank isn't taking on too much risk). At most major investment banks, the corporate finance and sales and trading functions are among the largest and most important.

The corporate finance department works to raise money for companies and other large organizations looking to expand or acquire new holdings. Generally, companies or organizations will approach a few different banks and then these banks compete for the deal. Teams of analysts, associates, VPs and MDs work to analyze the potential profit and risk for their own bank while creating pitches to entice the client. While good math and Excel skills are essential to being a successful I-banker, those who can buttress their quantitative skills with creativity when building pitch books and PowerPoint presentations tend to catch the eye of their superiors.

Sales and trading is a different story. An investment banking trading floor is chaos. There's usually a lot of swearing, yelling and shouting going on—a pressure cooker of stress. Traders must rely on their market instincts, and salespeople yell for "bids" when the market tumbles. Deciding what to buy or sell, and at what price to buy and sell, is difficult when millions of dollars are at stake.

However, salespeople and traders work much more reasonable hours than research analysts or corporate finance bankers. Rarely does a salesperson or trader venture into the office on a Saturday or Sunday, leaving the trading floor completely void of life on weekends. Any corporate finance analyst who has crossed a trading floor on a Saturday will tell you that the only noises to be heard are the clocks clicking every minute and the whir of the air conditioner.

The economic ripple

Many banks and financial firms actively invest in and trade debt (in these circles, being owed money is almost as good as having the money already) as a way to generate profit. In the summer of 2007, many homeowners across the United States found that they could no longer pay their mortgages due to increased interest rates and, as a result, home foreclosures skyrocketed—this is commonly referred to as the subprime mortgage collapse or subprime crisis. Banks and other financial firms with investments in these defaulted home loans have been rapidly losing money ever since.

Visit Vault at **www.vault.com** for insider company profiles, expert advice, career message boards, expert resume reviews, the Vault Job Board and more.

VAULT CAREER LIBRARY   115

Just months after record-breaking bonuses were doled out on Wall Street, the 2007 subprime mortgage collapse created a seismic rift through Wall Street as investment banks around the world are reporting total losses in the hundreds of billions of dollars for the first quarter of 2008. Entire groups in real estate, home lending and syndicated finance are being restructured or eliminated as banks announce lay-offs of 5 to 10 percent of their workforce. Multiple interest rate cuts by the Fed are confirming the prospect of a full-blown economic recession by late 2008 and the stock market continues to nose-dive every time a major multi-national corporation discloses significant losses. A spike in MBA and JD applicants is expected in the next admissions cycle as former bankers attempt to ride out the looming recession.

PERSONALITY MATCH	PERSONALITY MISS
• Analytical • Aggressive • Confident • Workaholic • Greedy	• Shy • Mellow • Cautious

Career Path

In corporate finance, undergraduates are generally hired into grueling two-year analyst programs that promise plenty of all-nighters and 90-hour weeks. The first couple of months include extensive training in accounting and Excel modeling—while a basic knowledge of accounting and economics is beneficial when interviewing for an analyst position, ambition and the willingness to learn are essential to succeeding. Long days entail reviewing financial statements of companies, modeling to generate projected numbers, creating pitch books and ultimately making recommendations on potential profits from investments in specific companies. Analysts may also start to determine the fair market value for a company looking to trade its stock publicly. In larger firms, analysts may specialize in a certain industry, like transportation or health care, or a certain market, such as government financing.

After completing the program, "graduating" analysts often leave to attend graduate school or to find another job. Some analysts able to stand the long hours and stress, will stay on for a third year (if it is offered) in order to gain more experience, more money, and a better shot at getting in a top MBA program. Firms have often promoted top analysts to associate positions after their third years. More recently, however, some firms have started to promote top analysts to associate after only two years.

Like analysts, associates in investment banking work virtually all the time, and their stress level can be higher as mistakes are not as easily tolerated. Associates gradually take on more and more client contact and move up to the vice president level in three to four years. After vice president comes director (or senior vice president) and then managing director. Established relationships and networking abilities determine the success of an MD who is often responsible for originating deals within his/her sector.

In sales and trading, the career path is not quite as structured. For example, analysts move more easily to the associate level without an MBA than they do in corporate finance. And associates can climb quickly to the VP and director levels, depending on the firm's need and the talent of the salesperson or trader.

HOURS	SALARY
• Average 80 per week	• Entry-level undergrads on Wall Street: $55,000 to $65,000 + $40,000 to $90,000 bonus • Entry-level MBAs on Wall Street: $100,000 + $100,000 to $200,000 year-end bonus.

Our Survey Says

Don't make the mistake of thinking that all investment banks are the same. While it's true that I-banks tend to fulfill the same functions, their cultures can be very divergent. At one major investment bank, employees say it can be "quite a forgiving place in many ways." A trader there explains: "There have been some people, mostly at the middle level, who have lost $30 million in a day. Nobody's happy about it, but it's not the end of the world, they keep them. I've had my losing days myself, and they haven't fired me. Sometimes I've even come to the office hung over." However, other firms are not so easygoing, featuring a "horrendous" bureaucracy which "can sometimes combine with office politics to make life miserable and incomprehensible." "Sometimes, for no apparent reason, you get blamed for things you didn't do, and get assignments you're not supposed to have, and there's no one to complain to—life becomes like a page from a Kafka novel," says one young insider.

Trading is its own world, complete with its own culture. One trader says: "Trading is like warfare. It can get very frantic and then very quiet, and flare again without warning. It's long periods of silence punctuated by fear and terror. That's what makes it stressful." Life off the floor isn't much less stressful, according to I-bankers. One associate says, "You burn out by the time you're 30. Most people last only until they're about 35, then go off and do something else. Some people move into managerial roles within the firm or at another firm, and some will just leave the business entirely because, frankly, they're tired."

SKILLS TO ACQUIRE

• Bachelor's degree with coursework in economics and accounting

• MBA or JD for certain positions

A Day in the Life: Investment Banking Associate

We've asked insiders at leading investment banks to offer us insight into a day in the life of their position. Here's a look at a day of an associate I-banker at Goldman Sachs.

8:15 a.m. : Arrive at 85 Broad Street. (Show Goldman ID card to get past the surly elevator guards.)

8:25 a.m.: Arrive on 17th floor. Use "blue card" to get past floor lobby. ("Don't ever forget your blue card. Goldman has tight security and you won't be able to get around the building all day.")

8:45 a.m.: Pick up work from Word Processing, review it, make changes.

9:00 a.m.: Check voicemail, return phone calls.

9:30 a.m.: Eat breakfast; read *The Wall Street Journal*. ("But don't let a supervisor see you with your paper sprawled across your desk.")

Visit Vault at **www.vault.com** for insider company profiles, expert advice, career message boards, expert resume reviews, the Vault Job Board and more.

V\ULT CAREER LIBRARY 117

10:00 a.m.: Prepare pitchbooks, discuss analysis with members of deal team.

12:00 p.m.: Conference call with members of IPO team, including lawyers and client.

1:00 p.m.: Eat lunch at desk. ("The Wall Street McDonald's delivers, but it's the most expensive McDonald's in New York City; Goldman's cafeteria is cheaper, but you have to endure the shop talk.")

2:00 p.m.: Work on restructuring case studies; make several document requests from Goldman library.

3:00 p.m.: Start to prepare analysis; order additional data from DRG (data resources group).

5:00 p.m.: Check in with vice presidents and heads of deal teams on status of work.

6:00 p.m.: Go to gym for an abbreviated workout.

6:45 p.m.: Dinner. ("Dinner is free in the IBD cafeteria, but avoid it. Wall Street has pretty limited food options, so for a quick meal it's the Indian place across the street that's open 24 hours.")

8:00 p.m.: Meet with VP again. ("You'll probably get more work thrown at you before he leaves.")

9:45 p.m.: Try to make FedEx cutoff. Drop off pitchbook to Document Processing on 20th floor. ("You have to call ahead and warn them if you have a last-minute job or you're screwed.")

10:00 p.m.: Order in food again. ("It's unlikely that there will be any room left in your meal allowance—but we usually order in a group and add extra names to bypass the limit.")

11:00 p.m.: Leave for home. ("Call for a car service. Enjoy your nightly meal on wheels on the way home.")

Librarian

UPPERS	DOWNERS
• Sharing information with people • Expertise in multiple topics and technologies	• Long workdays with little assistance • High stress level • Clueless customers

Overview

Taming the information hydra

As people have become exposed to more information than ever before, librarians' data-handling skills have become increasingly essential. Careers in the library have changed as the Internet has encroached upon the historic domain of the library, but the new breed of librarian, really a savvy information manager, has adapted right along with the times.

A veritable catalog of career options

Entry-level library workers are known as pages. Their duties include shelving books, checking volumes in or out and similar tasks. Most work part time, while in school or as a summer job. The next rung up on the ladder, library assistants or technicians, help and instruct patrons, retrieve materials from restricted areas and issue library cards; they may also specialize in a certain department such as reference or multimedia. They can also be involved in library outreach activities, such as a bookmobile or bringing books to the elderly. This position does not require a master's degree in library science, but may call for some post-collegiate study. Library assistants may work part or full time.

The duties of full librarians include acquiring books and other educational materials and entering them in the catalog, as well as the discarding of materials that are no longer useful. Librarians must be highly technologically literate, in order to cope with evolving data storage and retrieval technologies. Some librarians work specifically with speakers of foreign languages, with children or in schools. Depending on the size of the library, librarians' duties may be primarily administrative and/or managerial (in the case of large university or urban libraries that may employ hundreds of people), whereas within a small rural library, the librarian might be the sole employee.

Depending on the individual library's hours, a librarian may work weekends, evenings and even some holidays. Elementary and high school librarians, however, like teachers, often have off work while school is out. More than a fifth of librarians work part time, as libraries frequently hire part-time workers in order to allow for longer hours.

PERSONALITY MATCH	PERSONALITY MISS
• Analytical • Efficient • Literate • Technologically adept	• Disorganized • Unmethodical

Visit Vault at **www.vault.com** for insider company profiles, expert advice, career message boards, expert resume reviews, the Vault Job Board and more.

VAULT CAREER LIBRARY 119

Career Path

Mastering their art

Librarians generally have a master's degree in library science (MLS), preferably from a one- or two-year program accredited by the American Library Association (ALA); there are currently over 50 such programs in North America. Topics of study include the history of books and printing, theories and methods of information organization, censorship and more. Some librarians go on to acquire more advanced degrees in library science, in order to follow a career path in academia, or additional master's degrees in other topics, if they wish to work in a specialized library, such as in medicine or law. Librarians who work in schools may hold degrees in both education and library science.

Beyond the stacks

Contrary to popular perception, librarians don't just hang out with books—public libraries (i.e., not university) often function more like community centers than simply repositories of bound information. Frequently they host events that address literacy, censorship, fund-raising and specific groups such as children, young adults, retirees or the disadvantaged. Other events, such as bridge games, craft lessons or film festivals, are sometimes held at libraries.

Holders of an MLS or those with an interest in information management can also find success beyond traditional library settings with information brokers, private corporations and consulting firms. Many librarians have jumped from educational institutions to corporations, where they function as data experts and chief information officers (CIOs). Their research and data management skills are highly coveted, as is their familiarity with computer databases and networks.

Demand for librarians is expected to grow slowly between now and 2014, as technology takes the place of some human work. That said, the library job market is predicted to grow after that point, as three in five librarians working today are over the age of 45 and slated to retire in a decade or so, freeing up room for advancement. Strong growth has been predicted for nontraditional library activities in consultancies and corporations.

For your first assignment, find some resources

The ALA's web site (www.ala.org) is very informative in and of itself—but for those who are just starting to think about a career in the stacks, check out the ALA's separate, more introductory web site, www.librarycareers.org, which answers such questions as "What is librarianship about?" and "What kind of library offers the best match for my interests?"

As for librarian culture—again butting up against a common misconception—it's worth noting that those employed in the field are remarkably social outside of work. The ALA sponsors a number of conferences each year, and professional organizations for people in law, medical and theological libraries also host conferences that are ideal for networking.

HOURS	SALARY
• Average about 40 per week	• Median salary: $49,060
	• Median salary in the Federal Government: $70,060
	• Median salary for library technicians: $26,560

Our Survey Says

The few, the proud, the librarians

A librarian's day can consist of everything from "tracking down a 50-year-old, out-of-print monograph on government" to "explaining microfiche to a 10-year-old." The job is "hard" the first year and many librarians remember "wanting desperately to quit." However, after "proving [their] mettle" during this "weeding-out process," most find that "you gain so much more respect."

One insider says it takes a certain kind of person to be able to "commit [one's] life to creating order out of chaos." Librarians are not allowed to recede into a hermetically-sealed environment, "alone with those precious books;" rather, they must be "ambassadors of learning" and deal with some of the "most difficult personalities imaginable." The hours can be long and the pay "merely adequate" at first, but after a few years most librarians feel that "the money and the multitude of tasks" make all their hard work worthwhile.

SKILLS TO ACQUIRE

- BA or BS
- Master's degree in library science (MLS) required for advancement

Visit Vault at **www.vault.com** for insider company profiles, expert advice, career message boards, expert resume reviews, the Vault Job Board and more.

VAULT CAREER LIBRARY   121

Management Consultant

UPPERS	DOWNERS
• High pay	• Grueling travel
• Wide variety of projects	• Long hours
• Intellectual stimulation	• Too much jargon
	• Unpaid overtime

Overview

What is it you do?

Consulting may sound nebulous, but it's a booming industry, even if many aren't quite sure what consultants actually do. Basically, consultants are hired by a company (or sometimes, a government entity or a nonprofit) to help assess its problems, plan its future, or improve operational efficiency and profits. These companies believe that consultants are neutral outsiders, sometimes with more overall industry experience than the client itself. Teams of consultants then work on projects—usually called "engagements"—for the client that can last anywhere from a couple of weeks to several years.

Because consultants are always moving to new engagements and learning new information about their clients and their industries, management consulting—whether strategy, operations or information technology in nature—is a unique career that offers the chance to work within many industries and companies, rub shoulders with CEOs, and travel throughout the country and the world. Consulting firms sell knowledge, and the skill and expertise of their employees. Expect long hours, lots of travel, the inability to make firm weekend plans, and an insider's view of sick and hypochondriac companies and organizations around the world.

Popular profession

Consulting is one of the best-paid professions for recent grads, offering lucrative salary packages and the chance to hobnob with top management of Fortune 500 companies, while working on some of the most interesting issues that these clients face. At first glance it looks like a no-brainer.

But don't be hasty. A career in consulting has many positives, but it is certainly no walk in the park. Pressures are high, travel is onerous and the interview process can be painful. Before setting off down the consulting route, you should develop a good understanding of where the industry is going, what your role will be and how closely it fits with your needs and personality.

PERSONALITY MATCH	PERSONALITY MISS
• People-oriented	• Antisocial
• Well spoken	• Inflexible
• Analytical	• Afraid of flying
• Independent	
• Creative	

Visit Vault at **www.vault.com** for insider company profiles, expert advice, career message boards, expert resume reviews, the Vault Job Board and more.

VAULT CAREER LIBRARY   123

Career Path

While job titles may differ between consulting firms, the levels and promotion path across firms is remarkably similar. Students graduating from undergraduate institutions come into a firm at an analyst stage, while those with an MBA or similar degree enter at an associate (also called consultant) level. (At Booz Allen, recent grads of undergraduate programs are called consultants.) After one-and-a-half to three years as an associate, the next promotion is to manager. Consultants at this level have a day-to-day relationship with the client and responsibility for managing the activities of the team. The key difference in this role is the need to step back from the details more often, and an increased use of people management skills. Following manager, the senior manager position allows the consultant to begin to develop more off-engagement relationships with clients and to prospect for new business. At this stage, the senior manager is also given a broader range of projects to oversee at a somewhat higher level.

The ultimate aspiration of a career consultant is to achieve the partnership/director position. This level is about building and maintaining client relationships and developing the intellectual capital of the firm. As most consultancies are still partnerships, promotion to director normally involves a hefty increase in compensation, as directors begin to benefit directly from the firm's profits.

Analysts typically spend two to three years at a consulting firm before returning to get an MBA or abandoning the field of consulting altogether. Some consulting firms will now promote top analysts directly to the associate level. At most top consulting firms (Bain, Boston Consulting Group and McKinsey, for instance), the typical path for analysts includes business school before a promotion to associate. In rare cases, a sterling analyst may be given the option for promotion without an MBA. At other firms (e.g., Capgemini, Booz Allen Hamilton), analysts routinely win promotions to associate after two to three years. Not all firms are so cut-and-dry in their career paths, though, allowing for some flexibility and customization according to the individuals' needs and preferences (e.g., Deloitte Consulting LLP).

HOURS	SALARY
• Average about 65 per week	• Average salary for research analysts: $39,200
	• Entry-level consultants: $58,000
	• Management consultants: $76,300
	• Senior consultants: $100,300
	• Junior partners: $133,500
	• Senior partners: $259,500

Our Survey Says

Like separate countries, consulting firms have their own cultures. One associate at a consulting firm says, "The camaraderie here very appealing because this industry is somewhat cutthroat and it's good to have that human touch." Part of that competition is engendered by the "up or out" policy that many firms sport—which means that consultants must advance at a certain pace or find a new job that's more suitable for them. "At my former firm," says one consultant, "you're either promoted or told to leave after two years. That creates a lot of insecurity. It's survival of the fittest, and I don't know how much teamwork that culture can really support. My new consulting firm doesn't have that policy and that makes it a nicer place to work." Consultants are generally bright overachievers, and so it's no surprise that one consultant thinks his firm "attracts very aggressive businesspeople who are well-rounded and down to earth. The company values leadership and integrity." Another consultant says he's "surrounded by brilliant people," which "makes it harder to stand out."

Some consulting firms are defined by their socialization. "My firm will spend to create a friendly work environment," says one insider. Another insider reports that his firm's atmosphere is "totally convivial—like an elite fraternity or sorority." Firm culture can be affected by outside forces as well: "My firm had some problems two years ago, and people are still a little nervous and still look over their shoulders," says one consultant, while another Big Four consultant says: "The culture is still pretty much dominated by the accounting side, as you can tell by all the blue and gray ugly suits walking around here, even though the consulting side of the firm is increasingly profitable." Despite these separate traditions and quirks, all consulting firms emphasize and value teamwork. "The culture is very collaborative," say insiders. "People in Australia will get on a plane and fly to your client in the middle of the night to help you out with a project," says another consultant. "Most firms look "for extraordinarily smart people who have the ambition, the ability and the self-discipline to give 200 percent where only 100 percent would suffice. Consultants are experts in fields you've never heard of. They are mavericks and builders and it is a true joy to work with them," gushes one insider.

SKILLS TO ACQUIRE

• Bachelor's degree, often an MBA to advance

A Day in the Life: Strategy Consulting Associate

Greig Schneider is an associate at McKinsey's Boston office. He kindly agreed to share a "typical" workday at McKinsey with Vault, noting that no day at McKinsey or any consulting firm can be called typical.

6:15 a.m.: Alarm goes off. I wake up asking myself why I put "run three times per week" into the team charter. I meet another member of the team and we hobble out for a jog. At least it's warm out—another advantage of having a project in Miami.

7:15 a.m.: Check voicemail. Someone in London wants a copy of my knowledge building document on managing hypergrowth. A co-worker is looking for information about what the partner from my last team is like to work with.

7:30 a.m.: Breakfast with the team. We discuss sports, Letterman, and a morning meeting we have with the client team (not necessarily in that order). We then head out to the client.

9:00 a.m.: Meet with the client team. We've got an important progress review with the CEO next week, so there's a lot going on. We're helping the client to assess the market potential of an emerging technology. Today's meeting concerns what kind of presentation would be most effective, although we have trouble staying off tangents about the various analyses that we've all been working on. The discussion is complicated by the fact that some key data is not yet available. We elect to go with a computer-based slide show and begin the debate on the content.

10:53 a.m.: Check voicemail. The office is looking for an interviewer for Harvard Business School hell weekend. The partner will be arriving in time for dinner and wants to meet to discuss the progress review. A headhunter looking for a divisional VP. My wife reminding me to mail off the insurance forms.

11:00 a.m.: Depart with teammate for an interview. We meet with an industry expert (a professor from a local university) to discuss industry trends and in particular what the prospects are for the type of technology we're looking at. As this is the last interview we plan to do, we are able to check many of our hypotheses. The woman is amazing—we luck out and get some data we need. The bad news is now we have to figure out what it means.

12:28 p.m.: As I walk back in to the client, a division head I've been working with grabs me and we head to lunch. He wanted to discuss an analysis he'd given me some information for, and in the process I get some interesting perspectives about the difficulties in moving the technology into full production and how much it could cost.

Visit Vault at **www.vault.com** for insider company profiles, expert advice, career message boards, expert resume reviews, the Vault Job Board and more.

V/\ULT CAREER LIBRARY **125**

1:30 p.m.: I jump on a quick conference call about an internal knowledge building project I'm working on for the marketing practice. I successfully avoid taking on any additional responsibility.

2:04 p.m.: Begin to work through new data. After discussing the plan of attack with the engagement manager, I dive in. It's a very busy afternoon, but the data is great. I get a couple "a-has"—always a good feeling.

3:00 p.m: Short call with someone from Legal to get an update on the patent search.

6:00 p.m.: Team meeting. The engagement manager pulls the team together to check progress on various fronts and debate some issues prior to heading to dinner with the partner. A quick poll determines that Italian food wins—we leave a voicemail with the details.

6:35 p.m.: Call home and check in with the family. Confirm plans for weekend trip to Vermont. Apologize for forgetting to mail the insurance forms.

7:15 p.m.: The team packs up and heads out to dinner. We meet the partner at the restaurant and have a productive (and calorific) meal working through our plans for the progress review, the new data, what's going on with the client team and other areas of interest. She suggests some additional uses for the new data, adds her take on our debates, and agrees to raise a couple issues with the CFO, whom she's known for years. She takes a copy of our draft presentation to read after dinner.

9:15 p.m.: Return to hotel. Plug in computer and check e-mail, since I hadn't had a chance all day. While I'm logged in, I download two documents I need from the company database, check the Red Sox score, and see how the client's stock did.

10:10 p.m.: Pre-sleep voicemail check. A client from a previous study is looking for one of the appendices, since he lost his copy. The server will be down for an hour tomorrow night.

10:30 p.m.: Watch *SportsCenter* instead of going right to sleep, as I know I probably should.

Note: Had this been an in-town study, the following things would have been different: I wouldn't have run with another member of my team, and we'd have substituted a conference call for the dinner meeting, so we could go home instead. Also, I probably wouldn't have watched SportsCenter.

Nurse

UPPERS	DOWNERS
• Wide variety of career options	• Long hours
• Satisfaction from helping people	• Erratic schedule

Overview

More than an assistant

Nurses may be doctors' assistants, but they provide much more than just support to their MD counterparts. Registered nurses (RNs) not only care for their patients' physical condition, but they are also often the sole source of comfort to people in times of trauma, such as after an accident or just before going under the knife. Nurses spend more time with patients than doctors; sometimes they even spend more time with patients than the patients' families. Because of this close relationship with patients, there is immense physical and emotional strain associated with being a nurse, as well as many rewards.

With over two million jobs, nursing is the largest occupation in the field of health care, and the demand is growing. As the current crop of registered nurses advances towards retirement, not enough younger workers are entering the field to replace them. This shortage may result in greater perks in order to attract and retain qualified nurses. Generally speaking, registered nurses promote health, prevent disease, and help patients cope with illness. In more specific terms, this entails assisting physicians during treatments and examinations, administering medications and assisting in rehabilitation. RNs also provide instruction in health care and manage nursing care plans.

Different avenues

Nurses generally fall into several main groups, depending on where they work: in hospitals, in private practice, in private homes, etc. Hospital nurses, the largest group, are staff nurses who provide bedside nursing care and carry out the medical regimen prescribed by physicians. They also supervise licensed practical nurses and aides. Hospital nurses are typically assigned to one area such as surgery, maternity, pediatrics, emergency, ICU or oncology, but they sometimes rotate among departments.

As opposed to hospital nurses, office nurses work in private practice, clinics, surgicenters, emergency medical centers and HMOs, serving as right hands to doctors in these medical facilities. Home health nurses provide periodic services, prescribed by a physician, to patients at home. They also provide support to patients and their families, and at times work independently.

Nurses who work in nursing homes manage care for elderly residents. They spend most of their time on administrative tasks, but also assess the medical condition of residents and work in rehabilitation units, assisting patients recovering from strokes and injuries.

Public health nurses work for government and private agencies in clinics, schools, and retirement communities. They are professionals in disease prevention, proper nutrition and prenatal care. Occupational health or industrial nurses provide care at work sites to employees, either in the case of injury or for general wellness. Nurse practitioners are the most advanced nurses, with the power to write prescriptions and independently diagnose and treat patients.

Visit Vault at **www.vault.com** for insider company profiles, expert advice, career message boards, expert resume reviews, the Vault Job Board and more.

VAULT CAREER LIBRARY 127

Weird hours

It is common for hospital nurses to maintain long, irregular hours, often working double shifts or staying on call 24 hours a day. Occupational health and office nurses work more conventional 40-hour weeks. Nursing can also be a dangerous occupation, as nurses are sometimes exposed to highly infectious diseases and handle sharp objects, needles and blood.

PERSONALITY MATCH	PERSONALITY MISS
• Efficient	• Lazy
• Sympathetic	• Easily tired
• Caring	• Squeamish

Career Path

After graduating from an accredited nursing school and passing a state licensing examination, an entry-level registered nurse will have graduated from one of three programs: the associate degree of nursing (ADN) program, the bachelor of science in nursing (BSN) program, or a two-year nursing program from a community or junior college. An enrolled student in one of these programs can expect courses in such subjects as anatomy, microbiology and nutrition, as well as nursing. In addition, students receive supervised clinical experience in hospitals, ambulances or nursing homes. A bachelor's degree is generally necessary for administrative positions in hospitals and for positions in community nursing or teaching.

Experience and a good performance record bring a promotion to management, assistant head nurse or head nurse. The next advancement level is assistant director of nursing, then director, then vice president. Increasingly, management-level nursing positions require a graduate degree in nursing or health services administration. Graduate programs that prepare nurses for executive positions are one to two years long. If nurses want to advance within patient care positions, a one- to two-year graduate education is also needed to become a nurse practitioner, clinical nurse specialist or a certified nurse anesthetist. Another career option is to become a consultant for health care corporations in health planning and development, marketing and quality assurance.

HOURS	SALARY
• Average about 55 per week	• Median salary for RNs: $57,280
	• Licensed practical or vocational nurses: $36,546

Our Survey Says

Alphabet soup

Nursing educational requirements vary depending on the level of certification. Licensed practical nurses (LPs) require the least amount. For one, this was a "high school diploma, an approved 12-month nursing course, then certification through state boards"—though a colleague of hers said that her "LPN program was 18 months [and] very intense."

The next level, registered nurse (RN), requires a bachelor's or "an associate degree in nursing," says one RN. Another asserts that "the nursing classes are intense and require a lot of time; you take the same board exam whether you graduate with an associate's or a bachelor's degree." A clinical nurse specialist (CNS) says that her "position requires a master's degree in nursing with a clinical specialist track at a university level." Her colleague agrees: aspiring CSNs "need a master of science in nursing, preferably in the area [one wishes to] specialize in."

Nursing can be difficult to advance in, as one practitioner points out: "More experienced nurses are not always supportive of new nurses and sometimes try to take advantage of them. A new nurse will typically have to work the night shift for several years." Nurses must also keep up with the latest advances in medical science. Says one RN, "Nursing is a field that requires a lot of continuing education. I take classes in person and online to keep my skills up to date."

Seller's market

"The great thing about nursing is the possibilities and opportunities are almost endless," says an RN from Missouri. Pay varies by location, experience and education. "You should enter for the desire to do the work and not for the money," advises one nurse who works in the ER. On the other hand, not all nurses feel underpaid. "The salary is pretty good, the insurance benefits are fair, the bonuses are really good," notes one LP nurse. A nurse from New York says, "The pay is decent but it comes with a lot of stress." Her colleague, an RN, adds, "I have good benefits, including health insurance." One seasoned professional says, "We are in a nursing shortage; the older us Baby Boomers get, the more we need you younger nurses." "The job outlook is excellent for nursing as the population ages and has increasing health care needs," adds another nurse from the Empire State.

Not your daily grind

"You have to have a good heart and strong stomach," says a LP nurse from Trenton. Adds a Arkansas-based nurse, "This is a very rewarding career, [but] make sure your heart is in it. And don't over-do it. Burnout is very common in nursing." While the career may be rewarding, it's not always easy. An RN says, "Some patients and family are not appreciative of the care we provide. Some are even abusive. Sometimes even with a well-planned schedule, staff emergencies arise and our workload increases due to shortage." "Not all of our patients get better and it can be very hard when patients die," adds his colleague. "When you're a nurse," another says, "you often grab the obituary section of the newspaper first."

One nurse feels that the "worst part of [her] job is too little time to do everything that needs to be done. A nurse could never spend enough time with her patients." Her colleague adds, "It's hard to leave work [when] at home. The work is physically exhausting. I don't know any nurses without back pain!" The profession does offer rewards for all of the hard work that nurses put in, though. "It is not an easy job, but if you love what you do it is very rewarding," says one RN. "When it comes down to it, I wouldn't trade my nursing license for anything!" adds another. A third registered nurse says, "My job is not a job but a calling. I cannot imagine myself doing anything else as a profession other than nursing. Whether the patient gets better or not, knowing that I made a difference regardless of the outcome—it is fulfilling to me." Says a RN from Missouri, "If you care for people, this can work for you."

SKILLS TO ACQUIRE

- Degree from an accredited nursing school
- ADN, BSN, MS Nursing
- Nursing license

Visit Vault at **www.vault.com** for insider company profiles, expert advice, career message boards, expert resume reviews, the Vault Job Board and more.

VAULT CAREER LIBRARY 129

A Day in the Life: Family Nurse Practitioner

Carina Sanchez is a family nurse practitioner with 10 years' experience. She works at a migrant health center in rural North Carolina. The center receives grant funding from the federal government so that it can provide primary health care to uninsured families. Most of the patients are Spanish-speaking, so her bilingual skills are a huge asset to the practice. As a family NP, Carina sees people of all ages.

8:45 a.m.: Carina arrives and checks her schedule for the day. She has 10 patients scheduled for the morning session that runs from 9 a.m. to 1 p.m. Another 10 are scheduled for the afternoon, 2 to 5 p.m. About half of the patients keep their appointments. But, she will probably be busy because the center accepts walk-in patients who come without an appointment for an urgent problem. Carina has a student FNP working with her. The student sees every patient first, then presents the case to Carina who goes back with the student to complete the encounter. Carina is not paid for precepting the student, but she does get a clinical faculty appointment with the school of nursing and a discount on the continuing education courses they offer. She feels a professional obligation to contribute to nursing education in any way that she can.

9:00 a.m.: The first patient is a two-month old baby boy, Miguel, here for a routine checkup. He is weighed by the nursing assistant and Carina speaks to the mother about how he is feeding. She finds that he is breastfeeding and that the mother did not know she could receive WIC foods for herself while breastfeeding. (WIC is a federal program, funded through the Department of Agriculture, that provides food coupons for pregnant and nursing mothers and infants up to age five.) There is a WIC program next door to the health center so the mother is directed to go there after the checkup. Carina examines Miguel and orders routine vaccinations for him. She talks to the mother about safety, child development and family planning. Miguel will return in two months. His mother needs a family planning visit later in the week.

9:30 a.m.: Next is a 50-year-old overweight man who has back pain. Carina looks over his lab records to find that his blood sugar and blood cholesterol have been rising over the past couple of years. She speaks to him about the relationship between his weight and all of his problems. After giving him instructions for over-the-counter pain medications and back stretching exercises, she refers him to see the dietician down the hall.

10:00 a.m.: The next patient is a teenage girl, presenting with a vaginal discharge. Her mother has brought her to the health center but she graciously goes to the waiting room when Carina reminds her that the visit is confidential. Without her mother's presence, the teen admits to sexual activity so Carina does a pregnancy test and an exam checking for infection with a sexually transmitted disease. By looking at the discharge under the microscope, Carina diagnoses a simple yeast infection, treatable with over-the-counter medication. She prescribes the morning after pill and counsels the teen on safe sex and more effective birth control.

11:00 a.m.: The next three patients are here for routine follow-ups of high blood pressure. Carina checks their diets and medications and makes sure that they have routine lab work every six months. Two of them are overweight but only one agrees to see the dietician this time.

12:00 p.m.: Lunch time. Carina takes the time to check her telephone and e-mail messages and respond. She has time to review a couple of journals to keep up with new developments in health care. She eats lunch with the dietician and they begin to plan a group education series for diabetics who need to learn how to balance diet, exercise and medications to control their blood sugars. The FNP student will be involved with this also as part of her community project.

1:00 p.m.: Next is a well woman checkup for a 45-year-old. The patient wants to discuss symptoms of menopause. She also needs an exam with screening for cervical and colon cancer. Carina watches the student complete the exam and arranges a referral for mammogram. She counsels the patient on diet and exercise to stay healthy as she ages.

1:45 p.m.: Next are a couple of walk-in patients with cough and fever. Neither one is terribly ill but they are miserable and would like some medication. Because their illness is probably viral, no antibiotics will help and the best medication is over-the-counter. One of the patients is found to have large cavities in the lower right molars so is referred to the dental clinic also run by the health center.

2:30 p.m. : Another child comes in, a 12-year-old, here for a school physical. Carina has a supply of the forms needed to show that required examinations were done. She checks the immunization record to find that this child needs a booster of tetanus, diphtheria and pertussis vaccines. Also she counsels the preteen on sex, drugs and rock 'n roll to hopefully prevent future problems.

3:00 p.m.: An elderly woman comes in next. She has borderline diabetes, controlled by diet and one oral medication. She also has high blood pressure, well controlled. Her medications and her lab work are reviewed every three months. She is encouraged to keep up her daily walking schedule and to participate in activities she enjoys, such as her painting class.

3:30 p.m.: A young man comes in to have his stitches removed. He had gone to the emergency room a week ago after lacerating his knee. The wound healed well without any infection and the stitches come out easily.

4:15 p.m.: Carina checks her messages again to return calls and e-mails before the end of the day. She reviews the patient list for the next day and asks the nursing assistant to check that lab reports are available for those patients. Carina is "on call" tonight, so she checks with the other providers, two physicians and a pediatric NP, to see if they expect anyone to call.

5:00 p.m.: This is a good day, Carina leaves on time! However, she may need another hour or so to answer questions and arrange care for anyone who calls in during the night.

A Day in the Life: Medical-Surgical Hospital Nurse

Dan Bratton, RN, BSN, works rotating shifts at the medium-sized (220 beds) Good Samaritan General Hospital. For two weeks, Dan works 7 a.m. to 3:30 p.m., the next two weeks will be 3 p.m. to 11:30 p.m., and the next two weeks will be 11 p.m. to 7:30 a.m. (The 30-minute overlap between shifts gives the nurses that are leaving some time to report to the nurses taking over the important events that pertain to each patient.) Dan graduated six months ago and this is his first position in a medical-surgical unit. Today, Dan is working the day shift, 7 a.m. to 3:30 p.m. The day shift is busy because this is when physicians come in to see their patients and many diagnostic tests and therapies are scheduled.

6:45 a.m.: Dan arrives a few minutes early so he can change into his hospital-supplied scrub suit and get himself organized for the day.

7:00 a.m.: Dan's supervisor gives him a list of eight patients to care for. Dan knows two of the patients from his previous shift; six of the patients are new. They range in age from 25 to 85 and their diagnoses include: diabetes mellitus, congestive heart failure, two days post-stroke, and acute renal failure.

7:05 a.m.: Dan listens to the report of all the nurses going off shift, paying particular attention to his eight patients. Because the report is tape-recorded, any questions must be asked of the night shift leader.

7:30 a.m.: Dan goes to the patients' records to check each care plan, describing tasks and schedules for the day. Each patient's physician will be coming in early to go around to see his/her patients. Dan will check on any discharges scheduled and any therapy or diagnostic testing that requires the patient to travel to another area of the hospital. Then he plans his day around these events and the medication and care schedule for each patient.

8:00 a.m.: Dan accompanies the physicians to report on any changes in the past 24 hours and to gather information on what is next in the physician's plan. He discovers that the diabetic patient is to be discharged to home and he will meet with family members to reinforce the self-care needed to balance treatment for diabetes: exercise, nutrition and medication. Also, one of the post-stroke patients is going to be moved to a rehabilitation facility. Dan talks with those family members to answer questions, provide reassurance and explain the goals of rehab. He shows them an internet site, www.medlineplus.gov, where

Visit Vault at **www.vault.com** for insider company profiles, expert advice, career message boards, expert resume reviews, the Vault Job Board and more.

VAULT CAREER LIBRARY **131**

they can find specific information about stroke, appropriate rehabilitation, safety and homecare, and any medications that may be prescribed later.

9:00 a.m.: Dan receives and stores the single-dose medications for his patients that have been brought to the unit by a pharmacy technician. He has to check the physicians' documentation for new orders and authorize them and set them in motion for each of his eight patients. The day goes very quickly, even without any real crises arising. Medications and treatments must be given before patients go to their therapy with rehabilitation or before they go to have radiology testing or treatments.

10:00 a.m.: Most of the patient discharges occur before noon. The patients who are going home need to have specific discharge instructions as well as an escort to leave the hospital safely. As soon as one patient leaves, another is admitted, so Dan greets the new patient and completes paperwork setting up a nursing care plan.

11:00 a.m.: Dan "rounds" on his patients again before lunch to check blood pressures and other vital signs and to keep an eye on everyone.

12:00 p.m.: This is a good day, Dan gets to relax and eat lunch with a colleague. They discuss a continuing education program on diabetes that they will attend over the weekend. According to their state Board of Nursing regulations, they need 30 hours of continuing education every two years in order to renew their license to practice.

12:30 p.m.: Dan and his colleague return to work. He sees that one of his patients has called for help. When he goes to the patient's room, he finds that she became dizzy and has fallen on her way to the toilet. He helps her back to bed and assesses her condition. Fortunately, she appears to have no broken bones and the dizziness has passed. He cautions the patient not to stand up quickly but to give herself a couple of minutes sitting at the bedside before standing and walking. He also encourages her to seek assistance when she wants to get out of bed. After checking the patient's medication list, Dan phones the patient's physician and suggests some medication changes that may decrease the patient's tendency toward dizziness. Dan knows that the circumstances around this event are very important because his hospital is working to decrease the overall rate of falls and patient injuries.

1:30 p.m.: By this time, Dan must administer another round of medications and treatments to his patient group. He checks the physician orders to find new IVs, blood tests, and referrals were ordered. Dan checks with the unit secretary to see that these were ordered. Dan talks with one of the medical school students about patient falls and how to prevent them.

2:30 p.m.: Dan speaks with a nursing school faculty member on the telephone. She is looking for a clinical practice site for students in the summer rotation. He agrees to work with undergraduate student nurses and to recruit fellow staff nurses to take other nurses. He does a final round to check each patient's condition before he leaves for the day.

3:00 p.m.: Dan gives a report to the group of nurses coming on for the next shift. He speaks to his supervisor regarding his preference for next month's schedule that is being planned. (Some hospitals have made self-scheduling available to the nursing staff.) Then, Dan has a few moments to document the care he provided during the past eight hours. He enters data into a computerized record that contains easy templates for routine care. After that, it is time to relax for a moment!

Paralegal

UPPERS	DOWNERS
• Great ground-level experience for law school • Plentiful overtime pay	• Long hours • Many clerical tasks

Overview

A mixed lot

From freshly graduated English BAs to document-drafting veterans with training and certification, paralegals are really something of a mixed lot. Some have formal training, while others do not. Some have one of many certifications, while others have none. Paralegals, or legal assistants as they are sometimes called, come from a great variety of backgrounds and perform a wide range of tasks. As a result, compensation and working conditions vary to a large degree. Further complicating matters is that, while some legal assistants find they enjoy their paralegal careers, for others it is a stepping stone to a law degree.

Swimming in paper

Generally speaking, much of what paralegals do involves the large mounds of paperwork generated by large scale commercial litigation and corporate transactions. Legal assistants may find themselves sifting through these documents, organizing them, analyzing them or even drafting them. In addition, paralegals perform research and prepare reports based upon their findings. To do this, paralegals must have a good understanding of legal terminology and good research skills. When permitted by law, paralegals involved with community service sometimes even represent clients at administrative hearings. In short, paralegals can do everything a lawyer does, except the "practice of law:" presenting cases in court, setting legal fees and giving legal advice. Paralegals are free to do just about anything else, which is good if it involves using the brain, but possibly tedious if it involves rote clerical work.

Varying pay

Pay for legal assistants reflects the great variety of the work performed. Entry-level workers do not enjoy high salaries, but with increased experience and education, compensation becomes healthier. Paralegals in major metropolitan areas tend to earn more money than those in smaller locales. Similarly, working for a large law firm means higher pay. Major firms may also have perks in the way of bonuses, extra vacation time, and tickets to sports events and the like. At any rate, paralegals can almost always count on boosting their salaries with hefty overtime hours at the rate of time and a half. Some feel that obtaining a certification or a degree in paralegal studies can lead to greater compensation and responsibility. Two certifications are available to those in the profession, the Certified Legal Assistant exam (CLA) and the Paralegal Advanced Competency Exam (PACE). The two-day CLA exam is offered by the National Association of Legal Assistants three times a year. The PACE exam is affiliated with the National Federation of Paralegal Associations and is administered throughout the year by an independent agency. Once either of these certifications has been obtained, a paralegal may use the title registered paralegal (RP).

In addition to certification exams, many paralegal training programs are available (some are run through colleges and universities, while others are independent). Most of these degrees are either two- or four-year programs. Correspondence courses, which have grown increasingly popular due to the Internet, are also an option. Degrees recognized by the American Bar Association and the American Association for Paralegal Education tend to be the most reputable.

Visit Vault at **www.vault.com** for insider company profiles, expert advice, career message boards, expert resume reviews, the Vault Job Board and more.

VAULT CAREER LIBRARY 133

PERSONALITY MATCH	PERSONALITY MISS
• Organized • Detail-oriented • Resourceful	• Impatient • Thin-skinned

Career Path

There are various opportunities for paralegals, besides just the standard law firm. The legal departments in large corporations are in need of legal assistants, as well as departments in the U.S. government; not surprisingly, the Department of Justice is the biggest employer of paralegals. Once hired, paralegals are expected to follow the ethical guidelines standardized by the National Association of Legal Assistants and the National Federation of Paralegal Associations. Generally, though, for the first two years, a paralegal is a clerical functionary, preparing files and photocopying research materials. After about five years, a paralegal usually specializes in a particular field and is largely unsupervised.

For some, becoming a paralegal is a way of testing the waters without getting soaked. Many young graduates decide to do paralegal work for a year or two before making a decision about whether to undergo the financial burden of paying for law school. Legal assistant jobs allow these people to see the inner workings of a law firm on a day-to-day basis. These interim legal assistants frequently do not bother with certification or formal training, as their plans are short-term. Others move on to related fields such as law enforcement or public health regulation agencies.

For others, the paralegal trade is the law career that they seek. Paralegals can, and do, perform many of the same tasks as lawyers. Furthermore, as companies look to reduce costs, paralegals can expect to do more and more of the non-essential work normally allotted to attorneys.

HOURS	SALARY
• Average about 60 per week	• Average salary: $38,000 • Average bonus: $2,400

Our Survey Says

"I think becoming a paralegal is a great choice for those who like the law but who do not want to become married to it," says one paralegal from New York. Paralegals perform "grunt work, pure and simple," but as they gain tenure, "the casework is fascinating" and they "begin to feel needed and more respected."

Much of a good experience lies in being lucky enough to stumble upon attorneys who care about their paralegals. More than a few respondents warn of the "stultifying lifestyle" that involves "ludicrous hours," "monotonous work" and "sinking morale." A few warn of "overweening" partners "who will remind you that you are beneath them," and "who will make sure that you don't leave the office before 10 p.m." Says one respondent, "At my firm, they want you to get your work done—and do it perfectly. If you don't, they get angry." All of this translates into a profession in which "many of us would be doing something else if we had the chance." Despite this angst, however, a position as a paralegal is, for some, the best entry to the more lucrative life of a lawyer. Notes a paralegal from New York, "You will see what it is like to work at a law firm on a day to day basis, and in turn, see if this is a career for you. In addition, if you choose to go to law school, it will help you immensely in getting through your first year." For people with families, "the flexible hours are worth a mint." For those who are "analytical," "willing to take orders" and "anal, or at least willing to work with anal people," paralegal work may be a good choice.

SKILLS TO ACQUIRE

- Bachelor's degree or one of the three American Bar Association-recognized programs (National Association of Legal Assistants, the National Federation of Paralegal Associations and the American Alliance of Paralegals)
- Paralegal training program certification: CLA exam and PACE

Visit Vault at **www.vault.com** for insider company profiles, expert advice, career message boards, expert resume reviews, the Vault Job Board and more.

VAULT CAREER LIBRARY

135

Park Ranger

UPPERS	DOWNERS
• Getting to live in national parks	• No benefits for seasonal employees • Poor housing options

Overview

Nature calls

Forest rangers are the human face of America's national parks and wildlife. Their work demands that they spend long hours alone, but they must also be skilled communicators with superior interpersonal skills. While we tend to think of rangers as nature lovers, the life of a park ranger entails more than preventing forest fires and guiding tours. Rangers are trained law enforcement officers, first-aid administrators and ecologists.

From law to education

Park rangers are a diverse group of professionals. Some specialize in law enforcement and search and rescue, others in maintenance, administration, concessions management, resources management and interpretation. Interpreters are in charge of contact with the general public. They staff visitor centers, lead guided hikes, present talks, give evening programs, conduct environmental education in and out of schools, distribute literature and organize exhibits.

Full-time positions as rangers are difficult to come by, and only people with the right combination of experience and education (including college courses in environmental science, biology and forestry) are likely to get them. Many park rangers break into entry-level jobs after high school, starting out as seasonal rangers. Seasonal workers go from park to park, working at one in the winter and another in the summer. In these positions, they usually perform maintenance duties: cleaning up campsites, maintaining trails and working as information personnel and guides. Seasonal rangers receive few or no benefits outside of worker's compensation insurance and a minimal amount of sick leave. On top of that, rangers might have to endure very hot or bitterly cold conditions for extended periods. Rangers who live in park housing still pay rent (although it is often drawn from non-taxable income).

Permanent ranger positions are coveted, as rangers usually get to live in the most beautiful natural settings in the country. The pay is relatively low—it can start at around $10 an hour—but most park rangers feel sufficiently compensated knowing that they work for something in which they believe, with co-workers who are dedicated to the job. And after a few years, a park ranger can live comfortably on a salary of about $30,000. Permanent government jobs, usually offered by the Department of the Interior, also come with a comprehensive benefits package.

During recent years, budget cuts have hit the National Park Service. As a result, many park rangers need to be more resourceful, and some parks have experienced staffing shortages due to budgetary problems. In the coming decade, both the federal government and some state agencies expect lots of employees to retire, which could create job openings. However, many opportunities in the fields of forestry and conservation will be in consulting, as federal and state governments contract these services to private companies.

Visit Vault at **www.vault.com** for insider company profiles, expert advice, career message boards, expert resume reviews, the Vault Job Board and more.

VAULT CAREER LIBRARY 137

PERSONALITY MATCH	PERSONALITY MISS
• Resourceful	• Ambitious
• Socially conscious	• Impatient
• Tree-hugging	• Agoraphobic

Career Path

Although a college degree isn't required, college courses in life and environmental sciences can help someone with less practical experience get hired into an entry-level position. Experience in management and communications can also give someone an edge in the field. Another option is seasonal work in a state or national park, which can equip a potential park ranger with skills such as law enforcement, fire prevention and control, and basic knowledge of the park's trails and campsites. In addition, some cities, such as New York, hire "urban park rangers" to connect city dwellers to the natural world and encourage people to protect the environment.

Each year, the National Park Service hires as many as 10,000 seasonal and temporary employees to work in America's national parks. For example, Denali National Park in Alaska has employed extra park rangers during its peak summer season, which is from mid-May to mid-September. You might have to work as a seasonal personnel for a few years before landing a permanent position. Once you becomes a full-fledged park ranger, however, the job is stable, and most park rangers stay at the same park for many years.

HOURS	SALARY
• Average about 45 per week	• Average entry-level salary with a bachelor's degree: $28,862 to $35,752
	• Average starting salary with a master's degree: $43,731 to $52,912
	• Average government salary: $65,964

Our Survey Says

There is "dirty work" involved in being a park ranger, such as park maintenance. Other annoying aspects of the job, as reported by one ranger, include "putting up with stupid questions and irate campers, drunk college students, drunk teenagers, and let's not forget my personal favorite, drunk senior citizens." There are also some "cocky, know-it-all co-workers," and an "out-of-balance chain of command."

If that isn't enough, starting pay is low. And, because of shrinking budgets and staff, rangers often put in a great deal of overtime for which they are not compensated. Although pay is "not as high as one might earn in the private sector," there are things "in your pay envelope besides dollars," such as "the number of times a week someone says, 'How do I get a job like yours?'" Overall, the perks seem to outweigh the drawbacks. One ranger enjoys benefits such as "a healthy life, the ability to do things for pay that others pay to do, and going to bed at night without begrudging the fact that you have to get up in the morning to go to work." All respondents agreed that it is difficult to land a job, but a successful ranger advises aspiring rangers to "size up the competition and try to stand out."

The mission of the National Park Service is "to conserve the scenery and the natural and historic objects and the wildlife therein, and to provide for the enjoyment of the same in such manner and by such means as will leave them unimpaired for the enjoyment of future generations." On the whole, park rangers believe in that dual mission of preservation and public enjoyment, and feel that those who do not share the same commitment should not enter the field. Rangers who work in roles involving contact with the public are required to wear the National Park Service uniform of green pants, gray shirt and flat hat. Most "feel honored to wear it." They receive a small uniform allowance, but usually end up spending some of their own money to spruce up the outfit.

SKILLS TO ACQUIRE

• Bachelor's degree or high school diploma and at least three years' experience in park services

Visit Vault at **www.vault.com** for insider company profiles, expert advice,
career message boards, expert resume reviews, the Vault Job Board and more.

VAULT CAREER LIBRARY   **139**

Pharmacist

UPPERS	DOWNERS
• Good salaries	• Long hours
• Wide variety of career options	• Potential restlessness

Overview

Fill me up

These days it seems there is a prescription drug to cure anything and everything. That's why pharmacists are everyone's best friends: they advise and dispense drugs and give advice to consumers and physicians, making sure no one mixes anything they shouldn't. Their work treats diseases, saves lives and eases pain. However, the mortar and pestle compounding, or mixing of powders, tablets, capsules and ointments, is no longer the domain of the pharmacist because most medicines are manufactured by pharmaceutical companies.

Retail and hospital

There are two major types of pharmacists: retail and hospital. Retail pharmacists advise customers about prescription and over-the-counter drugs, and their possible side effects and interactions. Three out of five pharmacists work in community pharmacies, often managing them as well. The hours can be demanding, since many pharmacies are open all night and on holidays. Most full-time, salaried pharmacists work an average of 50 hours a week.

Pharmacists in hospitals and clinics not only dispense medications and advice, but also instruct medical staff on the selection and effects of drugs, monitor patients' drug regimens, and evaluate drug use patterns in the hospital. It is common for pharmacists to specialize in specific aspects of drug therapy, such as those used to treat psychiatric disorders, radiopharmaceuticals or oncology.

Pharmacists can work outside of retail pharmacies and hospitals, too. For example, some pharmacists apply their knowledge to narcotics investigations for law enforcement agencies. Research pharmacists work on teams with doctors and biologists to develop new drugs and seek out cures.

PERSONALITY MATCH	PERSONALITY MISS
• Precise	• Creative
• Focused	• Indiscriminate
• Circumspect	• Emotional
• Conscientious	

Career Path

All states require a license to practice pharmacy. To obtain a license, a pharmacist must graduate from an accredited college of pharmacy, pass a state examination, and serve an internship under a licensed pharmacist. Colleges of pharmacy train students to dispense prescriptions, communicate with patients and strengthen their understanding of professional ethics.

Visit Vault at **www.vault.com** for insider company profiles, expert advice, career message boards, expert resume reviews, the Vault Job Board and more.

VAULT CAREER LIBRARY   141

Instruction is focusing more and more on training pharmacists on the subtleties of direct patient care and consulting services to other health professionals.

Since 2000, all new pharmacists must graduate from a six-year program (two years pre-pharmacy and four years in pharmacy school). These pharmacists will all have Doctor of Pharmacy (PharmD) degrees. BS pharmacists will still be in the market, but aspiring pharmacists will all go through the six-year commitment.

In community (retail) pharmacies, pharmacists usually begin at the staff level. After they gain experience and secure the necessary capital, many become owners or part-owners of pharmacies. Pharmacists in chain drug stores may be promoted to supervisory pharmacist at the store level, followed by the district level, and later to an executive position within the chain's headquarters. Pharmacists in the pharmaceutical industry may advance in marketing, sales, research, quality control, production and other areas.

Pharmacy students interested in research must have a PharmD, though some enter fellowship programs that are designed to prepare students to do independent research.

HOURS	SALARY
• Average about 40 to 50 per week	• Median salary: $94,520

Our Survey Says

Many pharmacists are satisfied that their work is "important" and "rewarding." One respondent cites "demystifying drugs and their effects" for patients as part of what makes the job fun. For pharmacists in community pharmacies, "helping people and interacting with them in person" are the reason they do not move to administrative levels at companies. Adds one pharmacist technician, "Co-workers became like a family." Researchers have a different reason for remaining in their fields, and look forward to "the chance of becoming the next Dr. Salk."

While hours as a pharmacist can be long, they also can be flexible, and some pharmacists report the luxury of part-time schedules. There are downsides to the job, however, including "long hours on your feet" and aggravated customers. Says one pharmacist technician, "There are sometimes customers that are very difficult to handle, especially since in a pharmacy, one is typically dealing with individuals who don't feel well." There is always the chance to "drop a vial or inhale a substance that is potentially hazardous." For some, however, the element of danger makes some pharmacists feel like "kids playing with their first chemistry set, and it is still fun."

SKILLS TO ACQUIRE
• PharmD degree
• Pharmacy license

Photographer

UPPERS	DOWNERS
• Travel	• Deadline pressure
• Flexible hours	• Unpredictable hours
• Wide variety of career options	

Overview

Say "Cheese!"

We all take photographs, but some of us are paid to do it. And some of the professional photographers who are paid to take pictures also fly around the world, mingle with celebrities and are feted as celebrity artists themselves. But many others struggle to make ends meet as professional photographers: taking a picture of professional caliber requires more than the push of a button. Everything from camera angle to the type of lens can make the difference between a Pulitzer Prize and wasted film.

Specialities

About half of all photographers work independently and in specialized areas. Commercial photographers are the jet-setters of the profession; their work takes them to exotic locales for everything from the *Sports Illustrated* swimsuit issue in the Galapagos Islands to Sudan for *The New York Times*. Portrait photographers often work in their own studios, schedule appointments and coax smiles from cranky toddlers. Industrial photographers take trade pictures for companies such as automobile manufacturers or engineering firms, which the companies then use in their annual reports and advertisements.

Forty percent of photographers are self-employed freelancers. One of the major outlets for freelance photography is stock photo. Stock photos are used by advertising agencies when they don't have the budget to hire a photographer. If a photographer's work is accepted by a stock company, he or she receives a commission every time the photo is used. Newspapers, magazines and ad agencies also frequently hire freelance photographers.

Labor of love?

For many photographers, their primary concern is photography as art. For these ambitious artists, portrait or commercial photography may simply be a way to make ends meet. It is not unusual for struggling photographers to earn their living taking school pictures while they await their first gallery show. For those with artistic ambitions, the flexible hours afforded by freelancing are ideal, although the search for work can sometimes be as grueling as working an eight-hour day in an office.

New technology is offering even more outlets for the ambitious photographer. Digital cameras eliminate the need for film and make it easy to transmit photos directly over the Internet. Using digital technology, photographers can also electronically alter photos for a desired effect, or produce more accurate results for advertisements and scientific photographs than if the photographer had used regular silver-halide film. It certainly wouldn't hurt up-and-coming photographers to learn the ins and outs of computer technology and stay on top of new trends.

Visit Vault at **www.vault.com** for insider company profiles, expert advice, career message boards, expert resume reviews, the Vault Job Board and more.

VAULT CAREER LIBRARY   143

PERSONALITY MATCH	PERSONALITY MISS
• Creative	• Anal
• Determined	• Conservative

Career Path

Although no formal education is required of photographers, a strong technical understanding of photography techniques and familiarity with film processing are essential. Entry-level positions in photojournalism and in industrial, scientific or technical photography usually call for a college degree in photography, journalism, or the specific field being photographed (archaeology, botany, etc.). Many aspiring photographers get their start as assistants at a studio. As an assistant, they learn to mix chemicals, develop film, print photographs and various other skills vital to running their own businesses.

Aspiring photographers should subscribe to photographic newsletters and magazines, join camera clubs, and seek work in camera stores or photo studios. Interning or working part-time for a photographer, newspaper or magazine is an excellent way to make contacts that will be useful when the time comes to strike out alone. Photographers who want to operate their own businesses need to know how to submit bids, write contracts, hire models and gain access to private properties for shoots.

Photojournalists require more formal education, since they need to understand the history and the significance of an event to determine whether it is newsworthy. They must act as journalists to recognize a potentially good photograph and capture the moment quickly.

HOURS	SALARY
• Average about 40 per week	• Median salary: $26,170
	• Salaried photographers usually earn more than those who are self-employed

Our Survey Says

When they think about their careers, most photographers "feel as though it is not a job/work." "While the hours can be long, sometimes it goes by quick," says one photographer. Even though they may be taking photos of Mrs. Jones' sixth grade class for a paycheck, they are still doing what they love—taking photographs. And it's lucky, because in a client-driven industry like this one, one photographer notes, "a positive attitude is also very important. Clients can sense this easily."

Photography is a competitive field. "Anyone interested in photography had better be thick-skinned," says one photographer. "The competition is intense." So how do you stay ahead of the pack? "Learn, learn, learn!" Keep on top of technology trends and advances while honing your creativity. In the words of one photographer, "Be as diverse as possible."

SKILLS TO ACQUIRE
• Technical understanding of photography techniques
• Journalism or fine arts degree can be helpful
• A "good eye" is necessary

Physical Therapist

UPPERS	DOWNERS
• Good pay • Wide variety of career options • Can have flexible hours	• Physically demanding

Overview

Picking up where doctors leave off

When athletes tear tendons, dancers sprain their knees, and anyone injured in an accident needs more than a cast and some painkillers, a physical therapist takes over where a physician leaves off. Physical therapists prescribe and oversee a regimen of strengthening exercises, stretching and other non-surgical treatments, all as an attempt to bring their patients as far back to full strength as possible, sometimes as quickly as possible. Therapists also occasionally use electrical stimulation and ultrasound to relieve the pain associated with injuries or terminal illnesses, teach patients to use crutches, prostheses and wheelchairs, and help them to cope with their injuries on a day-to-day basis. Physical therapists combine their medical expertise with assessments of patients' medical histories and individual needs to develop treatment plans. Physical therapists can work in both general and specific areas. They can work with patients from ages 9 to 90 (pediatrics and geriatrics respectively) and from head to toe (neurology and orthopedics)—there are numerous possibilities for specialization.

In the office or at your home

Some physical therapists work in hospitals, schools, home health agencies, nursing homes and physicians' offices; others have strong enough client bases to open their own practices. Both those in private practice and those who work for agencies or other employers occasionally travel to the homes of patients who are unable to travel to hospitals for treatment. Many develop close, long-term relationships with their patients as they document their progress and modify treatment programs. Therapists typically work eight hours a day, but frequently find that their patients' needs extend into evenings and weekends.

In addition to technical expertise, physical therapists must possess compassion and tact, especially when dealing with a patient's family.

Physical therapists must be in top physical condition not only to lift and move their patients and heavy equipment, but also to spend a great deal of time on their feet, since their jobs require them to actively participate in their patients' treatment.

PERSONALITY MATCH	PERSONALITY MISS
• Patient • Outgoing • Sensitive	• Introverted • Controlling

Visit Vault at **www.vault.com** for insider company profiles, expert advice, career message boards, expert resume reviews, the Vault Job Board and more.

VAULT CAREER LIBRARY 145

Career Path

In order to practice physical therapy, therapists must complete a four-year undergraduate program. Most physical therapy programs start with basic biology, chemistry and physics courses. Later in the program, a student begins the study of biomechanics, neuroanatomy, human growth and development, manifestations of disease and trauma, evaluation and assessment techniques, research and therapy. Like physicians, therapists receive supervised clinical experience in hospitals. After the four-year program, most students with aspirations of working with patients or starting their own practices pursue a graduate level degree. In the past, a master's degree in physical therapy (MPT) was often sufficient to gain employment, but more schools now offer doctoral degrees in physical therapy (DPT). The American Physical Therapy Association (APTA), the largest professional association for the field in the United States, identified 205 accredited physical therapy programs in 2004; 94 of the programs offered MPTs and 111 offered DPTs, a disparity that should only increase in coming years. The APTA has also predicted that every physical therapist will have a DPT degree by the year 2020.

Competition for entry to physical therapy programs is tough, so top grades from reputable schools are imperative. Volunteer experience in hospitals or clinics is also extremely helpful in gaining admittance. In order to advance past an administrative or research position, a master's degree is usually required. Physical therapists who want to stay on top of developments in the profession take continuing education courses and workshops; some states even require a certain number of hours of continuing coursework to maintain licensure.

HOURS	SALARY
• Average about 40 per week	• Median salary: $66,200

Our Survey Says

Most physical therapists find their jobs "rewarding and exhausting." Advancement in the field requires people to "pay their dues." The field is "very competitive, and very cliquey," depending on the place, insiders say. Perks of the job include travel, as therapists are often employed at agencies that specialize in roaming therapists, whose "travel expenses and living accommodations are paid, on top of their salaries." The dress is "casual and comfortable," ranging from a "white lab coat" to a "jogging suit with a company logo." Therapists are exposed to a "diverse group of people with different problems." Says an Arizona-based PT, "You really get the chance to know your patients and really make an impact on their recovery and for the rest of their lives." A sense of personal accomplishment, combined with comfortable salaries for licensed therapists— "$60,000 to $75,000 is a lot of money"—make physical therapists a satisfied group of professionals.

SKILLS TO ACQUIRE
• Master's degree in physical therapy (MPT)
• Doctorate in physical therapy (DPT)
• Must pass a state licensing exam

A Day in the Life: Physical Therapist

Generally speaking, there is no "typical day" for a physical therapist, since career paths and daily routines vary so widely. After two or three years of general practice, a physical therapist may find a special area of interest and devote energy and training to a specific patient population or specific treatment technique. For example, a physical therapist in Reno, Nevada may find that his special area of interest is prevention of injuries in high school students involved in team sports and he may set up a private practice teaching adolescents and adults stretching and strengthening techniques and conditioning routines. A physical therapist living in New York City may have found her niche in evaluating and treating women living with breast cancer after total mastectomy procedures.

A day in the life of an entry-level physical therapist at an acute care hospital in a city will consist of seeing an assigned patient load that can range from eight to 12 patients a day in a quality facility. Too many patients a day equals an understaffed facility and compromises on care. Treatment times range from 20 minutes to 40 minutes, a much shorter time frame compared to the days before managed care, when typical treatment lasted 40 minutes to an hour. A physical therapist conducts her evaluations, treats her patients, documents all treatments (often written documentation can take 20 to 30 percent of the work day) attends inservices, which are educational training sessions for physical therapists by in-house and outside experts, and participates in interdisciplinary meetings. Physical therapy work is physically demanding, as therapists must use their own strength to transfer, gait train and exercise patients, and the new physical therapist will have to learn how to economize his/her own physical energy by scheduling time to document notes or other non-physically demanding activity in between exercise sessions.

It is important for an individual pursuing the field of physical therapy to understand how wide the opportunities for practice in the field are. There is always more to learn.

A Day in the Life: Outpatient Rehabilitation

Cara Mateo works in an outpatient rehabilitation center in New York City that treats stroke patients, head injury, spinal cord injury, multiple sclerosis, Parkinson's and other neurological diseases. Cara is one of five other physical therapists working in her department. She reports directly to the director of physical therapy, who reports to the director of rehabilitation. Cara has been working at the rehabilitation center for two years.

7:30 a.m.: Cara walks from her Upper West Side apartment to her job to arrive at 8 a.m. Her work day begins at 8:30 a.m. but she would like time to review her patient load and have a cup of coffee at her desk.

8:30 a.m.: Cara has reviewed her e-mails, phone messages and schedule for the day. She attends an interdisciplinary care meeting with the rehabilitation team from 8:30 to 9:30 a.m. to review two problem cases.

9:30 a.m.: Cara's first patient is called over the loudspeaker by the receptionist and Cara goes to the lobby area to receive her patient. He is a post-stroke patient and is wheelchair bound. He is accompanied by his wife. Cara works with her patient in gait training, or walking with a quad cane (a cane with four prongs). Her patient is excited about his progress in terms of the distance he can accomplish. Cara suggests that in another two weeks, she may progress him to a straight cane. Cara sits with her patient and his wife after the gait training to perform stretches on his upper extremity (arm) that have become tightened in a pattern typical of a stroke (called a synergy pattern). The three, therapist, wife and patient, work as a team to review home exercises. The session ends at 10:30.

10:30 a.m.: Cara documents treatment in the patient's chart and includes reports of pain by the patient or reports of difficulty performing the exercise program. Cara also includes all exercises and gait training that she performed with the patient. She concludes her documentation with goals for the next treatment and a plan to carry out these goals.

Visit Vault at **www.vault.com** for insider company profiles, expert advice, career message boards, expert resume reviews, the Vault Job Board and more.

VAULT CAREER LIBRARY   147

10:45 a.m.: Cara's second patient is called. This patient has multiple sclerosis and is also overweight. Cara's challenge, and the patient's, is to increase the patient's aerobic endurance without causing a relapse of fatigue (termed an exacerbation of symptoms cycle) typical of this condition. Cara checks the patient's vital signs, including blood pressure, heart rate and temperature. She also checks the patient's weight. Cara supervises the patient on aerobic circuit training, which includes the stationary bike, treadmill and upper body ergonometer. The patient is able to tolerate 15 minutes on each piece of equipment. Cara and the patient talk about when in the patient's day she feels most fatigued and what she does to alleviate this fatigue. Cara notes that the patient is wearing too much heavy clothing for the temperature of the gym and advises her about the effect of heat on the fatigue patterns of MS patients. Together they review the home exercise program. Cara walks her patient to the reception area after reviewing the next appointment time.

11:45 a.m.: Cara documents the treatment of the MS patient.

12:00 p.m.: Cara attends an interdepartmental inservice given by the director of the psychology department on cognitive deficits in stroke patients.

1:00 p.m.: Cara sees her third patient of the day, a spinal cord-injured patient, aged 25. Her goals for this patient are to improve the patient's ability to move from the wheelchair to the mat and to increase his abdominal strength using the Bobath Ball (large gymnasium ball) for core (trunk) exercises. After a vigorous treatment, Cara and her patient talk about the fact that her patient would like to go back to work at some point. Cara makes a note that she will talk to the rehab team about a referral to the vocational department for training to return to work.

2:00 p.m.: Cara documents her treatment.

2:15 p.m.: Cara has an hour staff meeting to talk about the schedule for accepting PT students for the year from neighboring educational programs. The director would like to assign these students to a therapist. This is Cara's first time supervising a student and she is looking forward to the experience. Cara receives her assignment for a student from NYU.

3:15 p.m.: Cara leads a group therapy session consisting of five post-stroke patients. The patients and Cara go through a series of exercises to improve balance. Cara has integrated some tai chi techniques into her group session and the patients enjoy this very much.

4:15 p.m.: Cara documents the group therapy session in all five patient charts.

5:30 p.m.: Cara reviews e-mails and phone calls that she received during the day and gets ready to leave for the day.

Physician/Surgeon

UPPERS	DOWNERS
• Intellectually and emotionally rewarding • Great financial compensation	• Long education and training path • High-pressure work • Matters of life and death

Overview

There is an element of prestige that comes with being a doctor. After all, these are the people who help save and prolong lives in both bold and mundane fashions. Essentially, physicians and surgeons diagnose and treat illnesses, as well as prescribe and administer help for people suffering from injury or disease. This ability to examine patients, order, perform and interpret diagnostic tests, counsel patients on diet, hygiene and preventive health care, and also wield a mean scalpel, are the result of having concluded one of the most rigorous formal education and training requirements of any occupation. As such, the salaries for physicians and surgeons rank among the highest.

The job market for physicians and surgeons will continue to grow, particularly in rural and low-income areas. There will be a 14 percent increase (higher than many other industries) in hiring through the year 2016, as the health care market expands and older professionals retire. That said, keep an eye on the upcoming political battles over health care reform. Future policies may dictate a consumer's willingness or ability to procure physician services. New business models, such as Wal-Mart's Retail Clinics, feature care given by nurse practitioners and physician assistants, but are not likely to diminish the demand for doctors.

It takes all kinds

When most people think of doctors, they tend to think of an MD, Doctor of Medicine (also known as allopathic physicians). But physicians are also just as likely to be a DO, Doctor of Osteopathic Medicine. Both types may treat via drugs or surgery, but DOs focus on the body's musculoskeletal system, preventative medicine and holistic patient care. Thus, many become primary care specialists, practicing general or family medicine, pediatrics and internal medicine.

Most physicians have one or more specialties, which include anesthesiology, family and general medicine, general internal medicine, general pediatrics, obstetrics and gynecology, psychiatry and surgery. Each of these categories can be further broken down into more specific specialties, such as cardiology, radiology, pathology, neurology, ophthalmology and so on.

Is there a doctor in the house?

Physicians can be found scattered throughout a neighborhood in small private offices or clinics, or increasingly, in groups or health care organizations. Group physicians often work as a team to coordinate care for a number of patients, and are less independent than the solo practitioners of the past. Hospitals and surgical outpatient clinics are more likely to employ surgeons and anesthesiologists.

Long, irregular hours can be expected. Sixty-or-more hour work weeks are expected of over one-third of full-time physicians and surgeons, and while on-call, a doctor will field many phone consultations and make emergency visits to hospitals or nursing homes.

Visit Vault at www.vault.com for insider company profiles, expert advice, career message boards, expert resume reviews, the Vault Job Board and more.

VAULT CAREER LIBRARY   149

PERSONALITY MATCH	PERSONALITY MISS
• Diligent	• Lazy
• Self-motivated	• Easily discouraged
• Caring	• Impulsive
• Emotionally stable	

Career Path

Becoming a physician takes patience and dedication. Consider that after four years of undergraduate school and another four years of medical school, there is still another three to eight years of internship and residency. All states, the District of Columbia and U.S. territories require licensing of physicians, which dictates that all physicians must have graduated from an accredited medical school, pass a licensing examination, and complete one to seven years of graduate medical education. Foreign physicians must pass an examination and complete a U.S. residency to be licensed to work in the United States.

Medical school

But first you have to be accepted into medical school. Medical programs are highly competitive, and most candidates will already have a bachelor's or advanced degree. Applicants must submit scores from the Medical College Admission Test (MCAT), transcripts and letters of recommendation. Prior premedical coursework in biology, chemistry, mathematics and English are required, which sets up the first two years of classroom and laboratory study in such subjects as biochemistry, pharmacology, psychology, anatomy, pathology, medical ethics and laws. The final two years of medical school involve supervised work with patients in hospitals and clinics; learning acute, chronic, preventive and rehabilitative care through rotations in various departments and disciplines.

Finally, MDs and DOs seeking board certification in a specialty may spend up to an additional seven years in residency training and must pass a final examination immediately after. Even further, subspecialties require yet another one to two years of residency. Though residencies are paid on-the-job training, more than 80 percent of medical school graduates are in debt for educational expenses.

Specialties and subspecialties help physicians and surgeons advance by gaining expertise in niche markets and developing a reputation for excellence or authority among their peers and patients. Some continue with research and education, while many others begin their own practices or join a group practice. Hospitals and clinics also provide opportunities to advance into managerial, administrative and supervisory roles.

HOURS	SALARY
• Long and irregular	• Primary care: $182,477
• One-third worked 60 or more a week in 2006	• Specialties: $261,396

VAULT CAREER LIBRARY   **151**

Service distribution

There are more than half a million physicians and surgeons working in the United States, with about 18 percent employed in hospitals. Fifteen percent are self-employed, and roughly half work in offices of physicians. The rest can be found in government positions, universities and professional schools, as well as outpatient care centers. Approximately half of all physicians engage in primary care without sub-specializing. It should be noted that there are currently shortages reported in specialties such as family practice, internal medicine and OB/GYN, especially in rural or low-income areas.

SKILLS TO ACQUIRE

- Degree from an accredited medical school
- Medical license

Visit Vault at **www.vault.com** for insider company profiles, expert advice,
career message boards, expert resume reviews, the Vault Job Board and more.

VAULT CAREER LIBRARY   **151**

Political Aide

UPPERS	DOWNERS
• Opportunity to work on issues making tomorrow's headlines	• Irregular hours
• Ability to create social change	• High pressure
• Exposure to high-profile politicians	• Modest pay
• Outstanding non-salary benefits	• Occasionally dry tasks
	• Hard to break into the job

Overview

Covering the world of issues

Behind every successful politician is an organized, multitasking aide—or several. Aides, a general term applied to most non-secretarial staff in an elected official's office, can fulfill a wide variety of roles, so adaptability is key. Aides who focus exclusively on one policy area typically have several years of experience working on that specific topic; entry-level aides generally attend meetings, hearings and banquets, and assist with any number of other tasks. Those who stick around long enough will gravitate toward their strengths—media-savvy aides may assist the press secretary (also an aide, technically) with press releases and public statements, while those with an aptitude for translating legalese tend to lean toward policy and legislation research. No matter which area an aide tends toward in the long run, however, the one thing he or she must always keep in mind is that the aide is an extension of the politician in many respects, so stay alert.

Political aides handle issues ranging from welfare to business, to the environment, and deal with constituents (the voters in the area the politician represents) from a wide range of backgrounds. Aides are not only responsible for keeping abreast of political trends among policymakers, but also for staying in touch with the needs and concerns of the constituents. Generally speaking, successful aides start out with a focus on constituent assistance (this can range from writing response letters to coordinating with a governmental agency, to helping locate a constituent's missing disability pay) and community outreach, then add the responsibility of legislative work as they gain experience and the trust of their boss (this can take years).

Who you know

Loyalty is of utmost value in the field, and an aide who lands a job with the next Obama should go along for the ride if he or she plays the cards right. That said, the shelf life of politicians varies greatly. Members of Congress aren't constricted by term limits (a major reason why there are so many grandparents serving on Capitol Hill), but many states, counties and cities do impose such restrictions. For many elected officials, term limits mean transition time to consulting, teaching or retirement, and aides typically don't get to join them on these endeavors. There is an upside, however: once you're in the building—whether that means the statehouse, city hall or the White House—you should be able to make enough connections to find another job should you need to.

It's not all work and no play

As for the perks, the public sector ain't rolling in dough—at least not the kind of dough that's going anywhere near an aide's pockets. Veteran aides can collect a decent salary, but entry-levels shouldn't expect riches. What's more—and as illogical as it may seem—the higher up you start on the totem pole of U.S. governmental hierarchy, the less you typically make. An entry-level aide to a county supervisor in a major metro area, for example, may earn twice as much as a Congressional novice. The non-salary benefits, however, can be extremely generous when compared to those offered in the private sector, from lucrative

Visit Vault at **www.vault.com** for insider company profiles, expert advice, career message boards, expert resume reviews, the Vault Job Board and more.

V∧ULT CAREER LIBRARY 153

pensions to top-flight health coverage. Aides must generally work at the same level of government for a set number of years, however, to qualify for that pension.

The demands placed upon an aide can be great: night and weekend work is usually required, many politicians (and other aides) have, umm, let's say "challenging" personalities, and bureaucratic red tape can often impede seemingly simple tasks. Additionally, while no politician with a shred of common sense will ever force a governmental aide to help with a fund-raiser or pass out lawn signs, aides are often pressured to spend nights and weekends on the campaign trail as Election Day approaches. This may not be what aides envisioned when they signed up for legislative work—in fact, campaigns sometimes cause legislative offices to empty as staffers take time off to help bring in the votes, leaving constituents high and dry—but conventional wisdom holds that they're probably expected to "volunteer" if they want to stay on the team come transition time. This can place aides in a moral quandary if the cause du jour conflicts with their personal beliefs, but, hey, that's why idealists are few and far between in the upper echelons of government.

For all the frustrations aides young and old experience, moments of accomplishment can make it all worth it. As cliché as it sounds, helping an old lady claim a tax refund sent to the wrong address has its rewards, and witnessing Congress pass a bill that you've worked on feels good. Aides at the state and federal levels can spend years researching, revising and promoting a single piece of legislation; watching as it's signed into law should evoke elation.

PERSONALITY MATCH	PERSONALITY MISS
• Efficient	• Insecure
• Organized	• Impatient
• Outgoing	
• Ambitious	

Career Path

A bachelor's degree is strongly recommended for all political aides; many have graduate degrees or relevant professional experience. Many political aides begin their careers near where they grew up or attended college, either in local or state politics, and there's no better way to build a relationship with someone who may eventually help you find a job than on the campaign trail.

Normally, aides start out as legislative assistants, learning the technical and legal aspects of their specialized fields. It is important that, during their first few years on staff, aides cultivate relationships with colleagues in other legislative offices. The turnover rate for political aides is relatively high, but those who establish themselves with a successful career politician or as an expert in a particular field are highly valued as advisors or consultants. These veteran aides have typically built extensive professional networks within their level of government, and often know many of the politicians personally from past work experience. Those who rise to the level of chief-of-staff (the politician's top in-house staffer) usually have years of experience "within the building" and can hold their own in negotiations with their bosses and other elected officials; many eventually run for office themselves. Then again, some higher-up aides are staffers of moderate ability who simply befriended the right people and rode their coattails all the way up.

HOURS	SALARY
• Average about 45 per week	• Varies • Average entry-level salary: $15,000 • After five years: $30,000 • After 10 years: $60,000

Our Survey Says

The position of an aide to an elected official is stressful but filled with variety. "My day is never the same," says one staffer. Aides are exposed to many aspects of society; one contact describes a top perk of the job to be "a great education on humanity." However, life as a political aide also "requires a lot of reading and can be boring at times."

Although aides work 40- to 50-hour weeks, those hours are irregular, as aides often have to put together meetings "during the early morning or after dinner." Most elected officials "are very good when it comes to comp time, which makes the weird hours worth it." The dress code for political aides is generally "conservative and professional, more so for meeting with constituents."

The best way to land a position working for an elected official, insiders say, is to help out with a campaign and "get involved in the political side of things." Positions with the government "are terrific resume builders for private industry" and are "excellent for law or communication degrees."

SKILLS TO ACQUIRE
• BA • Master's degree in public policy, international relations, communications or similar discipline

A Day in the Life: Staff Assistant on Capitol Hill

8:30 a.m.: Come in to open up the office. Since you are the first person a visitor sees upon entering the office, it is your responsibility to ensure that the reception area is neatly kept and that there are plenty of brochures about things to do in Washington, D.C.

8:40 a.m.: Catch up on the latest news by reading the *Washington Post*, *Roll Call* (the newspaper of Capitol Hill), and your home-town papers online.

9:30 a.m.: Open and sort the mail. It is amazing how many people take the time to write to their Congressman. As you read each incoming letter, you must determine which legislative assistant or legislative correspondent is responsible for answering the correspondence. Reading the mail gives you a chance to learn about the issues Congress is considering.

10:30 a.m.: Welcome a family from the Member's district visiting Washington with their three children. You have already arranged a tour of the Capitol with one of the office staff.

11:30 a.m.: Answer yet another call from a constituent expressing his opposition to a bill pending before Congress. This is the 10th call you have received today on the same topic, all before lunch. One of the interests groups must be ginning up a strong grassroots operation to defeat this bill!

Visit Vault at **www.vault.com** for insider company profiles, expert advice, career message boards, expert resume reviews, the Vault Job Board and more.

VAULT CAREER LIBRARY   **155**

12:30 p.m.: Finally, time for lunch. Find one of the interns to cover the front desk so that you can slip away for 45 minutes. Head down to the Rayburn Cafeteria with two other officemates to grab a quick bite and gossip about the latest scandal stirring in Washington.

1:15 p.m.: The bells signal the first vote of the day. Activity in the office picks up as the Member prepares to go to the floor.

2:00 p.m.: Research an issue for one of the legislative assistants. Request several documents from the Congressional Research Service (CRS).

3:30 p.m.: The strange person who claims that the CIA implanted a chip in his brain and is monitoring his thoughts calls yet again asking to speak to the Congressman. You tell him that your boss is not available, but that you will be sure to pass along the message.

4:00 p.m.: Head down to the basement of the Capitol Building to pick up flags that have been flown over the U.S. Capitol to send to constituents that have requested them. The tunnels under the Capitol are mazelike—you are always surprised when you don't get lost.

5:00 p.m.: Time to call it a day, and head out to happy hour. Members' offices are required to pay overtime to all "non-exempt" employees, including staff assistants, so unless there's something pressing, you can only work an eight-hour day.

Project Manager

UPPERS	DOWNERS
• In charge of a group of creative people	• Long hours
• Given credit when a project is successful	• High pressure environment
• Variety of projects	

Overview

On time and under budget

Being a project manager can mean many things—it all depends on what industry you're talking about. In the dot-com and advertising worlds, project managers are in charge of supervising writers, editors, developers, designers and advertising teams and are called upon whenever a company wants to launch a new product, redesign the site, add a new service or upgrade old systems. A big part of being a project manager requires the ability to understand the intricacies of a particular project and to micromanage a creative team to complete a project on time and within budget constraints.

While the project manager manages the day-to-day progress of the project, he/she is also the "first arbiter of quality." In short, the project manager is responsible for making sure the project is a success. Coordinating many different teams for one goal can be hard, especially if each team's vision is different. The project manager sees everything going on inside and in between the many teams on a project; and is therefore expected to know when things have gone awry. He/she is responsible for identifying the problem—such as a lack of commonality between the departmental visions or that the project has simply gotten off track—and creating a solution.

Project managers often state that the stress is the toughest part of the job. It's no easy feat navigating the choppy waters between upper management and the creative team and still producing quality results on time. The ultimate success or failure of a project falls to the project manager; regardless of who makes a mistake, the project manager is the one who will be held responsible for it in the end. Due to this, a project manager has to always remain on his/her feet, both literally and figuratively. As one contact says, "I spend much of the afternoon calling clients to get any revised specs and to bounce new ideas our creative team has come up with off them. We speak about how the project is going and try to resolve any outstanding issues while reviewing the overall strategy we are trying to present."

Walking the walk

Although the office environment may at times be a bit chaotic (especially in a start-up environment), project managers often have their own offices close to the creative or design teams that they supervise. One contact in a web consulting/design firm said: "My basic premise of project management is the theory of management by walking around, so I spend a large part of the day speaking with the various people on my projects. I ask them if they need anything or have any questions. I find that there are always issues and I try to take care of them as soon as I receive them."

Many times, project managers have to put in more than 40 hours a week, depending on the status of the project on which they are working and the pressures they are under to complete it. If a project manager does happen to find himself with some extra time during the day, it means he is probably not doing his job as well as he could. As one proactive insider points out: "If I have any down time during the day, I usually try to read up on new trends in the industry and stay up-to-date on technical issues so that I can talk the talk and walk the walk."

Visit Vault at **www.vault.com** for insider company profiles, expert advice, career message boards, expert resume reviews, the Vault Job Board and more.

VAULT CAREER LIBRARY   157

Much of the day will most likely be spent in client meetings streamlining various projects and giving progress reports to the client, as well as working hand-in-hand with management and marketing teams to ensure the overall success of the particular project.

Talking the talk

Project managers need to be able to coordinate between departments with very different specialties, each with its own lingo. The technical team, for example, will have a different way of talking about the project than the business stakeholders. One NYC project manager describes the ability to communicate with all departments as being "multilingual" and "translating" between departments.

Coordinating with the different departments can also be problematic because project managers are not direct managers of the teams whose work goes into the project. In addition, project managers usually don't have the hands-on technical skills and experience of the technical and creative teams. Encouraging and directing the different teams without the standard authority of management or specialized skill can be difficult, but project managers get it done. Says one project manager, "This takes clever politicking and personal credibility to establish de facto authority when, in fact, the project manager has no authority except over the project schedule."

Being on the outside has its perks. By not being a part of one particular team and section of the project, the project manager is, in fact, a part of all the teams and sections on the project. The project manager can be involved in any stage in which he/she takes an interest, and this offers many possibilities, including career advancement. Higher-level project managers are often called program managers and manage a number of projects, as well as a project management team.

In order to keep track of these often disparate elements, project managers must be super-organized. At all of the meetings project managers attend, they are expected to take detailed notes. Each project manager has his or her own way of keeping track of all the details of a project. Some rely on the CPM, or the Critical Path Method, an organizational model that outlines the sequence in which things must happen. Some useful software applications are Microsoft Project, Primavera, Scitor Project Scheduler, AEC FastTrack and CA-SuperProject. Other project managers use simpler systems, such as MS Word or Excel documents, or even whiteboards above their desks. However, in the words of one project manager, it doesn't really matter what system is used, "a good project manager rarely has to go back to their notes."

PERSONALITY MATCH	PERSONALITY MISS
• Detail-oriented	• Disorganized
• Good communicator	• Introverted
• Assertive	• A follower
• Analytical	• Anxious

Career Path

Educational requirements vary greatly for project managers depending on in which industry they work. Those who work for high-tech startups are usually expected to have a degree in a related field and/or some prior history in computer science or engineering. The Project Manager Institute (PMI) also offers a certification for project management. PMI is a good starting point to learn about industry trends and other professional developments. Regardless of industry, however, it is common for project managers to have a bachelor's degree in accounting or business administration, and those with an MBA will probably find it much easier to score that ever-elusive high-paying job.

Starting out as a full-blown project manager is unusual and difficult. Most project managers start as assistants, helping the project manager oversee his/her projects, and then transition to a smaller company as a project manager or to business school. After that first straight project manager job (often classified as junior project manager), one advances to a senior project manager position. One gains more projects and those projects become more challenging and intricate as one climbs the ranks.

Being a project manager can also open other doors. Project managers get a taste for all parts and stages of a project, and often decide that they want to learn more about a specific one. This can lead to an unforeseen career as anything from a Java expert to upper management.

HOURS	SALARY
• About 40 to 60 hours a week	• Median compensation (base + bonuses), project manager I: $65,272 • Project manager II: $83,384 • Project manager III: $98,901

Our Survey Says

Project managers bring the ideas of the creative design team to life. One project manager describes it as a "very fun and interesting field." Working well and "building personal relationships" with people—both the clients and your team—is "key." Another project manager says project managers have the "ability to work on issues that will make the efforts of the staff easier and better in the long run. You feel like you make a difference."

However, being a project manager isn't just about working with the team. "You are responsible for defining requirements, scheduling, budget, and reporting to management on the progress of the project," says a NYC project manager. Says another, "The worst part of being a project manager—depending on the technology available—is scheduling meetings." Advises another project manager from Texas, "Learn to handle stress and take one day at a time." And if something goes wrong, projects managers take the blame—the buck stops with them. "Your job is closely tied to the project. If the project is cancelled, you may be out of work." But while project management can feel thankless—even if the project is a success, the project manager shares the credit with all of the teams that went into the success—in the words of one project manager, "rest assured, a project manager's individual efforts rarely go unnoticed."

In the end, project managers love the challenge and variety of the work. "You are not just doing the same thing over and over. Every project is new and challenging."

SKILLS TO ACQUIRE
• Bachelor's degree, MBA • Strong leadership skills • Strong communication and multi-tasking skills

Visit Vault at **www.vault.com** for insider company profiles, expert advice, career message boards, expert resume reviews, the Vault Job Board and more.

VAULT CAREER LIBRARY **159**

A Day in the Life: IT Project Manager

8:00 to 8:30 a.m.: I like to get there early so that I have a jump on things. I like to have the miscellany out of the way by the time everyone else gets there. I start doing the basic e-mail/voicemail check to make sure there aren't any fires burning. Usually I put together a to-do list each day. That usually comes out of what I've planned for the week. The list for that day will have action items on it to touch base with various clients and partners.

9:30 a.m.: One-on-one meeting with my director, the VP.

10:00 a.m.: Programmers don't come in until 10 a.m. at least. I'll meet with each project team to get an idea of where they are and whichever deliverable we're putting out this week or next week. I'll also get the status of each of the internal project teams.

11:00 a.m.: I'll start following up on wherever the clients or partners are. During the course of the day, I constantly have to resolve issues that come up. Those meetings can go on for hours, depending on how many of them I have to do. They can also be very quick, depending on the stage I'm at in the project.

12:00 p.m.: Lunch at my desk. I occasionally go out, but usually I don't. I bring my own lunch. I go to Whole Foods all the time, which is right across the street.

12:30 p.m.: After those meetings, I usually go into scheduling to see if what I've learned will impact the projects I'm managing. If there's an impact, I'll have to rearrange everything else and coordinate. That's where the whole timeline management piece of the job comes in.

1:00 to 2:45 p.m.: I start digging into documentation, either researching, reading or writing. At my current job, I don't write that much, but I'll end up working with an application architect to develop documentation.

3:00 p.m.: Coffee break.

3:30 p.m.: I check the status of rescheduling items. I also see if people have gotten back to me with answers that I've requested

4:30 to 5:00 p.m.: A little bit of time prepping for the following day. Entering my hours for the day into the time tracking system.

5:30 p.m.: I'm out of there.

Psychologist

UPPERS	DOWNERS
• Wide variety of career options • Intellectually stimulating	• Emotionally demanding • Long career path

Overview

Tell me about your mother

Wanna talk? A psychologist is ready to listen. Psychologists are perceived as the kinder, gentler brand of "shrinks." They are distinct from psychiatrists in that they do not prescribe drugs and do not hold medical degrees. Psychologists are social scientists and behavioralists—they are students of human behavior. More specifically, they investigate the physical, cognitive, emotional and social aspects of human behavior. They formulate hypotheses and collect data, and gather information through controlled laboratory experiments, as well as through personality, performance, aptitude and intelligence tests.

The types

The most common specialty is clinical psychology—or the hands-on diagnosis and treatment of patients experiencing some kind of mental distress. The majority of clinical psychologists work either in a private group or individual practice, though many hold staff positions in hospitals or clinics. Clinical psychologists provide group therapy, such as bereavement counseling, marriage and child counseling, and drug or alcohol counseling. They may collaborate with physicians and other specialists in developing and implementing treatment and intervention programs. As part of their involvement, psychologists work to make these programs less alienating and complex to their patients.

Other specialties within psychology include cognitive psychology, health psychology and neuropsychology. Cognitive psychologists deal with memory, thinking and perception. Health psychologists promote wellness by providing health counseling programs that help people quit smoking, lose weight and battle chemical dependency. Neuropsychologists study the relationship between the brain and human behavior; they are particularly interested in head injuries and strokes.

Another major group is the developmental psychologists, who study the patterns and causes of behavioral change as people progress from infancy to adulthood. Some developmental psychologists specialize in behavior during infancy, childhood and adolescence, while others study changes that take place during maturity or old age. The study of developmental disabilities and how they affect people is a relatively new area within developmental psychology.

Psychologists aren't simply confined to the study of the disturbed or other special cases. As behavioralists, their work is applicable in every aspect of human life. For example, industrial-organizational psychologists apply psychological techniques to personnel administration, management and marketing problems. They are involved in applicant screening, training and development, counseling, and organizational development and analysis. An industrial psychologist might work with management to develop better training programs and to reorganize the work setting to improve worker productivity or quality of worklife.

Visit Vault at **www.vault.com** for insider company profiles, expert advice, career message boards, expert resume reviews, the Vault Job Board and more.

VAULT CAREER LIBRARY 161

Work from home

About half of all psychologists in the United States are self-employed. Clinical, school and counseling psychologists in private practice generally set their own hours and can work in comfortable offices—often even within their homes. They are, however, expected to be available to their clients on weekends and evenings. Psychologists on the faculties of colleges and universities divide their time between teaching, research and administrative responsibilities, while some even choose to do consulting on the side. The life of a psychologist, save for the occasional conference and the company of patients, is a solitary and studious one. They work alone, reading and writing reports and articles for trade journals. Although they set their own schedules, they are often under a great deal of time management pressure, while trying to juggle treating patients, doing research and writing all at once.

PERSONALITY MATCH	PERSONALITY MISS
• Logical	• Narrow-minded
• Rational	• Abrasive
• Sympathetic	
• Perceptive	
• Patient	

Career Path

Psychologists without PhDs are limited in their career options. They can work as organizational or industrial psychologists, or work as psychological assistants under the supervision of doctorate holders, conducting research or psychological evaluations. A few work as school psychologists or guidance counselors, or teach in high schools and community colleges. For entry-level positions, the federal government employs non-doctoral candidates with 24 semester hours in psychology and a statistics course. Competition is stiff for these jobs, since they do not require an advanced degree. Vocational and guidance counselors generally need two years of graduate study and one year of counseling experience.

Psychologists with PhDs qualify for a wide range of teaching, research, clinical and counseling positions in universities, elementary and secondary schools, private industry and government. Psychologists with a PsyD, or Doctor of Psychology, generally work in clinical positions. And those interested in becoming a school psychologist need look no farther than an Educational Specialist (EdS) degree.

Earning a doctoral degree usually requires five to seven years of study; the PhD degree culminates in a dissertation based on original research. The PsyD is usually based on practical work and examinations rather than a scholarly dissertation. The doctoral degree generally requires at least a year of internship.

Psychologists in independent practice and those who offer clinical patient care or counseling must meet certification or licensing requirements. Clinical and counseling psychologists generally require a doctorate in psychology, completion of an approved internship, and one to two years of professional experience. In addition, most states require that applicants pass a standardized test. The American Board of Professional Psychology recognizes professional achievement by awarding certification, primarily in clinical psychology, clinical neuropsychology, counseling, forensic, industrial, organizational and school psychology. Candidates need a doctorate in psychology, five years of experience, professional endorsements and a passing grade on an examination.

HOURS	SALARY
• Average about 40 per week	• Median income (clinical, counseling, school): $59,440 • Median income (industrial-organizational): $86,420

Our Survey Says

Psychologists work "without knowing if [they] are being successful a good share of the time." Thus, in addition to being a deeply satisfying experience, the job can be at times "difficult and frustrating." Psychologists must be self-disciplined in that they cannot "give in to their feelings" and speak their mind, as "only the patient gets to do that." Psychologists are irked by the misconception that "doing therapy" is "just a matter of having a friendly, kind and helpful conversation." Therapy is grueling and requires "the most comprehensive clinical training you can find." One downside to being a psychologist is that they are often "affected by hearing other people's problems all the time."

According to a school psychologist, that specialty is becoming more challenging because psychologists are dealing with "more and more students with all types of emotional baggage." Psychologists who work in the public sector, like school counselors, "must like challenges and cannot require pats on the back."

SKILLS TO ACQUIRE
• Master's degree • PhD or PsyD for private practice • Certification from the American Board of Professional Psychology

Visit Vault at **www.vault.com** for insider company profiles, expert advice, career message boards, expert resume reviews, the Vault Job Board and more.

VAULT CAREER LIBRARY   **163**

Public Relations

UPPERS	DOWNERS
• Exciting environment • Access to events	• Long hours • Hectic schedule

Overview

Relating to "the people"

Can you think analytically? Do you work well under pressure? Does imagination and creativity ooze from your every pore? Combine these traits with great communication skills, self-confidence, diplomacy and superb organizational and planning skills and you just might have what it takes to be a public relations professional.

PR reps understand public perception and can structure their efforts to address whatever type of audience they're addressing, whether it's a minority group, disgruntled shareholders, or parents concerned about Product X's sugar content. Public relations firms have a larger purpose than publicity agencies, and often manage all the communication efforts—both external and internal—of a client company. This entails trumpeting successes, releasing news and figures, softening scandals and spinning failures or disappointments to maintain a positive company image.

Along the way, it's also important for a PR professional to build relationships with tech and new media reporters. Doing so will keep them on top of current events, especially those concerning Internet-based companies where industry trends change often and with little warning. The up-and-coming next-best-thing online increasingly turns to a public relations firm to manage its "brand," both before and after attracting investors. Some PR firms deal solely with Internet-based companies, applying the usual skills to promote an online service or a site.

Inside the PR machine

An agency can specialize in one or more disciplines such as consumer relations, corporate communications, brand marketing, crisis management, event marketing, media relations, product placement or reputation management. A PR firm may also specialize by industry, working with companies in financial services, health care, high tech and the Internet, or sports.

Long hours, including evenings and weekends, are common. In 2006, the U.S. Department of Labor reported that more than 65 percent of advertising, marketing and public relations managers worked upwards of 40 hours a week, so be prepared to put in the time. Substantial travel may also come with the territory; for example, you may need to be present at meetings sponsored by clients or their industry groups, or fly to meet with special interest associations or government officials in times of crisis.

PERSONALITY MATCH	PERSONALITY MISS
• Outgoing • Well-rounded	• Unassertive

Visit Vault at www.vault.com for insider company profiles, expert advice, career message boards, expert resume reviews, the Vault Job Board and more.

VAULT CAREER LIBRARY 165

Career Path

Info, please

Many colleges and universities have established public relations degree programs. Graduating with an English or communications degree can also be useful. You can contact a local or campus chapter of the Public Relations Society of America (PRSA, at www.prsa.org) to latch onto further information about working in this field. It's also a good way to locate internships and personal contacts that may be helpful in a future job search. The Public Relations Student Society of America and the International Association of Business Communicators are other fine sources. The PRSA offers an accreditation program for specialists who have at least five years of field experience and have passed a comprehensive six-hour evaluation. Most employers look highly on candidates who hold the merit badge of a PRSA certificate which signifies a degree of professional seriousness. For other information online, try About.com or Chief Marketer (www.chiefmarketer.com).

Up the ladder, slowly

A big part of your job will be writing press releases, reviewing published articles (to make sure your company is accurately portrayed in the media), pitching story ideas to reporters, fielding requests from writers, setting up interviews and creating and distributing media kits to the press. The more established PR firms have honed their methods over many years, and have developed structured learning opportunities and a clearly-defined career path.

Grab bag

PR is a very hot industry right now, especially for technology and web-based firms. The U.S. Bureau of Labor Statistics reports that the PR field will grow faster than average, by 18 percent through 2016, in part due to the increasingly competitive business environment. The number of applicants for entry-level positions is expected to continue to outpace the job supply, making those with education or experience more valuable commodities.

HOURS	SALARY
• About 40 to 60 per week	• Median salary for public relations specialists: $47,350
	• Mean annual salary for public relations managers: $92,250
	• Top earners: $145,600 and above

A Day in the Life: Public Relations Executive

According a former executive at Ogilvy PR Worldwide (New York), a typical day goes something like this.

7:00 a.m.: Scan/watch the national morning shows and read *The Wall Street Journal* and *New York Times*.

9:00 a.m.: Check and respond to huge numbers of e-mails from the following night.

9:30 a.m.: Conference call with Client A and team re: project and budget updates.

10:00 a.m.: Attend a creative "brainstorm" for a new business opportunity.

11:00 a.m.: Budget meeting with team leader for a new project for Client B.

12:00 p.m.: Meet with marketing group management regarding staffing and billable hours.

12:30 p.m.: Lunch with a health and nutrition reporter from a leading consumer magazine.

1:30 p.m.: Respond to new business inquiries and investigate opportunities.

2:00 p.m.: Client C meeting to discuss messaging and strategy for new product launch.

4:00 p.m.: Check mega-e-mails again before the end of the day.

4:30 p.m.: Respond to Client D regarding alternative media strategy for their launch.

5:00 p.m.: Review new business target list and allocate action items for next day.

6:00 p.m.: Think about dinner.

6:30 p.m.: Dent expense reports for the past month.

7:30 p.m.: Finally leave the office to eat—check e-mail one last time.

SKILLS TO ACQUIRE

- Strong writing and speaking skills
- Creative thinking
- Research skills

A Day in the Life: Assistant Public Relations Executive

Lisa Cottini, Assistant Account Executive at Porter Novelli

7:30 a.m.: Arrive early at work to get a jump on the day before my colleagues arrive. Change my voicemail to the current date and day's events. "If a client wants to get a hold of me, they need to know where I am and how to reach me." Look over my calendar and to-do list then read headlines in major daily newspapers to keep up-to-date on any issues that affect my clients.

8:30 a.m.: As my colleagues arrive, I check in with my supervisors and teams to see if we have any new direction or priorities for the day or week. "I always need to look a few steps ahead in order to prioritize and anticipate what is coming up around the corner." Check in with other staff and interns to see if they have questions on projects I have delegated and what the status is.

9:30 a.m.: Call clients to check in.

10:00 a.m.: Call reporters to check in on stories under development and ask if they need any other information.

11:00 a.m.: Our teams are constantly developing programs, strategies and contingency plans for things we know will happen and to prepare for things that may happen and could impact our clients business negatively. I am always working toward executing action items starting with the most urgent first—until I near the bottom of my never-ending to-do list.

12:30 p.m.: Lunch with peers in the PR industry or related trade industries, such as attending League of Cities meeting.

Visit Vault at **www.vault.com** for insider company profiles, expert advice, career message boards, expert resume reviews, the Vault Job Board and more.

VAULT CAREER LIBRARY **167**

1:30 p.m.: Prepare for client meeting tomorrow by editing team's presentation outlining the status of our current project. Depending on the day, I typically prepare for and attend client meetings. If I'm not in meetings, I am working towards completing strategic projects. Towards the end of the day, I start planning for projects with deadlines a week or month out.

3:00 p.m.: Attend internal client meeting and provide information on the status of the tasks that were assigned to me. We have numerous account teams. Each team meets once a week to keep current on projects and stay ahead of deadlines.

5:30 p.m.: Before I leave, I make my to-do list for the next day. Anything I missed or did not have time to get to won't be forgotten tomorrow. Leave work and head for yoga class to unwind.

Publicist

UPPERS	DOWNERS
• Contact with high-profile clients • Travel	• Long hours • High stress level • Low pay

Overview

Any publicity is good publicity

Publicists are the cheerleaders for obscure personalities and the spokespeople for high-profile clients. They must generate press coverage for their clients to get them maximum exposure. They also must maintain positive relationships with journalists to ensure that the media will be receptive to their pitches. Radio and television special reports and magazine feature articles can often be traced back to an independent publicist or public relations firm. Specialists also plan events and programs such as speaking engagements, and may be called upon to write speeches for politicians and business executives.

Hobnobbing with celebrities is one of the draws of being a publicist, but most entry-level workers soon find out that before they can enjoy such perks they have to endure long hours of grunt work. Though the pay is not high compared to other industries, they find the fast pace and interesting work stimulating. Good publicists are courted by the press and by potential clients, and the pros enjoy a degree of celebrity themselves.

Different type of publicity employers

One of the most popular ways for a publicist to break into the business is to work in a public relations firm. (PR firms are broader in scope than publicity agencies, and are often charged with juggling a firm's entire communication profile, relating to both the public and its own workers.) Most major ones have departments that serve different industries, and smaller firms often specialize in several related businesses. Public relations firms tend to pay pretty well—more than book publishers or nonprofit companies—and usually offer structured learning and a clearly-defined career path.

If you know you're interested in a specific company, you can work for its in-house corporate communications, investor relations or publicity department. You get a different kind of satisfaction working from inside the company you are promoting. For instance, working in publicity for a publishing house is a perfect job for people who love books and reading. Book publicists schedule book tours, work to get authors' books reviewed and think up ways to get writers and their work featured in as many media outlets as possible.

PERSONALITY MATCH	PERSONALITY MISS
• Creative • Aggressive • Extroverted	• Disorganized • Shy

Visit Vault at **www.vault.com** for insider company profiles, expert advice, career message boards, expert resume reviews, the Vault Job Board and more.

VAULT CAREER LIBRARY   169

Career Path

In larger corporations or decent-sized public relations firms, there are formal training programs for new hires. In smaller firms, the newbies will work closely with a supervisor or as part of an experienced team. Each environment has its advantages: publicists in smaller firms generally get a broader career education while specialists who work for multi-million-dollar organizations receive deep training in one highly-specific area. Anywhere one starts, the early tasks are largely simple ones (maintain company activity files, scan printed and web-based accounts for appropriate articles, compile facts for speeches and brochures); later on, after gaining some experience, recent hires may write news releases and articles, or assist in various ways on more involved campaigns. After years building their reputation and amassing industry and client contacts, many publicists start their own agencies.

Compensation is said to be better for publicists working in educational institutions than at an average company or nonprofit. Median salary is higher in Los Angeles—and higher still in San Francisco—than in New York City.

HOURS	SALARY
• Average about 50 per week	• Average entry-level salary: $32,000 • Average salary after five years: $52,800

Our Survey Says

"Basically, in agencies, we work in teams," explains an account executive in a high-tech PR firm, "so there are people from every level, from account coordinator to VP. It really helps you learn about the business and understand how your work fits into the big picture." Responsibilities might include writing press releases, preparing for product launches, and setting up conferences.

"To do well in this business," adds another agency contact, "you have to be very detail-oriented. You have to catch things before the client does, and you have to keep track of a lot of administrative things. You have to document every phone call, remember everything you said to everyone, and remember what they said to you. PR manages communications and deals with crises—so you can't be the ones making the mistakes." PR professionals also have to be sensitive and relationship-oriented—not only with clients, but with the media. "You have to respect journalists," warns a contact. "Some journalists hate PR people. They even have journalists come in during our training program to discuss their pet peeves about the process." Another thing you need to work in PR is a sense of humility. "You are always behind the scenes," says a book publicist. "You need to be comfortable with that."

SKILLS TO ACQUIRE
• English or communications degree   • Writing skills   • Creative thinking

Radio DJ

UPPERS	DOWNERS
• Work with creative people • Some amount of celebrity	• Long (and sometimes unusual) hours • Low starting pay • Little job security

Overview

Don't touch that dial!

Talk about deadline pressure: radio DJs, announcers and newscasters have about five to 10 seconds to capture your attention before you switch the dial. The job requires a lot more than playing music and giving traffic updates. To attract listeners, DJs have to put a spin on the news and the weather, too. As one DJ puts it, "In radio, you're only as good as your audience thinks you are."

Radio DJs have to be able to think on their feet and ad-lib much of the commentary to make smooth transitions between songs, commercials and other show segments. No formal education is required, but writing and researching skills figure largely into a DJ's job, whether she is interviewing Maroon Five or a local political candidate. In fact, the lively and (occasionally) witty banter that disc jockeys lob at one another is often scripted, and they frequently write promotional and news copy themselves.

The number of jobs available for traditional radio DJs is shrinking in the ever-shifting modern media landscape—for instance, one DJ can service several terrestrial stations at once, thanks to digital technology that records several hours' worth of talk time in just a few minutes and then distributes it to several stations. However, more and more radio personalities are making the leap to opportunities in satellite radio and the Web. Several independent radio stations operate entirely via streaming audio over the Internet airwaves (WOXY in Cincinnati and East Village Radio in New York are two notable examples), while public radio affiliates offer expanded online audio content and podcasts.

More than music

DJs are rarely limited to playing music; they are usually assigned a specialty like sports, weather, general news or traffic reports. Radio announcers also work at news radio stations where they are newscasters, anchors and co-anchors. Broadcast news analysts are called commentators, and they present news stories, interpret them, and integrate them into a broad discussion of how they will affect the audience they serve.

Not your normal hours

The hours for DJs and announcers can be long and irregular, which can affect their social and personal lives. Popular DJs are expected to turn up at promotional events and concerts, which can be considered a perk or a downer. The schedule constraints of the job can be physically and mentally strenuous, but of the rewards for the strange and long hours is the ability to be creative. Furthermore, radio DJs—with the exception of a few stars such as Howard Stern and major market morning show hosts—do not make a lot of money. Successful DJs can, however, gain personal satisfaction from their local celebrity status.

Visit Vault at **www.vault.com** for insider company profiles, expert advice, career message boards, expert resume reviews, the Vault Job Board and more.

VAULT CAREER LIBRARY 171

PERSONALITY MATCH	PERSONALITY MISS
• Creative	• Sensitive
• Extroverted	• Need structure
• Charismatic	
• Spontaneous	

Career Path

Getting hired in radio broadcasting is competitive and can be difficult. A degree in broadcast journalism or communications does not guarantee that you will be hired; station managers are more impressed by taped auditions that showcase an applicant's delivery and style—however, experience at college stations and internships also helps. DJs usually start out at a local station to gain experience and gradually move to larger and larger markets. Competition for jobs at national networks and satellite radio firms is stiff, and employers seek out college grads with years of radio experience.

Anyone considering enrolling in a broadcasting school should contact personnel managers of radio stations as well as broadcasting trade organizations to determine the school's reputation for turning out qualified candidates. Announcers who operate transmitters must obtain a Federal Communications Commission (FCC) restricted radiotelephone operator permit.

HOURS	SALARY
• Average about 40 per week	• Median salary for radio news announcer: $25,000
	• Range for smallest to largest markets: $7,100 to $102,676

Our Survey Says

Radio is generally "very relaxed." One DJ candidly admits that "the business is more pure entertainment than anything else." For example, dress code is "irrelevant—your persona is what counts." As far as those personas are concerned, insiders say, "broadcasting attracts a larger than normal share of egotists."

Breaking into the field requires "persistence, some experience and knowing a few key people." The workload is "variable," depending on the station. For example, a DJ in Arkansas says that she "is never very busy," while a DJ in Miami feels as if he "is a professional juggler at times" because he works so many shifts and has his own radio show. The "real money" in radio is as a producer, but the die-hard DJs are in the business, as one such devotee vouched, "for love, not money."

SKILLS TO ACQUIRE
• In-depth knowledge of music and popular culture
• Good speaking voice and interviewing skills

Real Estate Agent

UPPERS	DOWNERS
• Flexible hours	• Long hours
• You get out what you put into it	• High rate of rejection

Overview

Selling the farm

It isn't easy to sell someone what could be the biggest investment of their lives: their home. A real estate agent or broker has to be convincingly trustworthy and knowledgeable in order to put a prospective homeowner at ease. In many ways, the agent acts as a counselor to individuals and families about to embark on a huge commitment. And when selling or establishing a price for real estate, people seek out brokers and agents to do the dirty work.

Agents and brokers

Real estate agents and brokers are closely related, but they are different types of professionals. Brokers are independent businesspeople who sell real estate and rent managed properties for a fee. Brokers also arrange for meetings between buyers and sellers. They manage their own offices, advertise properties and handle other business matters. Some combine insurance sales or a law practice with their real estate endeavors, since both fields are integral to the sale and management of real estate.

Real estate agents are independent sales employees who provide their services to licensed brokers on a contract basis. In return, the broker pays the agent a portion of the commission earned from property sold through the firm by the agent. Today, relatively few agents are salaried by a brokerage or realty firm; instead, they derive their income solely from commissions.

Not just residential

Real estate agents can also work in commercial real estate, helping companies buy or lease space to house their business operations. Commercial real estate agents work with businesses to makes sure that the space in question—whether a temporary downtown office, a boutique storefront in a trendy neighborhood or a manufacturing facility in a sprawling office park—fits the business' needs and wants.

Tiring days

A huge amount of legwork goes into a real estate agent or broker's day. They meet with clients—often multiple times—to show different properties. They must also tailor their sales approach to each individual client; the pitch must fit the client as closely as the property the agent is showing. For example, a young family in search of its first home has very different expectations than a potential investor seeking out a rental property or an owner of a rapidly-expanding business looking for larger office space.

Since they always need properties to sell, brokers spend a large portion of their time obtaining listings. When listing different properties for sale, agents and brokers compare each to similar properties previously sold in that area to determine a competitive market price. Agents and brokers are also to some degree financiers, since they direct their clients to mortgage loan brokers and negotiate prices between buyer and seller.

Visit Vault at **www.vault.com** for insider company profiles, expert advice, career message boards, expert resume reviews, the Vault Job Board and more.

VAULT CAREER LIBRARY   173

Many real estate agents and brokers work an average eight-hour day, but one in four work 50 hours or more (including evenings and weekends) to suit their clients' schedules. Because they work on commission, their salaries are commensurate with the amount of time they spend showing properties, meeting with prospective clients, analyzing properties for sale and inspecting properties for appraisal.

Most real estate firms are relatively small, but some large real estate firms like Century 21 have thousands of real estate agents operating out of numerous branch offices. Individual brokers often have franchise agreements with national or regional real estate organizations. Under these arrangements, the broker pays a fee in exchange for the privilege of using the more widely known name of the parent organization.

Changing world

In 2001-2005, the U.S. experienced a "housing bubble." This meant that the demand for housing rose to excess, as did the cost of homes and real estate commissions and salaries. It seemed everyone was rushing to buy, partly because credit was so easy to come by and because mortgage interest rates were so low. However, in 2006, the "bubble" began to burst as interest rates climbed and homeowners were unable to pay their rapidly-increasing monthly mortgages, leading to foreclosures. Today, home sales continue to fall, loans are becoming impossible to get, and ripples can be seen throughout our economy.

PERSONALITY MATCH	PERSONALITY MISS
• Aggressive	• Sensitive
• Friendly	• Introverted
• Optimistic	• Not self-motivated
• Persistent	
• Trustworthy	
• Tactful	

Career Path

The best place to start is a bachelor's degree. After that, real estate agents and brokers must obtain state licenses to sell and rent properties. This often entails 30 to 90 hours of classroom instruction for agents, and 60 to 90 hours of formal instruction plus one to three years experience selling real estate for a broker's license. Most states require that licenses be renewed every one to two years.

Beginners often apply for jobs locally, since familiarity with a neighborhood is an asset—agents need to know such things as local zoning and tax laws when advising clients. Many local real estate associations sponsor courses covering the fundamentals and legal aspects of the field. As for sales skills, large brokerage firms offer formal training programs for both beginners and experienced agents.

Advancement opportunities for agents generally take the form of higher commission rates and an increase in the number and size of sales. This occurs as agents gain expertise and contacts, and become more efficient in closing a greater number of transactions.

Experienced agents can also advance in many large firms to managerial positions. And those who have received their broker's licenses (different from a sales license) can open their own offices. Also, agents, brokers and appraisers who gain general experience in real estate and a thorough knowledge of business conditions and property values in their localities may enter mortgage financing or real estate investment counseling.

While the majority of agents and brokers work with residential properties, there is also a small number who work in specialty areas, such as commercial, agricultural and industrial real estate.

HOURS	SALARY
• Average about 45 per week	• Median salary for real estate agents, including commission: $39,760
	• Median salary for brokers, including commission: $60,790

Our Survey Says

Although it is a demanding profession, real estate offers the freedom that "no other career could offer" in terms of work hours. The pay and the hours depend on the agent's motivation and skills. There are not many who are "driving expensive foreign cars," however. And one respondent feels that "those who do don't have much of a life." In order to last as an agent or broker, one must be willing to "accept rejection and understand that it is not a personal reflection." The work varies from day to day and "no transaction is the same." As one real estate agent puts it, "sometimes you feel as though you are working in the ER, and other [times] you feel you are working at a playground." Building a client base is a slow process and an "emotional roller-coaster" at times.

However, agents feel most gratified when they see a family "totally happy with their new home." A few respondents advise that anyone going into the field should have at least two to three months' savings, since it "takes a while to get paid." Finding a job in the field once you pass the real estate sales exam, however, is hardly difficult. One contact notes: "You don't have to worry about finding a company—they find you."

SKILLS TO ACQUIRE
• Bachelor's degree
• Passing score on real estate licensing exam

A Day in the Life of a Residential Real Estate Agent

9:00 a.m.: Get in the office, check voicemail and e-mail. Create to-do list for the day.

9:30 a.m.: Place calls on behalf of a client looking to buy a house to set up a tour for this weekend. Ask the sellers' agent to fax over the property listing sheets that contain all the vital information on the house. Confirm the asking price and try to figure out if the property is in demand and determine the flexibility of the sellers.

10:15 a.m.: Check in with some of co-workers to find out what deals they are working on and if they have any market scoop (i.e., trade sale comparables).

11:00 a.m.: Lob a call into a client buyer's attorney to see if everything is going smoothly with a pending property purchase. Find out that items discovered on the property inspection are being addressed. Call client to relay the information and reassure her the closing will happen later that week as planned. Have a brief discussion about mortgage rates.

12:00 p.m.: Break for a lunch with a mortgage broker. Talk about what is happening with mortgage rates and receive thanks for all the referrals you've passed on to him.

Visit Vault at **www.vault.com** for insider company profiles, expert advice, career message boards, expert resume reviews, the Vault Job Board and more.

VAULT CAREER LIBRARY   175

1:30 p.m.: Check and return voicemail and e-mails. Organize marketing materials for delivery that day. Hand the deliverables to an administrative assistant to mail.

3:30 p.m.: Head to the title company to close a deal. Your client is the buyer. Huddle up with the attorney and the client to make sure everyone is happy. Everything runs smoothly. Get a cashier's check made out to the broker. Thank client and tactfully remind them to refer your services to their friends.

5:00 p.m.: Back to the office. Give the check to your manager and give self a pat on the back. Ask about timetable for payment of the commission and return to desk. A co-worker gives a high five.

5:30 p.m.: Check e-mail and voicemail one more time. Put out fires and check commissions for the past year to see how your sales compare to those of your co-workers.

6:00 p.m.: Make sure everything is set for your upcoming home tours. Open up prospect list, record the closed deal and see what deals you expect to close in the near future.

7:00 p.m.: End of the day. Co-worker who gave the high five reminds you that you promised to buy drinks once your deal closed.

Statistician

UPPERS	DOWNERS
• High salaries	• Long hours
• Challenging tasks	• Can be tedious
• Influential work	

Overview

Tell me what these numbers mean

Statisticians break down mounds of mathematical data into digestible percentages and the "big picture." In other words, they look at numbers and draw conclusions about those numbers—finding out what those numbers mean. For example, it is the work of statisticians that tallies up Nielsen television ratings to determine whether *Grey's Anatomy* should call it quits. They do so by surveying TV-watchers to see how many of them are watching the show and then deciding whether enough of them are watching to keep the show on the air.

Statisticians work in such diverse fields as biology, finance, psychology, medicine and insurance. While sometimes statisticians' work is urgent—for instance, statisticians might assesses the likelihood that at outbreak of the Ebola virus might strike the United States—statisticians spend a great deal of time crunching numbers for manufacturers and other private companies to evaluate their products and to propose improvements based on experiments using statistical models. Statisticians can gather data for many different departments, and for different purposes; their conclusions influence many levels of the company, from product development and quality control to pricing and marketing.

Working with others

Statisticians do not have the luxury of working in a vacuum; they must constantly decode their statistical findings for their managers and other non-statisticians, many of whom are only concerned with the bottom line. Because of this, statisticians must recognize that numbers on a page mean little to many people. They have to be good writers and strong communicators to translate their data into concrete, simple ideas. The training involved in becoming a statistician should consist of at least 15 undergraduate hours of statistics, along with liberal arts and science courses.

About 30 percent of the almost 20,000 statisticians in the country work for the federal government. Among the largest employers are the Bureau of the Census, the Department of Agriculture and the Department of Health and Human Services. For its statisticians, the U.S. government requires 24 semester hours of mathematics and statistics with a minimum of six semester hours in statistics and 12 more in advanced mathematics.

PERSONALITY MATCH	PERSONALITY MISS
• Analytical	• Artistic
• Orderly	• Shortsighted
• Deductive	• Inattentive

Visit Vault at **www.vault.com** for insider company profiles, expert advice, career message boards, expert resume reviews, the Vault Job Board and more.

V\ULT CAREER LIBRARY 177

Career Path

Although a bachelor's degree in statistics is sufficient for some entry-level jobs, more and more employers are expecting statisticians to have master's degrees. Moreover, research positions in institutions of higher education and many positions in private industry require a doctorate—in statistics. A bachelor's degree in stats is not required for acceptance into a graduate statistics program, but a strong mathematics background is a prerequisite.

Many statistician positions do not have "statistician" in the titles, such as epidemiologist or biometrician. Usually these are just names for specialized statisticians; their work uses statistical methods on certain kind of data. Entry-level statisticians spend their time crunching numbers and assisting senior statisticians. After a few years, they may advance to positions that require more technical skills and management responsibility. However, opportunities for promotion are best for those with advanced degrees, and statisticians who hold master's degrees or PhDs enjoy more autonomy in their field and have the credentials to do research, develop new statistical methods or strike out as consultants, especially once they have earned a strong reputation in a specialized area.

HOURS	SALARY
• Average about 40 per week	• Average starting salaries: $65,720 • Average salary for statisticians in the federal government: $85,690 • Mathematical statisticians: $96,121

Our Survey Says

Most statisticians recognize that they are in "one of the top few professions," with beginning salaries that are "second only to engineers." However, "there aren't really any special perks," except the option of joining the American Statistical Association (ASA)—"they have good conferences."

One of the benefits of being a statistician is the fact that the field isn't a hectic one. As one statistician puts it, "there aren't usually any statistical emergencies." Statisticians admit that "statistics can be really boring," but they can also be "extremely lucrative." One statistician reveals that she was "terrible in math, actually," and that the real key to being a good statistician is "understanding the relationship between numbers and [having] an ingrained passion for them—and a good stats computer package."

SKILLS TO ACQUIRE
• Bachelor's, master's or PhD

Teacher

UPPERS	DOWNERS
• Summers off	• Long hours
• Personally fulfilling	• Emotionally challenging
• Variety	• Low pay

Overview

The good life?

Although it's not generally acknowledged with a large paycheck, teaching is an extremely important profession. According to a Japanese proverb, "Better than a thousand days of diligent study is one day with a great teacher." Teachers play a valuable role in children's lives, and parents and society trust educators to produce intelligent, successful individuals. However, the requirements to become a teacher and the subsequent demands of the profession aren't always fully understood. Is teaching really an eight-hour-a-day job with summers and weekends off? In reality, 40-hour workweeks are just a myth in teaching, as in most careers.

Teaching positions range from kindergarten to the elementary, to the secondary level. Most teachers get to work at around 7:30 a.m., if not earlier, and stay well past the end of the school day, until 4 or 4:30 p.m. On average, teachers spend an allotted one-hour "prep period," as well as their evenings and weekends, grading papers and preparing lessons for the next day or even the next week. The rest of the day is devoted to classroom time. Lunch hours can be occupied with administrative duties such as supervising the cafeteria or playground. Depending on the situation, teachers are responsible for the education of 30 to 150 children each school year.

Above and beyond these central duties, teachers must be available before and after school to meet with students, parents and administrators. Some evenings, schools have "open houses," where teachers meet with parents, preview the coming year's curriculum and syllabus and discuss the current status of the children's work. Outside of the classroom, teachers sponsor clubs, advise publications, coach sports teams and assist with school plays and musicals. All in all, teachers typically put in a solid 60-hour workweek. Wages for some of these other responsibilities, in addition to positions at summer schools or as tutors, can help augment the traditionally low payscale for teachers.

Yes, teaching is a rigorous occupation. So where are the rewards? A love for the subject matter and, moreover, the desire to help others succeed will produce a successful and fulfilled teacher. Educators have a lot of responsibility, and teaching demands a great deal of time, effort, energy and emotion. However, the privilege of leading children into the world and impacting their lives can be awe-inspiring.

What does it take?

Teachers in the kindergarten and lower elementary levels usually teach all subjects, including math, reading, language arts, science and history. Starting around the fourth grade and through the secondary school level, teachers specialize in one or two subjects. At all levels of the education system, special education professionals must be well versed not only in the specifics of the subject matter but also in the unique methods for teaching students with special needs. The teachers for art, music and physical education classes must also possess a facility with the art of teaching and with their subject matter.

Although subject knowledge is important, the crux of teaching lies in communication. Using methods such as humor, creativity, enthusiasm and technology, teachers must be able to reach and motivate every student in the classroom. This

Visit Vault at **www.vault.com** for insider company profiles, expert advice, career message boards, expert resume reviews, the Vault Job Board and more.

V∧ULT CAREER LIBRARY 179

requires an understanding of the age group and sensitivity to each student's individual learning needs. An unanticipated and often challenging role of teaching is that of disciplinarian, which is inevitable in the classroom environment.

PERSONALITY MATCH	PERSONALITY MISS
• Patient	• Easily frustrated
• Good people skills	• Unyielding
• Nurturing	• Unmotivated
• Creative	
• Organized	
• Dependable	

Career Path

All 50 states and the District of Columbia require public school teachers to be certified, generally in one or more related subjects. A state board of education can provide the requirements for this certification, and some states have reciprocal certification agreements. All states do agree on some things, though. Prospective teachers must hold a bachelor's degree and have completed an approved teacher training program, which includes a certain number of subject and education credits, in addition to supervised practiced teaching.

Teachers are permitted to instruct either early childhood grades (the nursery level through grade three), elementary grades (grades four through six or eight), a special subject (such as reading or music), or the secondary (high school) level. Many states require teachers to hold a master's degree in education; teachers who are hired with only a bachelor's degree often pursue their master's degrees during the summer and in night classes throughout the year.

Due to the current teacher shortage, many states have developed alternative teacher certification programs for people who have bachelor's degrees in the subject but not the necessary education courses required for certification. In some cases, individuals begin teaching under a provisional plan and, after working under the supervision of experienced teachers for one or two years while they take education courses, receive regular certification.

In addition, the National Board for Professional Teaching Standards (NBPTS) has begun offering voluntary national certification for teachers. The NBPTS offers 25 certificate areas that cover 15 subject areas and are sorted into seven student age groups, and the certification allows teachers to find a job in any state. Requirements include a portfolio demonstrating classroom work and a written assessment and evaluation of teaching knowledge.

Many states offer "career ladder" types of incentive programs, which offer salary bonuses to teachers who have taught in a district for a certain number of years or who obtain additional degrees. Most school systems consider teachers for tenure after two or three years of quality service. Tenure, a secure but not guaranteed position, was originally devised to protect teachers from dismissal based on political or personal views. It is important to remember that in some areas of the U.S., the teaching profession is highly unionized.

Teaching in the 21st century

The 21st century began with a pervasive, nationwide teacher shortage. The greatest needs lie in the areas of special education, bilingual education/English as a second language (ESL), and mathematics and science. Minority teachers, who reflect the diversity found in the schools and in the nation, are also needed. Although the number of education degrees granted in the

United States has increased during recent years, a demand for teachers remains in many areas, and schools will need new teachers to replace educators who are retiring. The Bureau of Labor Statistics expects the employment of teachers to increase by 12 percent between 2006 and 2016. Due to the number of the professions in this group, this growth will generate 479,000 new teacher positions.

An overwhelming number of vacancies is driving school systems to hire long-term substitutes and non-certified educators who are allowed an emergency license. Teachers are also being recruited directly out of college and from other careers, under the auspices of various provisional certification arrangements. For instance, New York City, Washington, D.C. and other cities staff schools through teaching fellows programs, and Teach for America recruits recent college graduates and professionals to teach in urban and rural schools for two years.

People who are entering education at a later point in life and after significant years of experience in other industries are bringing exciting new perspectives and approaches into the classroom. Influenced by these new teachers and by new goals in education, the traditional role of teacher is evolving. There is increasing emphasis on the teacher as mentor and guide. Innovative techniques are enhancing the educational landscape beyond the school building and the classroom in order to prepare students for the workforce. Teachers are challenged to find new ways to help students develop the ability to interact with other people, adapt to new technology and solve problems logically.

HOURS	SALARY
• Average about 50 to 60 per week	• Average starting salary: $31,753 • Average salary in public elementary and secondary schools: $43,580 to $48,690

Our Survey Says

Teachers like the fact that they can "be a positive role model in children's lives" and help "shape the future." One educator says teaching is "very rewarding," and that there is "great vacation time—off on all holidays and eight weeks during the summer!" In addition, the source says, teaching "can be fun," and teachers describe the work atmosphere as "casual." Another insider says, "Kids are definitely the best part of my job. Being a part of the progress of the nation's youth is very rewarding." The teacher adds, "The variety of my days is a sure 'upper' too. No two days are the same. In as much as I teach many of the same things over and over, the teaching situation changes day in and day out."

On the down side, one teacher says that the field has "low pay, high stress and too much work outside of school hours." Another contact says, "I have a friend who is a dentist; I like to tell him, 'You earn more than $100K annually to fill teeth, and I earn a mere $50K to fill heads.'" One teacher explains, "The money has gotten better but still lags behind other professions." Sources also say that dealing with school administrators and parents can be challenging.

Insiders feel that, in order for people to excel as teachers, they should love teaching and kids, have a selfless personality and "be patient and have a great sense of humor." One source says, "I do not suggest anyone to go into education unless they have 200 percent of their heart in it." Another teacher recommends that people who are interested in going into the field should "do some student teaching, or at least help out in a classroom." The insider adds, "Get to know a teacher, and see what the job really entails. There's a lot more to teaching than people think. Make sure you know what you're getting yourself into." Another teacher advises, "Be sure to choose a content area that suits you well."

Visit Vault at **www.vault.com** for insider company profiles, expert advice, career message boards, expert resume reviews, the Vault Job Board and more.

VAULT CAREER LIBRARY 181

SKILLS TO ACQUIRE

- College degree
- State teacher's certification
- Communication skills
- Organizational abilities

A Day in the Life: Teach For America Third Grade Literacy Teacher

7:30 a.m.: I arrive at school. I use this extra hour in the morning to make copies and grade papers, get my classroom put back in order, write the morning message on the board, and talk with other teachers in my school. The message of the day usually involves a greeting (Good morning class!), the date, the special period of the day—art, computers, gym, music or library—and something to get my students excited about a lesson. For example, "Today we're going to learn about how sharks breathe."

8:25 a.m.: I pick up and greet my students. We listen to the morning announcements on the PA and recite the flag salute and the National Anthem. Each student also has a specific morning task. For example, a student might be in charge of taking roll or collecting and stamping homework. (Homework is stamped so that I know it was done on time.)

8:35 a.m.: Now the day really begins. I teach my first group of students reading, writing and social studies. We do some direct instruction, guided practice (with some help from the teacher) and center work. Center work involves rotating among three different stations. At one station, students work with a teacher on a guided reading; at another station, students work independently at one of several skill-building centers—computers, writing, reading and sentence building; and at the final station, students do worksheets on their own.

10:45 to 11:40 a.m.: Lunchtime. I'm supposed to be able to leave my classroom during this time, but the lunch aides are a little loose on discipline so I usually eat my lunch in the room with my students to keep an eye on things.

11:40 a.m.: I switch classes and get my second group of students who spent their morning with their math and science teacher. These are the CHIPS (honors) students, so the afternoon leaves room to take lessons to a more advanced level if they get the basics down faster than the morning students. Again, we go through reading, writing and social studies lessons.

For example, one week, I might be teaching adjectives. I start off the lesson by playing a game, a good way to get the students involved. I describe objects around the room, saying, "I see a purple folder. I see a blue chair. I see a round table." The students join in by mimicking me. This leads into a discussion of what is means to be an adjective.

2:10 p.m.: The school day is almost over and it's time for my prep, a free period when I get a chance to grade papers, plan lessons, or call parents about missing homework and discipline issues, or sometimes about high scores and improved behavior. This time is also spent speaking with my students' math/science teacher as well as our literacy coach about unit and theme planning, test scores and other information regarding our students.

2:55 p.m.: Now it is student dismissal time. I go back to the classroom and help get my students packed up and out the door. I often have short in-person conversations with some of the parents picking up their students. I also get another chance to talk to other teachers about what is happening in their classrooms and upcoming school events. On Mondays we usually have a school meeting. Most days of the week teachers can't sign out until 3:30 p.m., except Friday when we can leave at 3 p.m.

4:00 p.m.: I don't really leave school until just after 4 p.m. most days. I have lesson plans to write, student work to grade and post in the classroom, bulletin boards to change, and there's always plenty to clean up! Despite the extra hour of work at school, I often bring home more work to grade and supplies to get lessons ready for the next day at school. A teacher's work is never truly done!

In addition to the normal work of a regular teacher, as a TFA corps member, I attend a weekly education class from 4 to 9 p.m. We talk about educational issues such as learning styles—How do you figure out what your students' learning styles are? How do you adapt? How has it been a problem in your classroom?

On other evenings, I might talk with other TFA teachers and directors about ideas to ensure my students are moving forward and making necessary gains, or ways in which I might improve my school through initiatives such as after school programs or professional development. As a TFA teacher, I'm not only concerned with becoming a good teacher, but also with affecting change.

A Day in the Life: ESL Teacher, South Korea

6:00 a.m.: Get up and jump in the shower. It's early, too early, but you've got to get to downtown Seoul and beat through the early morning traffic. Your first class is at 7 a.m. You catch the bus right outside your door and hop on for a rip-roaring ride through the dark streets of Seoul. Even though it's early, the bus is crowded.

6:50 a.m.: Arrive at the Institute and get a cup of hot instant coffee. The newer teachers are already there, anxiously preparing their lesson plans for the morning. Just like you when you first arrived. You've been doing this for six months now, and you know most of your lesson plans by heart. Goodbye, preparation time!

7:00 a.m.: Greet your first class, a group of eager "salarymen" and "salarywomen." They are anxious to get in their hour of English before they start their jobs at various banks and corporations. It's an advanced class, and most of the students have been at the Institute for several semesters. It's a relaxed and friendly class, despite the early hour. The topic for today? It's a "free talking" class, and one of the students has selected to talk about military conscription.

10:00 a.m.: Time for a short break. You've already taught three 50-minute classes. You hang out with the other teachers in the teacher's lounge, and grab a quick game of cards with a couple of Brits. With 10 minutes before your next class, you stop playing to prepare a bit: it's heavy on grammar, and you need some technical research.

11:30 a.m.: Say goodbye to your last class for the morning, a group of students studying for their university entrance exams. You've just spent an hour with them discussing the difference between "had" and "has had"—luckily most of the teaching at this Institute is not as dry.

12:00 p.m.: Grab a quick lunch with an Australian co-worker at the little restaurant round the corner. You've become addicted to the food in Korea, and slurp your cold chili noodles happily. And at only $1.50 a bowl, it's the best deal in town.

1:00 p.m.: Time to catch a bus across town to your first private tutoring lesson. This is where the real money is, and although your "split shift" at the Institute is a real pain (you have morning classes and late evening classes, but nothing in between), it leaves your afternoons free for private lessons, where you can earn three times your Institute salary per hour.

2:00 p.m.: You're having a conversation about cosmetics with a group of housewives on their weekly lesson. You don't think they learn too much (only an hour a week!) and you guess it's more about the experience for them. For you, too. You've made some good friends this way—one of the women has invited you out to visit her husband's mushroom farm in the country this weekend.

Visit Vault at **www.vault.com** for insider company profiles, expert advice, career message boards, expert resume reviews, the Vault Job Board and more.

VAULT CAREER LIBRARY   183

3:30 p.m.: Your last private lesson of the day is over. You've got a few hours to kill before your next class at the Institute at 7 p.m. Too short a time to go home, too long to do anything else. You stop in at an Internet café to catch up on the latest news from home, then you hang out in the park for a while, creating a game for a group of kindergarten students you will teach tomorrow.

9:00 p.m.: The long teaching day is over! You head out with a group of foreign teachers to a nearby bar. You relax and have a few beers. There are a couple of Canadians, two Brits and a Swede with impeccable English. Some are new, though most have been in the country for a while. Meeting all the different teachers, as well as the students, is one of the best perks of the job. In the noisy bar, tables of Korean businessmen are drinking and celebrating. If it were Friday, you'd probably continue drinking and then onto a nightclub or a Korean karaoke bar. But it's Wednesday, and everyone has an early start tomorrow. You take a cab home—it's almost as cheap as the bus.

Travel Agent

UPPERS	DOWNERS
• Discounted travel	• Long hours
• Make people happy	• High stress level
	• Low pay

Overview

A traveler's best friend

A travel agent is a harried traveler's best friend. Amateurs who have attempted to arrange their own airfare, hotel accommodations or vacation schedule know that can be frustrating and fruitless without the insider savvy of a travel agent. But travel agents don't just book reservations. They give advice, weather forecasts and restaurant suggestions, too.

The training required to become a travel agent is highly specialized; many agents have certifications from long courses. Even with their training and indispensability to their clients, travel agents aren't very well paid. Airlines have "capped" the commissions that they used to pay travel agents to a flat rate for fares over $500; previously an agent received 10 percent of the total fare, regardless of the price. It's not as if travel agents have a light work schedule, either. They often stay at their desks until at least 7 p.m. or later if a client should call with a missed flight or a lost passport. Travel agents generally choose their career path out of a love of travel and customer satisfaction, rather than expectations of fame and wealth.

Moving online

With the popularity of travel web sites like Orbitz, Expedia and Priceline soaring, some may think the job outlook of travel agents would be dim. But no! According to the Bureau of Labor Statistics, travel agent employments are expected to increase slightly in upcoming years. Travelers don't want to have to worry when they're vacationing, and having a travel agent watching their back provides a lot of comfort, especially as travelers visit more and more exotic locations.

However, while there is a wealth of job opportunities for travel agents right now, it is something that is never stable for agents entering the job market, since the travel industry is easily upset by economic fluctuations and international political crises.

PERSONALITY MATCH	PERSONALITY MISS
• Friendly	• Impatient
• Organized	• Ambitious
• Extroverted	
• Meticulous	

Career Path

While some colleges might offer degrees in travel and tourism, or industry-related courses, other degrees may help, as well. Employers sometimes look for potential agents who have graduated with degrees in communication, geography, foreign language or even computer science. Courses in accounting and business management are also a wise investment, as many agents consider starting their own agencies (in fact, according to the BLS, 13 percent are self-employed). Six- to 12-week

Visit Vault at **www.vault.com** for insider company profiles, expert advice, career message boards, expert resume reviews, the Vault Job Board and more.

VAULT CAREER LIBRARY   185

programs offered at community colleges and continuing education programs are comprehensive and are usually sufficient training for beginning travel agents.

Travel agents work in a variety of environments. Most work for traditional travel agencies, while others work for tour operators, visitor's bureaus, cruise lines and other reservation offices. Some agents start as reservation clerks or receptionists in agencies, advance to office manager or other managerial positions, and eventually move on to become full-fledged agents. Agents in larger firms often specialize by type of travel (leisure vs. business), or by destination (The Galapogos Islands vs. Iceland).

Travel agents who wish to advance quickly can take advanced courses from the Institute of Certified Travel Agents. Upon completion of the courses, an agent becomes a certified travel counselor. The American Society of Travel Agents (ASTA) offers a correspondence course, as well. These certifications can be helpful for those wishing to start their own businesses, as is gaining formal supplier or corporation approval (airlines, ship lines and rail lines), since approval is necessary before travel agents are authorized to receive commissions. Certain states also require some form of registration or certification of retail sellers of travel services.

HOURS	SALARY
• Average about 45 per week	• Median salary: $29,210

Our Survey Says

Although many travel agents receive "a rude awakening" when they find their hopes of "glamour and jet-setting" have exceeded the reality of the job, others do not seem to mind the "evenings behind the desk" because they feel a "genuine obligation" to their clients. As one respondent explains, "It is an ego boost to know that someone halfway around the world needs you." There are also perks in the job, like "discounted or free travel," although an agent's demanding schedule leaves "hardly any time to use all the free tickets."

It is easy for travel agents to become frustrated and "overburdened," especially because some clients consider them to be responsible for every aspect of their vacations. As one agent puts it, "They expect me to control the weather." The commission caps "have devastated the morale" of many agents, though many continue to work in the industry because they "love working with people and the travel is some consolation for the stress."

SKILLS TO ACQUIRE
• High school diploma or equivalent
• Certified travel counselor or ASTA certification
• Good writing, computer and sales skills

Veterinarian

UPPERS	DOWNERS
• Good salary	• Long hours
• High satisfaction	• Many years of training

Overview

A special breed

Veterinarians are a special breed of doctor. They do not command the huge salaries that doctors who treat humans do, but they boast a level of job satisfaction that surpasses that of more lucrative fields.

Vets work in different environments, from farms to penthouses to labs. Most vets, however, are in private practice, where they usually treat small house pets. Other vets treat large farm animals, like cattle and horses. Veterinarians who treat "companion" or domestic animals provide services in over 20,000 animal hospitals or clinics across the country. Those who treat large animals not only handle their treatment and care, but also advise farmers and ranchers on the breeding and maintenance of their livestock. In addition, many veterinarians work with physicians and scientists on research to treat and prevent the outbreak and spread of diseases such as rabies.

The working conditions are slightly more adversarial at animal clinics than normal hospitals—humans do not usually bark, bite or chirp (though there are exceptions) while receiving treatment. Veterinarians are susceptible to infection and disease, particularly since they can be bitten or scratched by their patients.

PERSONALITY MATCH	PERSONALITY MISS
• Compassionate	• Short-tempered
• Patient	
• Animal lover	

Career Path

All states require that veterinarians be licensed to practice and that they hold DVMs (Doctorate of Veterinary Medicine) from accredited colleges. The DVM requires at least six years of education, including two years of preprofessional study in the physical and biological sciences. Applicants to four-year veterinary programs usually hold a BS or a BA. In addition to academic preparation, the program consists of clinical training in the diagnosis of animal diseases, surgery training and laboratory work in anatomy and biochemistry.

Admission to one of the 27 colleges of veterinary medicine in the country is competitive, as these schools accept only one third of those who apply. Applicants must take the Veterinary Aptitude Test, the Medical College Admission Test (MCAT) or the Graduate Record Examination (GRE), as well as submit evidence that they have worked with animals. Colleges give preference to in-state applicants because most schools are state-supported.

To receive a license, prospective vets must have their DVM and complete the day-long North American Veterinary Licensing Exam (NAVLE), which replaced the National Board Exam (NBE) and the Clinical Competency Test (CCT) in April 2000.

Visit Vault at **www.vault.com** for insider company profiles, expert advice, career message boards, expert resume reviews, the Vault Job Board and more.

VAULT CAREER LIBRARY 187

Along with a license and the DVM, most states also require a state jurisprudence exam covering state laws and regulations. However, many states have different policies, making it difficult for vets to move around the country without first completing the new state's requirements. Hard to avoid is the continuing education requirement for licensed vets held by 39 states.

Fresh out of school, vets have a variety of career options, including becoming U.S. government meat and poultry inspectors, disease-control workers, epidemiologists, or commissioned officers in the U.S. Public Health Service, the U.S. Army or the U.S. Air Force. However, most vets get their start working in established practices while they decide on a specialty. After a few years, many seek the independence of their own practice. Some veterinarians also work in teaching and research fields, for which they obtain a PhD or a master's degree in addition to the DVM. Other veterinarians work with zoo, aquarium or laboratory animals.

HOURS	SALARY
• Average 50 per week in private practice • Average 40 per week in non-clinical areas	• Median salary: $71,990

Our Survey Says

Veterinarians count themselves "among the happiest" physicians. Not only do they "genuinely love their patients,"but they also find medicine rewarding. As one vet says, "There is such a feeling of personal satisfaction and urgency because animals are so helpless and appreciative of treatment." The salary is still "enough to make anyone comfortable," particularly in private practice.

Still, veterinary medicine is "neither as lucrative nor as prestigious" as other fields, and the job "can be very unglamorous," particularly when you "get kicked in the shoulder by a disgruntled patient." The hours average between 40 and 50 a week, and vets in private practice work nights and weekends.

SKILLS TO ACQUIRE
• Doctor of Veterinary Medicine (DVM)   • Successful completion of state board examination

Writer

UPPERS	DOWNERS
• Dynamic lifestyle	• Long hours
• Wide variety of career options	• Scarcity of jobs
• Creativity	• Fierce competition

Overview

Good writers are those who keep the language efficient. That is to say, keep it accurate, keep it clear.

—*Ezra Pound*

Writers are a vital part of our culture. In fact, this sentence you're reading right now was written by a writer. The image of a writer as someone who scribbles away in a darkened library is out of date, as there are jobs for writers in every industry. Writers now have more career options open to them than those who toiled with the pen in the time of Shakespeare—or even in the time of Fitzgerald and Hemingway.

The exploding high-tech industry seeks out technical writers with knowledge of a certain field to infuse dry, complex material with clarity and style. Copywriters at advertising agencies write content for print, broadcast and television media, and command slightly higher salaries. And many burgeoning content web sites are finding that writing talent is a hard-to-find and precious commodity.

Traditions die hard

Still, the high-profile writing jobs at national magazines and newspapers are alive and well. They remain hard to get without a long publishing history and an "in" at the magazine. And the "day job/night job" class of writers, who spend their days waiting tables or, like Kafka, clerking at an insurance agency, is far from extinct. These writers are often working on novels, screenplays and television scripts while they wait for an agent or a studio to "option," or agree to consider, their work. The most successful writers are those whose passion for their work pushes them to keep writing and keep submitting, even if it takes years to see their work in print.

Freelance writing

Not all people who choose writing as a career have 9-to-5 jobs. Some work as freelancers, and are hired for specific projects. It's a wide-open proposition—one day you can write a brilliant treatise on the effect Voltaire's *Candide* has had on modern satire and the next you'll be knee-deep in product write-ups for pet chew toys. Freelance writing is often a difficult world in which to become established, as many companies work through full-time ad agencies or have an in-house creative team that handles promotional and copywriting. Even after you land the first couple of jobs and get your foot in the door, there are no guarantees. It's hard work tailoring your own particular impulses to fit clients' needs while turning copy over on time and to their particular specifications. On the plus side, one need look no further than the Internet for a whole world of opportunities.

PERSONALITY MATCH	PERSONALITY MISS
• Creative	• Undisciplined
• Empathetic	• Procrastinator
• Inquisitive	
• Self-motivated	
• Persevering	

Visit Vault at **www.vault.com** for insider company profiles, expert advice, career message boards, expert resume reviews, the Vault Job Board and more.

VAULT CAREER LIBRARY 189

Career Path

Writers seeking employment with a general newspaper or magazine should have at least a bachelor's degree in journalism, English, communications or literature. Those applying for a technical writing position should be either well versed in their subject matter or hold advanced degrees in the field. Newspaper journalists need a good portfolio of published work to get in on the ground level as reporters.

Writers in entry-level positions at small companies may get writing opportunities almost immediately, but moving up the corporate ladder is a whole other story. On the other hand, writing opportunities at large firms only come after putting in the time doing research, fact checking and copyediting, but the chance for advancement is much higher and quicker. Many writers also take jobs as editors, either starting out (such as editorial assistants at magazines) or after their work has earned acclaim (editor at a major book publishing house).

Freelancing for prestigious publications is difficult for an unestablished writer. Submitting to small, regional papers and magazines (for free) is a good way to get published. In order to get a story published in a newspaper or magazine as a freelancer, a writer must either be an expert on the topic, or conduct extensive research and interviews. Writers have to be adroit salespeople to pitch their services. Rejection is par for the course, and can take a toll on a writer's sense of worth.

HOURS	SALARY
• Average about 40 per week	• Median salary for writers and authors: $48,640
	• Median salary for technical writers: $58,050
	• Salary for freelance writers varies

Our Survey Says

There is no "magic formula" for making it as a writer, whether as a journalist or as a poet. Most aspiring novelists would have a better chance of transmuting base metals into gold than of signing a book deal. Others write bestsellers their first time out. In general, though, it takes a long time, ("sometimes years and years and—you get the picture," says one contact) to make a living as a writer, whether your milieu is "science or science fiction." An English or journalism degree "doesn't mean you can write," insiders point out, and many authors worked in other industries before they began writing. Some writers must "force themselves to set aside writing time," which takes an "enormous amount of dedication."

An old cliché says that a writer should "write only what s/he knows," which is true only to the extent that anyone who wants to write needs to have a "cache of personal experiences and a way of making the world microcosmic." In other words, traveling, reading, talking and listening to other peoples' stories strengthens a writer's ability to "illuminate, educate and entertain." The job can be stressful, if only because of the "emotional difficulty," the "bouts of self-doubt and rejection," and "deadline pressure from slave driving editors." However, the payoff for persevering through draft after draft and one "ding" letter (trade speak for a rejection) after another is "a little piece of posterity—your name in print."

If you decide to work as a writer in a salaried job, things are looking up. Most writing departments have a "relaxed dress code" and reasonable hours. Working at an office also means that you're surrounded by other writers. Says one copywriter, the best thing about his office is "collaborating with interesting, creative people."

SKILLS TO ACQUIRE
• Bachelor's degree, MFA
• Sharp writing and organizational skills
• Excellent grammar

APPENDIX

About the Editor

Vault Editors

Vault is the leading media company for career information. Our team of industry-focused editors takes a journalistic approach in covering news, employment trends and specific employers in their industries. We annually survey 10,000s of employees to bring readers the inside scoop on industries and specific employers.

Much of the material in *The High School Career Bible* is excerpted from Vault titles to specific industries or career titles. Vault publishes more than 100 titles for job seekers and professionals. To see a complete list of Vault titles, go to www.vault.com.